THOMSON'S
SPANISH-ENGLISH
ENGLISH-SPANISH

ILLUSTRATED
AGRICULTURAL DICTIONARY

BY

ROBERT P. RICE JR. Ph.D.

THOMSON'S
ESPAÑOL-INGLÉS
INGLÉS-ESPAÑOL

DICCIONARIO AGROPECUARIO
ILUSTRADO

POR

ROBERT P. RICE JR. Ph.D.

COPYRIGHT 1993 BY THOMSON PUBLICATIONS

Printed in the United States Of America

ISBN - Number 0-913702-56-0

Library of Congress Catalog No. 93-060117

NOTES – NOTAS
ABBREVIATIONS – ABREVIACIONES

f   feminine noun – nombre feminino
m   masculine noun – nombre masculino

Verbs can be recognized by their characteristic endings in Spanish of "er", "ir", or "ar".

Adjectives are presented in their masculine form but must agree with the modified noun in gender.

Nouns can be recognized by the presence of either an "m" or an "f" in their Spanish translation which indicates the gender of the noun.

I am pleased to acknowledge Dr. William Little, Chair of the Department of Foreign Languages and Literatures at Cal Poly, San Luis Obispo, California for his valuable expertise in proofreading the Spanish-language aspects of this dictionary.

PART ONE

PRIMERA PARTE

ILLUSTRATED TERMS BY SUBJECT

CONTENTS/CONTENIDO

pig/el cerdo

goat/el chivo

horse/el caballo

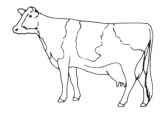

cow/la vaca

bull	el toro
cat	el gato
chicken	el pollo
chicken, hen	la gallina
chicken, rooster	el gallo
colt	el potrillo
cow	la vaca
dog	el perro
duck	el pato
fish (live)	el pez / pescado (food)
goat	el chivo
goose	el ganso
heifer	la becerra
horse	el caballo
livestock	el ganado
llama	la llama
mare	la yegua
mule	la mula
pig	el cerdo
rabbit	el conejo
sheep	la oveja
turkey	el pavo

chicken/el pollo

turkey/el pavo

FARM EQUIPMENT/EQUIPOS DE LA FINCA

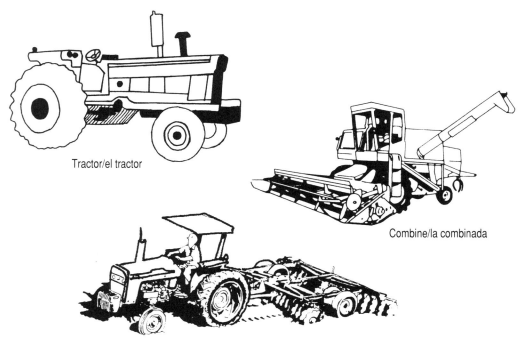

Tractor/el tractor

Combine/la combinada

Tractor and disc harrow/un tractor y una rastra de discos

baling machine	la embaladora	mower, rotary	la segadora rotativa
baling machine	la enfardadora	pick-up truck	la camioneta
belt conveyer	la correa transportadora	pick--up truck	la vagoneta
combine	la cosechadora-trilladora	plow	el arado
combine	la combinada	plow, disk	el arado de discos
compressor	el compresor	plowshare	la reja del arado
conveyor belt	la cinta de transporte	plowsole	el piso del arado
cultipacker	el rodillocompactador	potato digger	el arrancador de papas
defoliating machine	la máquina deshojadora	PTO	la toma de fuerza
disc coulter	la reja circular	ripper	el chísel
ditchdigger	la zanjadora	rotary cultivator	el cultivador rotativo
drill, coulter	la reja de sembradora	scraper	la escrepa / niveladora
drill, fertilizer	la abonadora mecánica	seeder	la sembradora
drill, seeder	la sembradora de surcos	soil injector	el enyector para el suelo
earthmover	la trailla mecánica	sprayer	el pulverizador
harrow	la rastra	subsoiler	el arado de subsuelo
harrow, disk	la rastra de discos	tractor	el tractor
knapsack sprayer	el atomizador de espalda	tractor, caterpillar	el tractor de oruga
land plane	la niveladora, la planadora	tractor, crawler	el tractor de oruga
		truck	el camión o el camión de carga

FRUITS

Fruits/las Frutas

Mango/el mango

Grape/la uva

Apple/la manzana

Cherry/la cereza

almond	la almendra
apple	la manzana
apricot	el chabacano
apricot	el albaricoque
avocado	el aguacate
banana	la banana
banana	el guineo
banana	el plátano
blackberry	la zarzamora, *mora*
breadfruit	el fruto del pan
cashew	el anacardo
cherimoya	la cherimoya
citrus	el cítrico
coconut	el coco
date	el dátil
fig	el higo
grape	la uva
grapefruit	la toranja, *pomelo*
guava	la guayaba
lemon	el limón
lime	el limero agrio, la lima
loquat	el níspero del Japón

lychee	el lychee
mandarin	la mandarina
mango	el mango
mulberry	la mora
nectarine	la nectarina
olive	la aceituna, *oliva*
orange	la naranja
papaya	la papaya
passionfruit	la granadilla
passionfruit	la maracuya
passionfruit	la chinola
peach	el durazno, el melocotón
pear	la pera
pineapple	la piña
pistachio	el pistacho
plantain	el plátano
plum	la ciruela
pomegranate	la granada
raspberry	la frambuesa
soursop	la guanábana
strawberry	la fresa
walnut	la nuez

Garden Tools/Herramientas del járdin

Shovels/las palas

Pruning knife/
cuchillo de poder

Spading fork/la horquilla cavadora

axe	el hacha	pick	el pico
broom	la escoba	pot	el envase
bucket	el balde	pruning knife	el cuchillo de podar
dibble	el escardillo	pruning saw	la sierra de podar
edger	la recortadora	rake	el rastrillo
fan	el abanico	respirator	el respirador
flat	la cajonera	rototiller	la cultivadora giratoria
grafting knife	la navaja para injerto	secateurs	las tijeras
grass catcher	el receptor de pasto	shover, square point	la pala cuadrada
greenhouse bench	la tabla	sledge hammer	el marro
hand pruners	las tijeras	spade	la pala
heater	el calentador	sprayer	el rociador
hedge shears	la tijera para setos vivos	string	la cuerda
hoe	el azadón	trowel	el desplantador
lawn mover	la máquina de cortar	wheelbarrow	la carretilla

Garden Tools/Herramientas del járdin

Pitchfork/la horquilla para heno

Trowel/desplantador

Broom/la escoba

Hoe/la azada
Hoe/el azadón

Rake/la rastra , rastrillo

Grafting knife/
la navaja para injerto

Garden Tools/Herramientas del járdin

Lawnmower/segadora de hierba

Secateurs/tijeras de podar

Hedge shears/tijeras para setos vivos

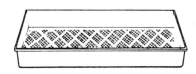

Flat/la cajonera

Loppers/tijeras de podar con mangas largas

Pruning saw/la sierra de podar

Insects/los Insectos

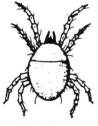

Mite/el acaro

Thrip/el trip

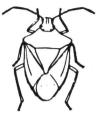

True bug/el chinche

Grub/el gusano

Beetle/el escarabajo
Pupae/la ninfa

Aphid/el áfido

Snail/el caracol

aphid	el áfido	mealybug	el pulgón lanígero
ant	la hormiga	mosquito	el mosquito
bee	la abeja	moth	la polilla
beetle	el escarabajo	nematode	el nematodo
bug (true)	la chinche	phylloxera	la filóxera
butterfly	la mariposa	pupae	la ninfa
caterpillar	la aruga *oruga*	scale	el cóccido
earthworm	la lombriz	scale	el cochinillo
earwig	la tijereta	slug	la babosa
flea	la pulga	spider	la araña
fly	la mosca	thrip	el trip
grasshopper	el saltamontes, el chapulín	tick	la garrapata
grub	el gusano	wasp	la avispa
lady bug	la mariquita	weevil	el gorgojo
leaf miners	el minador	white fly	la mosca blanca
leafhopper	el chapulín	worm	el gusano
mealybug	la cochinilla harinosa		

Irrigation/La Irrigación

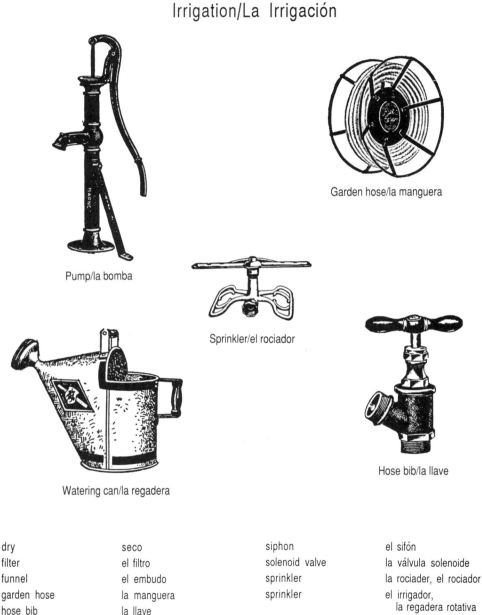

Pump/la bomba

Garden hose/la manguera

Sprinkler/el rociador

Watering can/la regadera

Hose bib/la llave

dry	seco	siphon	el sifón
filter	el filtro	solenoid valve	la válvula solenoide
funnel	el embudo	sprinkler	la rociader, el rociador
garden hose	la manguera	sprinkler	el irrigador,
hose bib	la llave		la regadera rotativa
injector	el inyector, el dosímetro	sprinkler head	el aspersor, la
nozzle	la boquilla		boquilla de regadera
pipe	el tubo	tank	el tanque
pump	la bomba	valve	la válvula
rain gear	los impermeables	washer	el disco
		wet	mojado

Elbow/el codo

Reducing coupling/
la conexión de reducción

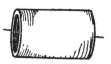

Coupling/la conexión

Elbow/el codo

Tee/el 'T'

Cap/el casquillo de tubo

Plug/el tapón

Nipple/el niple

brush	la brocha	pipe, copper	el tubo de cobre
cap	el casquillo de tubo	pipe, iron	el tubo de hierro
coupling, 45 degrees	el codo de cuarenta y cinco grados	pipe, plastic	el tubo plástico
		pipe, threaded	el tubo roscado
coupling, 90 degrees	el codo de noventa grados	plug	el tapón de tubo
deep	profundo	pressure	la presión
ditch	la zanja	pressure regulator	la reguladora de presión
drying time	el período de endurecimiento	pressure test	la prueba de la presión
		primer	el primario
elbow	el codo	pump	la bomba
emitter	la boquilla, el goteo	PVC cement	el pegamento PVC
emitter, clogged	el goteo tapado	sandpaper	el papel de lija
filter	el filtro	shallow	poco profundo
flux	el fundente	solder	la soldadura
gated pipe	el tubo con puertas	tee	el 'T'
hacksaw	el serrucho	teflon tape	la cinta teflon
leak	la filtración	timer	el reloj automático
nipple	el niple	torch	el soplete
pipe	el tubo	tubing	el tubo
pipe cutter	el cortador para tubería	valve	la válvula
pipe thread	la rosca del tubo		

MIST PROPAGATION SYSTEM/EL SISTEMA DE MULTIPLICACIÓN CON NIEBLA ARTIFICIAL

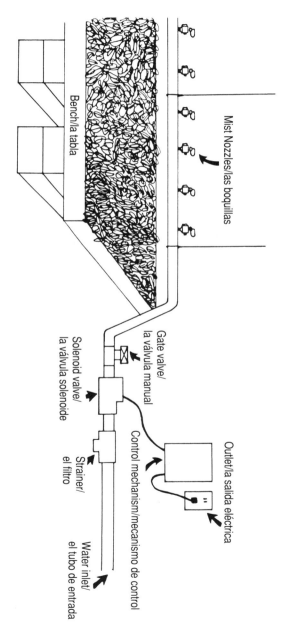

Mist Proagation System/Sistema de multiplicación con niebla artificial

Bench/la tabla

Mist Nozzles/las boquillas

Gate valve/ la válvula manual

Solenoid valve/ la válvula solenoide

Strainer/ el filtro

Control mechanism/mecanismo de control

Water inlet/ el tubo de entrada

Outlet/la salida eléctrica

PLANTS/LAS PLANTAS

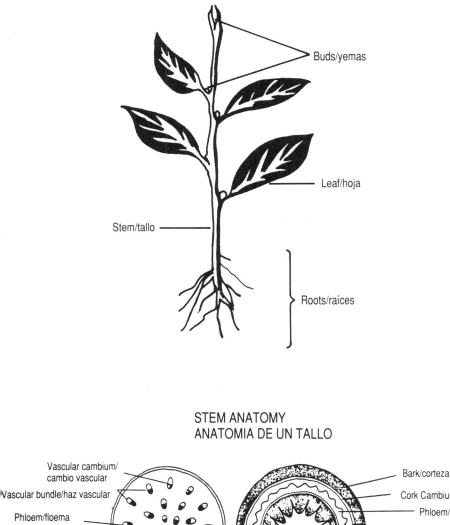

Buds/yemas

Leaf/hoja

Stem/tallo

Roots/raíces

STEM ANATOMY
ANATOMIA DE UN TALLO

Vascular cambium/
cambio vascular

Vascular bundle/haz vascular

Phloem/floema

Xylem/xilema

Epidermis/
epidermis

Bark/corteza

Cork Cambium/cambio de corcho

Phloem/floema

Xylem/xilema

Pith/medula

Vascular cambium/cambio vascular

(a)
Monocot/
planta monocotiledonea

(b)
Dicot/
planta dicotiledonea

PLANTS/LAS PLANTAS

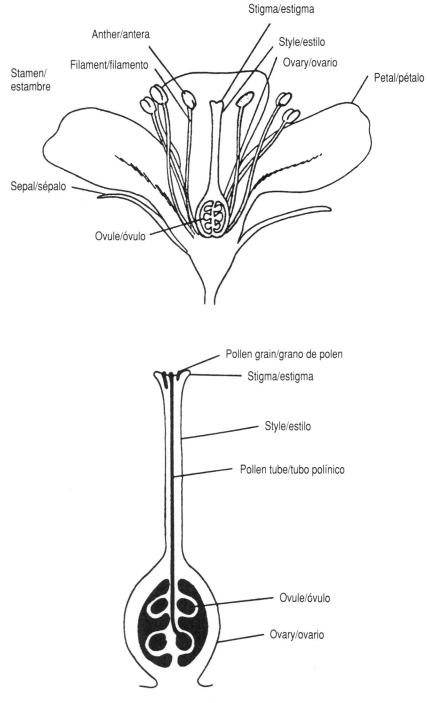

Stigma/estigma

Anther/antera

Style/estilo

Filament/filamento

Ovary/ovario

Stamen/
estambre

Petal/pétalo

Sepal/sépalo

Ovule/óvulo

Pollen grain/grano de polen

Stigma/estigma

Style/estilo

Pollen tube/tubo polínico

Ovule/óvulo

Ovary/ovario

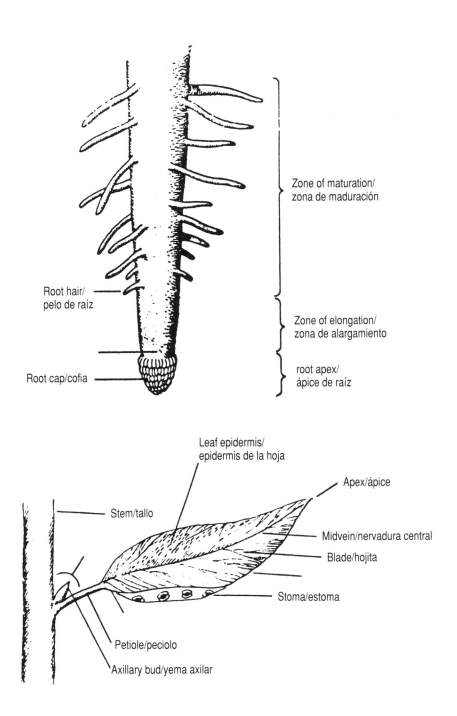

Zone of maturation/
zona de maduración

Root hair/
pelo de raíz

Zone of elongation/
zona de alargamiento

root apex/
ápice de raíz

Root cap/cofia

Leaf epidermis/
epidermis de la hoja

Apex/ápice

Stem/tallo

Midvein/nervadura central

Blade/hojita

Stoma/estoma

Petiole/peciolo

Axillary bud/yema axilar

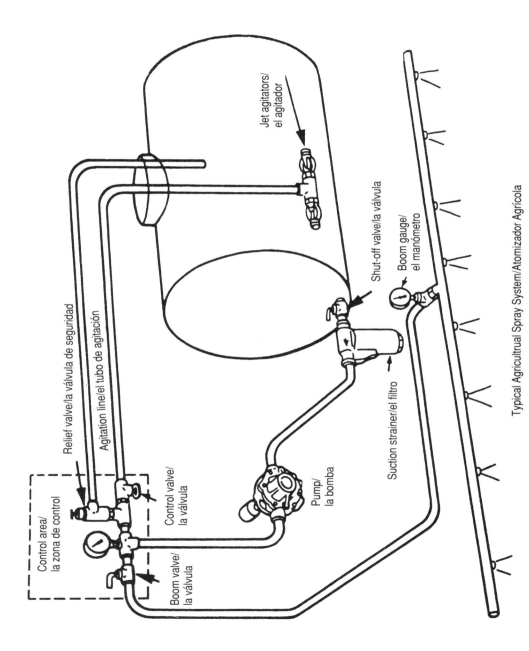

Jet agitators/
el agitador

Shut-off valve/la válvula

Boom gauge/
el manómetro

Relief valve/la válvula de seguridad

Agitation line/el tubo de agitación

Control valve/
la válvula

Suction strainer/el filtro

Pump/
la bomba

Control area/
la zona de control

Boom valve/
la válvula

Typical Agricultrual Spray System/Atomizador Agrícola

TOOLS/LAS HERRAMIENTAS

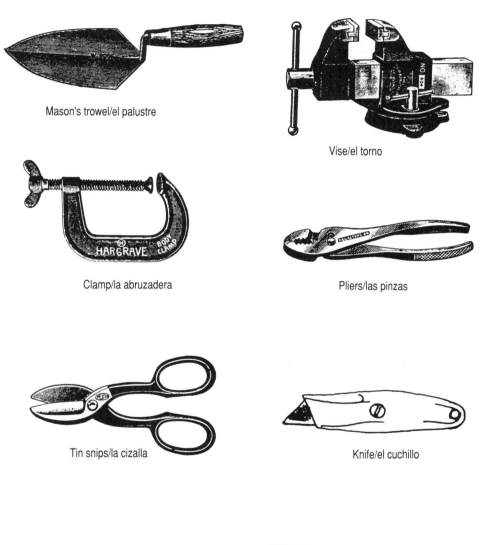

Mason's trowel/el palustre

Vise/el torno

Clamp/la abruzadera

Pliers/las pinzas

Tin snips/la cizalla

Knife/el cuchillo

Electric drill/el taladro eléctrico
Electric drill/la taladradora eléctrica

TOOLS/LAS HERRAMIENTAS

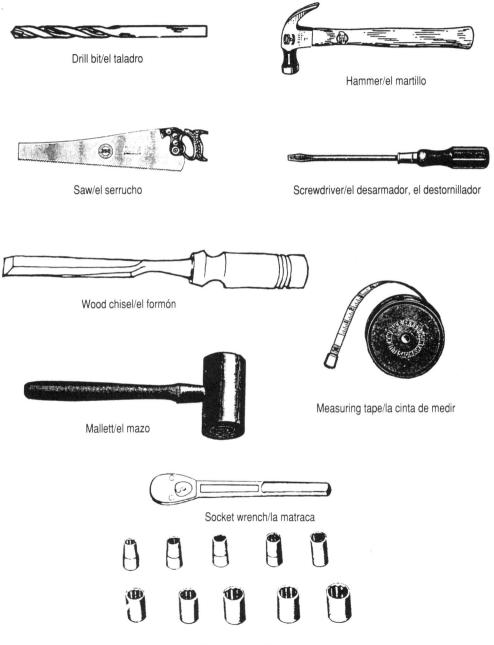

Drill bit/el taladro

Hammer/el martillo

Saw/el serrucho

Screwdriver/el desarmador, el destornillador

Wood chisel/el formón

Measuring tape/la cinta de medir

Mallett/el mazo

Socket wrench/la matraca

Sockets/los dardos

Plane/el cepillo de carpintero

Drill/el taladro

bolt	el perno	pliers	las pinzas
chain	la cadena	punch	el sacabocado
chisel, stone	el cincel	rope	el mecate
chisel, wood	el formón	screwdriver	el desarmador/
clamp	la abrazadera		el destornillador
drill	el taladro	screwdriver, Phillips	el desarmador de crux
drill bit	la broca	socket	el encaje
file	el afilador, la lima	soldering iron	el cautín
hacksaw	la seguenta	tape	la cinta
hammer	el martillo	tin snips	la cizalla
hasp	la aldabilla	trowel, builders	el palustre
knife	el cuchillo	turnbuckle	el tensor de alambre
level	el nivel	vise	el torno de banco
meter, electric	el contador eléctrico	welding machine	la soldadora
meter, water	el contador del agua	wingnut	la tuerca palomilla
nail	el clavo	wire	el alambre
nut	la tuerca	wrench	la llave
plane	el cepillo de carpintero	wrench, pipe	el estilson

VEGETABLES/LAS LEGUMBRES

Asparagus/el espárrago

Cabbage/el repollo

artichoke	la alcachofa
bean	las habichuelas, el frijol
beet	el betabel
beet	la remolacha
broccoli	el bróculi, *brécol*
brussels sprouts	las coles de bruselas
cabbage	el repollo
cauliflower	la coliflor
celeriac	el apio nabo
celery	el apio
chard	la acelga
chile pepper	el chile
chives	las cebollines
cilantro	el cilantro
cucumber	el pepino
eggplant	la berenjena
endive	la escarola, *endivia*
fennel	el hinojo
garlic	el ajo
green beans	los ejotes
kale	la col rizada
kohlrabi	el colinabo
leek	el puerro
lettuce	la lechuga
lima bean	el haba
melon	el melón
onion	la cebolla

Carrot/la zanahoria

Celery/el apio

Garlic/el ajo

palm, hearts of	el palmito
parsley	el perejil
peas	los guisantes
bell pepper	el chile ancho
chile pepper, green	el chile verde
potato	la papa
pumpkin	la calabaza
radish	el rábano
red bell pepper	el pimiento
red chile pepper	el chile colorado
rhubarb	el ruibarbo
rutabaga	el nabo sueco
spinach	la espinaca
squash, winter	la calabaza
sweet potato	la ~~patata~~ batata
tomato	el tomate
turnip	el nabo
watermelon	la sandía
zucchini	el zuquino
zucchini	el calabazín, la calabacita

Onion/la cebolla

PART TWO
SEGUNDA PARTE

ENGLISH – SPANISH
INGLÉS – ESPAÑOL

ENGLISH - SPANISH EQUIVALENTS

ENGLISH	SPANISH	ENGLISH	SPANISH
		aerial survey	reconocimiento m aéreo
		aerobic	aeróbico
- A -		aerobic	aeróbio
abortion	aborto m	aerobic bacterias	bacterias f pl aerobias
abrade, to	raer	aerology	aerología f
abscess	absceso m	aerosol	aerosol m
absentee owner	absentista f	aerosol spray	aspersión f a base de aerosol
absorb, to	absorber		
absorbent cotton	algodón m absorbente	African violet	santipaula f
absorption	absorción f	African violet	violeta f africana
accelerator	acelerador m	after-ripening	maduración f
accessory	aditamento m	after-ripening	post-maduración f
acclimation	aclimatación f	aftermath	segunda siega f
acclimatize, to	aclimatizar	agar	agar m
acetate	acetato m	agave	agave m
achene	aquenio m	Ageratum	agerato m
achillea	botón m de plata	aggregate	agregado m
acid	ácido m	aggregation	agregación f
acidify	acidificar	aging	envejecimiento m
aconitum	acónito m	agitator	agitador m
acorn	bellota f	agricultural	agraria
acreage	área (en acres)	agricultural chemicals	productos m agroquímicos
across	a través de	agricultural credit	crédito agrario
active ingredient	ingrediente m activo	agricultural engineer	ingeniero m agrícola
active ingredient	sustancia f activa	agricultural research	investigaciones agronómicas
add, to	agregar		
added value	valor m añadido	agriculture	agricultura f
adhesive	adhesivo m	agrobiology	agrobiología f
adsake bean	frijol m arroz, poroto m arroz	agronomist	agrónomo m
adsorb, to	adsorber	air conditioner	acondicionador m del aire
adsorption	adsorción m	air conditioning	climatización f
adsorption capacity	poder m de adsorción	air discharge	salida f del aire
advance (pay)	adelanto	air dried	secado al aire
advancement	adelanto m	air drying	secado m al aire
adventitious	adventicio	air duct	canal m de aireación
adventitious bud	yema f adventicia	air layering	acodo m al aire
advice	asesoramiento m	air pollution	contaminación f del aire impurificación f del aire polución f del aire
advisor	asesor m		
aerate, to	airear		
aeration	aereación	air supply	entrada f del aire
aerial	aéreo	air survey	reconocimiento m aereo
aerial dusting	espolvoreo m aéreo	air-layering	acodo m aéreo
aerial root	raíz f aérea	airplane	avión m
aerial seeding	siembra f aérea	airtight	hermético
aerial spraying	pulverización aérea, aspersión área	akee	seso m vegetal
		akee (Blighia sapida)	akí m

ENGLISH - SPANISH EQUIVALENTS

ENGLISH	SPANISH	ENGLISH	SPANISH
alanine	alanina f	analytical balance	equilibrio m analítico, balanza f
albumen	albúmina f	anaphase	anafase m
aleurone	aleurona f	anatomical	anatómico
aleurone layer	capa f aleuronífera	anatomy	anatomía f
alfalfa	alfalfa f	anchor, to	anclar
alfalfa field	alfalfar m, alfalfal m	andromonoecious	andromonoico m
alfalfa leaf meal	harina f de hojas de alfalfa	anemometer	anemómetro m
alkali	álcali m	anemone	anémona f
alkaline	alcalino	aneuploid	aneuploide m
alkaline	básico	angiosperm	angiosperma f
alkalinity	alcalinidad f	angular	anguloso
allelomorph	alelomorfo f	angular leaf spot	mancha f angular de la hoja
allelopathy	alelopatía f	anhydrous ammonia	amoníaco m
alley	callejon m	animal feed	alimento m para animales
allopolyploid	alopoliploide m	animal health	higiene f animal
alloy	aleación f	animal industry	ganadería f, producción f pecuaria
alluvial	aluvial	animal product	producto m animal
alluvial soil	aluvión m	animal production	zootecnia f, producción pecuaria
allysum	alhelicillo m	animal protein factor	factor m de proteína pecuaria
allysum, sweet	alhelicillo m	animal research	investigaciones f pecuarias
almond	almendra f	anion	anión m
almond tree	almendro m	anise	anís m
alstroemeria	peregrina f de Lima	Annatto tree (Bixa orellana)	achiote m
alternate	alternado	Annona sp.	anón m
alternate bearer	vecero m	annual	anual m
alternate bearing	añerismo m	annual ring	anillo m anual
altitude	altitud m	anopheles	anófeles
alum	alumbre m	ant	hormiga f
alveole	alvéolo m	antagonism	antagonismo m
alveolus	alvéolo m	anther	antera f
amaranthus ·	amaranto m	anthesis	antesis f
amaryllis	amarilis f	anthocyanin	antociano m
amendment	correctivo m	anthracnose	antracnosis f
amino acid	aminoácido m	anthrax	ántrax m
ammonia	hidróxido m amónico	anthurium	anturio m
ammonia	amoníaco	antineuritic	antineurítico m
ammonium	amonio m	antirrhinum	antirrino m
ammonium nitrate	nitrato m amónico	antiscorbutic factor	factor m antiescorbútico
amortization	amortización f	antiseptic	antiséptico m
amphidiploid	anfidiploide m	antitoxin	antitoxina f
anaerobic	anaerobio	anus	ano m
analogue	análogo m		
analysis	análisis m		
analysis report	boletín m de análisis		

ENGLISH - SPANISH EQUIVALENTS

ENGLISH	SPANISH	ENGLISH	SPANISH
aphicide	aficida f	arthropods	artrópodos
aphid	áfido m	artificial bee	abeja f mecánica
aphid	pulgón m	artificial light	luz artificial
apogamy	apogamia f	arum lily	aro m
apogamy	apogamia f	ascending	ascendente
apomixis	apomixis f	ascorbic acid	ácido m ascórbico
apomixis	apomixia f	aseptic	aséptico
apron (rubber)	delantal m de hule	asexual	asexual
apparent density	densidad f aparente	asexual	agámico
apparent specific gravity	peso m específico aparente	asexual propagation	multiplicación f asexual
appendix	apéndice m	ash	ceniza f
appetite	apetito m	asparagus	aspárrago m
appetizing	apetecible	asparagus bean	segadilla f
apple	manzana f	asparagus fern	espárrago m ornamental
apple aphid	áfido m verde de manzana	asparagus, ornamental	espárrago m ornamental
apple aphid	pulgón m verde de manzana	assay	ensayo m
		assimilate, to	asimilar
apple juice	jugo m de manzana	assimilation products	productos m de asimilación
apple sauce	pasta f de manzana	assortment	surtido m
apple syrup	jarabe m de manzana	aster	aster m or reina Margarita f
apple tree	manzano m	atmosphere	atmósfera f
application	aplicación f	atmospheric pressure	presión f atmosférica
applicator	aplicadora f	atomic weight	peso m atómico
apply, to	aplicar	atomize, to	atomizar
appraisal	avalúo m	atomizer	atomizador m
apricot	albaricoque m	attach	acoplar
apricot	chabacano m	attached	adjunto m
apricot tree	albaricoquero m	attachment	accesorio m
aquaculture	acuicultura f	attack	ataque m
aquatic	acuático	attack, to	atacar, infestar
aquatic plant	planta f acuática	attractant	atrayente m
arable	arable, cultivable	auction	remate m, subasta f
arable land	tierra f labrantía	auction clock	reloj m de subasta
arbor	parral m	auction costs	costes m de subasta
arboriculture	arboricultura f	auction market	subasta f
arborist	arbolista m	autoclave	autoclave m
area (surface area)	área f	autogamous	autugama f
arid	árido, seco	automatic	automático
aridity	aridez f	autopolyploid	autopoliploide
armyworm	gusano m cortador	autumn crocus	cólquico m de otoño
aromatic	aromático	auxin	auxina f
arsenical compound	compuesto m arsenical	available	aprovechable
arteriole	arteriola f	available	asimilable
artery	arteria f	available (nutrients)	asimilable
arthropod	artrópodo m	available (nutrients)	disponible

ENGLISH - SPANISH EQUIVALENTS

ENGLISH	SPANISH	ENGLISH	SPANISH
avalanche	alud m	baling machine	enfardadora f
avenue tree	árbol m de paseo	ball (i.e. root ball)	cepellón m
average price	precio m medio	ball valve	válvula f de bola
average yield	rendimiento m medio	balsam	balsamina f
avocado	aguacate m	bamboo	bambú m
awn	arista f, barba de la espiga	banana	banana f, plátano m
awning	toldo m	banana	guineo m
axe	hacha f	band	tira f
axil	axila f	bank loan	crédito m bancario
axillary	axilar	barbed wire	alambre m de púas
axillary bud	yema f axilar	barberry (Berberis spp.)	arlo m
axle	eje m	bare ground	terreno m limpio
axle, front	eje m delantero	bareroot	raíz f desnuda
axle, rear	eje m trasero	barge	lanchón m
azalea	azalea f	bark	corteza f
		bark beetle	escarabajo m de la corteza
		barley	cebada f
		barn	establo m
- B -		barn	galpón
		barnyard	corral m
back-cross	retrocruza f	barnyard grass	mijo m japonés
back-cross, to	retrocruzar	barrel	tonel m, barril m
backcross	retrocruzamiento m	barren	estéril
backfurrow	contrasurco m	barrow	cerdo m castrado
bacon	tocino m bácon m, báicon m	basal plate (bulb)	base f del bulbo
bacteria	bacteria f	base exchange	intercambio m de bases o cationes
bacterial	bacterial		
bactericidal	bactericido	basic commodities	artículos m de primera necesidad
bactericide	bactericida f		
bacteriologist	bacteriólogo m	basic crops	cosechas f principales
bacteriology	bacteriología f	basic crops	cultivos m básicos
bacteriophage	bacteriófago	basil	albahaca f
bag	saco m	basin irrigation	riego m en casuela
Bahiagrass	hierba f Bahía	basin irrigation	riego m por compartimientos
bait	cebo m		
bake, to	hornear	basket	canasta f
balance (financial)	saldo m	basket	cesta f
balanced diet	régimen m alimenticio equilibrado	basket	cesto m
		beaker	vaso m con pequeño pico
balcony plant	planta f de balcón	bean	frijol m
bale loader	cargador m de balas	bean	habichuela f
bale of straw	bala f de paja	bearings	baleros m
bale of straw	fardo m de paja	bed (garden)	cama f
baling	embalaje	bed (river)	cauce m
baling machine	embaladora f	bed rock	roca f madre

ENGLISH - SPANISH EQUIVALENTS

ENGLISH	SPANISH	ENGLISH	SPANISH
bee	abeja f	birch	abedul m
beehive	colmena f	bird	ave m
beekeeper	apicultor m	bird (small)	pájaro m
beekeeping	apicultura f	birdsfoot trefoil	cuernecillo m
beet, redbeet	remolacha f	birth	nacimiento m
beetle	escarabajo m	birth rate	natalidad f
begonia	begonia f	biscuit	galleta f
bell jar	campana f de cristal	bisexual	bisexual
	fanal m,	bitter	amargo
bell shaped	campaniforme	bitter pit	enfermedad no parasítica
bellows	fuelle m		de la manzana
belly	barriga f	bittersweet	agridulce
belly	panza f	bivalent	bivalente m
belt	correa f de transmisión	bivalent	divalente m
belt conveyor	correa f transportadora	black bean	habichuela f negra
	cinta f de transporte	black cherry	cereza f negra
bench	banco m	black currant	grosella f negra
bench (greenhouse)	tabla f, banco m	black mold	fumagina f
bench terrace	terraza f de banco	black mold	negrón m
bench terrace	terraza f de escalones	black nightshade	hierba m mora
berm	berma f, cheque m	black radish	rábano m negro
Bermudagrass	pasto m bermuda	black rot	pudrición f negra
Bermudagrass	hierba f Bermuda	black walnut	nogal m negro
berry	baya f	blackberry (fruit)	zarzamora f
BHC	hexacloruro m de benzeno	blackberry plant	zarza f
bibliography	bibliografía f	blackleg	carbunco m sintomático
bid	oferta f	blade (botanical)	limbo m
bid, to	ofrecer	blade (of grass)	hojita f
bid, to	proponer	blanket application	aplicación f total
biennial	bienal	blast	abortamiento m
biennial bearing	producción f alterna	bleaching	blanqueo m
bin	cajón m	bleeding heart	corazón m sangrante
bin, to	guardar en cajones	bleeding heart plant	dicentra f
binder	agavilladora f	blight	tizón m
binder	atadora f	blister	ampolia f
bindweed	correguela f menor	blister	vejiga f
bindweed	volúbilis m	blister rust	roya f vesicular
bioclimatology	bioclimatología f	blizzard	tormenta f de nieve
biological	biológico m	bloat, to	hincharse
biological control	control m biológico	bloat, to	inflamarse
biology	biología f	block (as in nursery)	bloque m
biometry	biometría f	blood lily	lirio m de sangre
biotin	biotina f	blood meal	harina f de sangre
biotype	biotipo m	blood orange	naranja f roja
bipinnate	bipinado	blood orange	naranja f sanguínea

ENGLISH - SPANISH EQUIVALENTS

ENGLISH	SPANISH	ENGLISH	SPANISH
bloodmeal	harina f de sangre	box, to	encajonar
bloom (wax on fruit)	pruina f	brace, to	apoyar
blossom	flor f	brackish water	agua m salobre
blower	sopladora f	bract	bráctea f
blower	ventilador m	brake	breca f
blowtorch	soplete m	brake drum	tambor m
blue tongue	fiebre f catarral	brake lining	cinta f breca
blue tongue	lengua f azul	brake shoe	zapato m
bluegrass	pasto f azul de Kentucky	bramble	zarza f
bluegum	ocalo m	brambleberry	zarzamora f
blueprint	cianotipia f	bran	afrecho m
blueprint	fotocalco m	bran	salvado m
blueprint	plano m	branch	rama f
bluestem	andropogón m	branch out, to	ramificarse
blunt	obtuso	branched	ramificado
board	tabla f	branding iron	hierro m de marcar
bog	pantano m	brass	latón m
bog	turbera f	bread	pan m
boil, to	hervir	break, to	romper
boiler	caldera f	breakdown	avería f
boll	cápsula f de algodón	breakdown (decomposition)	descomposición f
boll weevil	picudo m del algodón	breakdown, to	dañarse
bone meal	harina f de huesos	breaking	rompimiento m
bonus	pago m extraordinario	breed, to	criar
book value	valor m contable	breed, to	reproducirse
boot	bota f	breeder	criador m
borage	borraja f	breeding	majoramiento m genético
borax	bórax m	Brewer's dried yeast	levadura f de cerveza desecada
Bordeaux mixture	caldo m bordelés	bridging	pontoneado m
borer	barrenador m	bright	claro
borer	perforador m	brine	salmuera f
boron	boro m	bristle	cerda f
borrow, to	tomar prestado, pedir prestado	broad-leafed tree	árbol m frondoso
boss	jefe m	broadcast (ag.)	al voleo
botanical	botánico	broadcast application	distribucíon f al voleo
botany	botánica f	broadcast seed, to	sembrar al voleo
botfly	moscardón m	broadcast seeding	siembra f al voleo
botfly	tórsalo m	broccoli	bróculi m
botrytis	botritis m	broiler (chicken)	pollo n para asar
bottom heat	calor m del suelo	broker	corredor m
bouquet	ramillete m	brome grass	bromo m
bouquet of flowers	ramo m de flores	bronze	bronce m
bowel	intestino m	broom	escoba f
box elder	negondo m	broomrape	orobanca f

ENGLISH - SPANISH EQUIVALENTS

ENGLISH	SPANISH	ENGLISH	SPANISH
broomrape	orobanche m	bull	toro m
browning	pardeamiento m	bulldozer	explanadora f
browse	ramonear	bulldozer	niveladora f
brucellosis	brucelosis m	bulletin (extension)	folleto m, boletín m
bruise	magulladura f	bulrush	tule m, junco m
bruise, to	magullar	bumble bee	abejón m
brush	cepillo m	bumble bee	abejorro m
brush (plants)	broza f	bunch (grapes)	racimo m
brush killer	matabrozas f	bunsen burner	mechero m Bunsen
brush, to	cepillar	bur clover	trébol m de carretilla
Brussels sprouts	col f de Bruselas	burdock	bardana f
bryobia	ácaro	burette	bureta f
buchner funnel	embudo m Buchner	burlap	harpillera f
buck (goat)	cabro m	burner	quemador m
bucket	cubeta f, balde m	burning	agostamiento
buckwheat	alforfón m	burning	quema f
bud	yema f	burst, to	romper
bud scale	escama f de la yema	bush	arbusto m
bud sport	mutación f en los brotes	butcher's broom (Ruscus)	rusco m
bud, to	brotar	butterfly	mariposa f
bud, to (graft)	injertar	by-product	derivado m
budding knife	cuchilla f de injertar	by-product	subproducto m
budding, chip	injerto m de astilla		
budding, flute	injerto m de flauta		
budding, inverted T	injerto m en "T" invertida		
budding, patch	injerto m de parche	**- C -**	
budding, ring	injerto m anular		
budding, T	injerto m de yema en "T"	cabbage	repollo m
budget	presupuesto m	cactus	cacto m
budsport	mutación f de yema	caecum	ciego m
budwood	portayema f	caimo (Pouteria caimito)	abiú m, caimo m
budworm	gusano m de las yemas	caladium	caladio m, malanga f
buffalo grass	yerba f búfalo	calcareous	calcáreo
buffer	amortiguador m	calcareous soil	tierra f calcárea
buffer	tampón m	calceolaria	calceolaria f
buffer strip	faja f de contención	calcium	calcio m
bug	insecto m	calcium carbonate	carbonato m cálcico
bug (true bug)	chinche f	calcium cyanamid	cianimido de calcio m
bulb (botanical)	bulbo f	calcium nitrate	nitrato de calcio m
bulb (light)	bombilla f	calendula	caléndula f
bulb scale	escama f de bulbo	calf	ternero m
bulbous	bulbiforme	calibrate, to	calibrar
bulbous plant	planta f bulbosa	caliche	caliche m
bulk	volumen m	California pepper tree	turbinto m
bulk bin	paleta f caja	caliper	calibrador m

ENGLISH - SPANISH EQUIVALENTS

ENGLISH	SPANISH	ENGLISH	SPANISH
calla	lirio m calla	carbohydrate	hidrato m de carbono m
callus	callo m	carbon	carbono m
callus	callosidad f	carbon bisulfide	bisulfuro m de carbono m
calm	calma f	carbon dioxide	dióxido m de carbono
calorie	caloría f	carbonate	carbonato m
calorimeter	calorímetro m	carcass	cadáver m de animal
calving season	época f en que las vacas paren	carcass (dressed)	canal m
		carcass weight	peso m en canal
calyx	cáliz m	cardboard	cartón m
cam (engine)	lleva f	cardboard	cartón m ondulado
cambium	cambium m	cardboard box	caja f de cartón
camellia	camelia f	cardboard, corrugated	cartón m ondulado
camphor	alcanfor m	cardoon	cardo m
camshaft	árbol de levas m	carnation	clavel m
can	lata f	carob fruit	algarroba f
can, to	enlatar	carotene (biochem.)	caroteno m
can, to	poner en latas	carotene (chem.)	carotina f
canal	canal m	carpel	carpelo m
canary grass	alpiste m	carpetgrass	hierba f alfombra
candytuft (annual)	zarapico m anual	carrier	sustancia f portadora
candytuft (perennial)	zarapico m	carrot	zanahoria f
cane of bamboo	caña f de bambú	carry over	remanente m
canker	cancro m	caryopsis	cariópside m
canna	caña f de las Indias	case, to (mushroom growing)	cubrir
canned fruit	frutas f conservadas en lata	cash	dinero m efectivo
cannery	enlatadora f	cash crops	cultivos m comerciales
canopy	dosel m	cash crops	cultivos m industriales
cantaloupe	melón m	cashew	anacardo m
canvas	lona f	cashew	cajuil m, nueces f de la India
cap	cachucha f		
cape gooseberry	uchuba f	casings	envolturas f
caper	alcaparra f	cask	tonel m
capillarity	capilaridad f	cassava	yuca f
capillary action	acción f capilar	castor bean	semilla f de ricino
capillary tension	tensión f capilar	castor plant	palmacristi f
capillary vessel	vaso m capilar	castrate, to	capar
capillary water	agua m capilar	castrate, to	castrar
capital cost	gastos m iniciales de establecimiento	catch crop	cultivo m intermedio
		catchment area	cuenca f colectora
capital turnover	evolución f del capital	catchment basin	vaso m de captación
capon	capón m	caterpillar	oruga f
capsicum	ají m	caterpillar tractor	oruga f
capsule (bot)	cápsula f	caterpillar tractor	tractor m de oruga
caraway	alcaravea f	catmint	nébeda f
carbohydrate	carbohidrato m	cat's ears (weed)	orejas f de gato

ENGLISH - SPANISH EQUIVALENTS

ENGLISH	SPANISH	ENGLISH	SPANISH
cattle	ganado m vacuno	cheat	bromo m secalino
cattle	vacunos m	check, to	verificar
cattle industry	industria f pecuaria	cheese	queso m
cattle ranch	estancia f	chelate	quelato m
cattle ranch	hacienda f ganadera	chemical	químico m
cattle sanitation	sanidad f pecuaria	chemical compound	compuesto m químico
cattleman	ganadero m	chemical reaction	reacción f química
cauliflower	coliflor f	chemist	químico m
caustic	cáustico m	chemistry	química f
caustic soda	soda f cáustica	chemotropism	quimiotropismo m
cave	cueva f	cherry	cereza f
ceanothus	ceanoto m	chervil	perifolio m
cedar	cedro m	chestnut	castaño m
celery	apio m	chew	masticar
cell	célula f	chick	pollito m
cell divison	división f de célula	chick	polluelo m
cell membrane	membrana f de la célula	chicken manure	gallinaza f
cell sap	protoplasma m	chickpea	chícharo m
cell wall	pared f celular	chickpea	garbanzo m
cell wall	pared m de la célula	chickweed	oreja f de ratón
cellar	sótano m	chickweed	pamplina f pajarera
cellulose	celulosa f	chicle	chicle m
cement	cemento m	chicory	achicoría f
cementing materials	materiales m de cementación	chigger	nigua f
		chimera	quimera f
census	censo m	chimera, mericlinal	quimera f mericlinal
centiliter	centilitro m	chimera, periclinal	quimera f periclinal
centipede	ciempiés m	chimera, sectorial	quimera f sectorial
central leader	tronco m guía	chimney	chimenea f
centrifugal	centrífugo	China aster	reina f margarita
centrifugal pump	bomba f centrífuga	Chinese cabbage	col f de China
centrifuge	centrífuga f	Chinese cabbage	repollo f de China
centrosome	centrosoma f	chisel	escopio m
cereal	cereal m	chisel	formón m
chafer	escarabajo m roedor	chisel-subsoiler	arado m de subsuelo
chafer, garden	abejorro m	chive	ceboleta f
chaff	cáscara f	chive	cebollín f
chain	cadena f	chloride	cloruro m
chain saw	sierra f de cadena	chlorine	cloro m
chalk	tiza f	chlorophyll	clorofila f
character	carácter m	chloropicrin	cloropicrina f
chart	gráfica f	chlorosis	clorosis f
chart	lista f	cholera	cólera f
chart	tabla f	choline	colina f
chayote	tayota f	chop	chuleta f

ENGLISH - SPANISH EQUIVALENTS

ENGLISH	SPANISH	ENGLISH	SPANISH
chopper	desmenuzadora f	clip, to	esquilar
chore	tarea f	clivia	lirio m kafir
chromatid	cromátida f	cloche	compana m
chromatin	cromatina f	clod	mota f
chromophore	cromóforo m	clod	terrón m
chromosome	cromosoma f	clod (soil)	terrón m de tierra
chrysanthemum	crisantemo m	clod, (soil)	mota f
chufa	chufa f	clone	clon m
churn	mantequero m	closet	armario m de pared
churning action	acción f de batimiento	clover	trébol m
chute	canal m de descarga	clubroot	hernia f de la col
chute	manga f	clump	grupo m,
cider	cidra f	cluster	macollo m
cider	sidra f	cluster (bot)	ramillete m
cider factory	sidrería f	clutch (i.e. car)	embrague m, cloche m
ciliate	ciliado	co-op	cooperativa f
cinchona	quino m	co-ordinates	coordenadas f
cineraria	cineraria f	coarse	grueso
cinnamon	canela f	coastal marsh	marisma f costera
circuit (electrical)	circuito m	coating	enlucido m
circular	circular	cobalt	cobalto m
circulation	circulación f	cobweb	tela f de araña
citric acid	ácido m cítrico	cochineal	cochinilla f
citrus fruit	frutas f cítricas	cock	gallo m
citrus meal	harina f de agrios desecados	cocklebur	bardana f menor
		cockscomb	cresta f de gallo
clabber	cuajada f de leche agria	coconut	coco m
cladding	revestimiento m	cocoon	capullo m
clamp	mordaza f	cocoyam	yautía f
clary	tárrago m	cod liver oil	aceite m de hígado de bacalao
clary sage	ormino m		
clay	arcilla f	coefficient of variability	coeficiente m de variación
clay soil	suelo m arcilloso	coenzyme	coenzima f
clayey	arcillosa	cogongrass	cogón m
clean, to	limpiar	cohesion	cohesión f
clear, to	socolar	colchicine	coquicina f
clearing house	centro m de distribución	colchicum	cólquico m
clematis	clemátide f	cold chain	cadena f de frío
climate	clima m	cold chisel	cincel m
climate control	control m climático	cold frame	cajonera f
climatic conditions	condición f climatológica	cold frame	cajonera f fría
climatology	climatología f	cold storage	conservación f frigorifico
climb, to	trepar	cold storage	conservación f por el frió
climbing	trepador m	coldframe	cama f fría
clime	clima m	coleus	coleo

ENGLISH - SPANISH EQUIVALENTS

ENGLISH	SPANISH
collar	cuello m
colloid	coloide m
colloidal	coloidal
colon	colon m
colony	colonia f
color	color m
colt	potrillo m
colt	potro m
columbine	aguileña f
columbine	pajarilla f
column	columna f
combine	combinada f
combine	cosechadora-trilladora f
combining ability	aptitud f combinatoria
combustion chamber	cámara f de combustión, competición f rivalidad f
commodity	producto m
commodity exchange	intercambio m de mercancías
communal farming	explotación f agrícola colectiva
communal land tenure	régimen m comunal agrario
communal pastures	pastos m comunales
community	comunidad f
compact	apelmazado
compact, to	condensar
compactness	apelmazamiento m
companion crop	cultivo m asociado
comparative costs	costos m comparativos
compass	brújula f
compatibility	compatibilidad f
compete, to	competir
competition	competencia f competición f rivalidad f
complementary genes	genes m complementarios
complete fertilizer	abono m completo
completion	terminación f
compost	compost m
compost heap	montón m de abono vegetal
compost pile	montón m de mantillo
compost, to	fermentar
compound	compuesto m
compound (bot.)	compuesto
compound (chemical)	compuesto m químico
compound fertilizer	abono m compuesto
compress, to	apelmazar

ENGLISH	SPANISH
compressed air sprayer	pulverizador m de aire comprimido
compressibility	compresibilidad f
compressor	compresor m
concave	cóncavo
concentrate	concentrado m
concentrate	pienso m concentrado
concentration	concentración f
condensation	condensación f
condense, to	condensar
condenser	condensador m
conduit	conducto m
confinement	encierro m
congestion	congestión f
conical	cónico
conifer	conífera f
connecting rod	biela f
connective	conectivo
conservationist	conservacionista f
consistency	consistencia f
construction	construcción f
consumer	consumidor m
consumer goods	artículos m de consumo
consumption	consumo m
contact action	acción de contacto
contact poison	tóxico m de contacto
contact poison	tóxico m de contacto
container	envase m
container	recipiente m
containers	embalaje m
contaminate, to	contaminar
contamination	contaminación
content	contenido m
contour	contorno m
contour	curva f de nivel
contour planting	siembra f a nivel
contour plowing	aradura f en curvas de nivel
contract work	trabajo m contratado
contractil root	raíz f contráctil
contraction	contracción f
control	control m
control measure	medida f de control
control sample	muestra f testigo
controlled atmosphere storage	conservación f en atmósfera controlada

ENGLISH - SPANISH EQUIVALENTS

ENGLISH	SPANISH	ENGLISH	SPANISH
controlled droplet application	sistema m de aspersión de tama	cotton picker	cosechadora f de algodón
		cotton stainer	chinche m tintóreo
controlled flooding	inundación f regulada	cotton stripper	recogedora f de algodón
convex	convexo	cottonseed	semilla f de algodón
conveyer belt	cinta f de transporte	cottonseed cake	torta f de algodón
convolution	circunvolución f	cottonseed meal	harina f de algodón
cool, to	enfriar	cottonwood tree	álamo m
cooler	refrigerador m	cotyledon	cotiledón m
cooling	refrigeración f	couchgrass	grama f del Norte
coop	gallinero m	cougar	puma
cooperation	cooperación f	coulter	reja f del arado
cooperative	cooperativa f	count, to	contar
copper	cobre m	counter (i.e. in a shop)	mostrador m
copper sulphate	sulfato m de cobre	country	campo m
copra	copra f	county	condado m
cordate	cordiforme	county agent	agente m de extensión
cordon	cordón m	coupling	enganche m
core	corazón m	cover	cobertura f
core (of apple etc.)	antro m	cover, to	revestir
coreopsis	coreopsis m	cover crop	cultivo m de cobertura
coriander	cilantro m	cover slip	cubreobjeto m
cork	corcho m	cover up, to	tapar
corm	tubérculo m caulino	cover with a top, to	tapar
corn chamomile	manzanilla f silvestre	coverage (of a pesticide)	cobertura f
cornbelt	zona f del maíz	covering material	material m de cobertura
corncob	tusa f de maíz	cow	vaca f
cornflower		cowboy	vaquero m
__(Centaurea cyanus)	azulina f	cowpea	caupí m
corolla	corola f	cowpea	frijol m de vaca
corona	corona f	cowpea	rabiza f
corporation	sociedad f anónima (S.A.)	cowshed	vaquería f
correlation	correlación f	crack	quiebra f
corrosion	corrosión m	cracking	agrietamiento m
corsage	ramillete m	cracklings	chicharrones m
corymb	corimbo m	cranberry	arándano m agrio
cosmos	cosmos m	crank	manivela f
cost accounting	contabilidad f sobre la producción	crank handle	cigüeña f
cost of production	costo m de producción	crankcase	caja f del motor
costly	costoso	crankshaft	cigüeñal m
costs	costes m	crate	jaula f
costs of establishment	coste m de instalación	crate, to	embalar en jaula,
cotter pin	chaveta f	crawler tractor	oruga f
cotton belt	zona f algodonera	crawler tractor	tractor m de orugas
cotton field	algodonal m	credit	crédito m

38

ENGLISH - SPANISH EQUIVALENTS

ENGLISH	SPANISH	ENGLISH	SPANISH
creek	arroyo m	crystallize, to	cristalizar
creek	zanjón	cucumber	pepino m
crenate	dentado	culinary herbs	hierbas f de cocina
cress	lepidio m	cull, to	entresacar
crested wheatgrass	agropiro m crestado	culm	caña f
crew (work)	cuadrilla f	culm	talla f de los cereales
crib	pesebre m	cultipacker	rodillo compactador m
crinkle virus	rizadura f	cultipacker	rolo m
crisp	crespo	cultivate, to	cultivar
crocus	crocus m	cultivation	cultivo m
crooked	chueca	culture	cultura f
crop	cosecha f	culture, pure	cultura f pura
crop	cultivo m	culture, starter	cultura f iniciadora
crop	sembrado m	culture, to	cultivar
crop failure	pérdida f de la cosecha	cuneate	cuneiforme
crop insurance	seguro m de cosechas	cup	taza f
crop records	registro m de cultivos	cup shaped	vasiforme
crop residue	residuo m de cosecha	curd	cuajado m
crop rotation	rotación f de cultivos	cure	cura f
crop row	surco m	cure, to	curar
cropland	tierra f cultivable	curl, to	encrespar
cropping delay	retraso m de la cosecha	curling	abarquillamiento m
cropping plan	plan m de cultivo	curling	ensortijamiento m
cropping system	sistema m de cultivos	curly	crespo
cross	cruce m	curly	rizado
cross pollination	polinización f cruzada	curly top	abarquillado m de las hojas
cross, to	cruzar	currant	grosella f
cross-fertilization	fertilización f cruzada	current (electrical)	corriente m
crossbred	cruzado m	cut back, to	rebajar
crossbreeding	cruzamiento m	cut flower	flor f cortada
crossing over	entrecruzamiento m	cut foliage	hoja f ornamental
crow	cuervo m	cutaway disk	rastra f de discos recortados
crown	corona f		
crown (tree)	copa f	cutting (propagation)	estaca f
crown gall	agalla f de los pomos	cutting edge	filo m
crucible	crisol m	cutting, hardwood	estaca f de madera f dura
crude	basto	cutting, leaf	estaca f de hoja
crude	crudo	cutting, leafy	estaca f foliáceas
crude fiber	fibra f cruda	cutting, semi-hardwood	estaca f de madera f semidura
crush, to	triturar	cutting, softwood	estaca f de madera f suave
crushed grain	grano m triturado	cutworm	gusano m cortador
crushed limestone	piedra f caliza molida	cyanamide	cianamida f
crusher (grapes)	estrujadora f	cyclamen	ciclamen m
crust	costra f	cyclamen	pamporcino m

ENGLISH - SPANISH EQUIVALENTS

ENGLISH	SPANISH	ENGLISH	SPANISH
Cyclamen spp.	artanita f	daylily	lirio m de San Juan
Cyclamen spp.	ciclamen f	de-alkalize, to	desalcalizar
cycle	ciclo m	dead weight	peso m limpio
cyclic lighting	iluminación f cíclica	debris	desecho m
cylinder	cilindro m	debt	deuda f
cyme	cima f	decade	decenio m
cyst	agalla m	decay	putrefacción f
cyst	quiste m	decay, to	pudrir
cyst nematode	nematodo m cecidio	decayed	carcomido
		deciduous	caduco
		deciduous	de hojas f caducas
		deciduous tree	árbol m deciduo
		declination	declinación f
	- D -	decompose, to	descomponerse
		decomposition	descomposición f
		decorative plant	planta f de adorno
daffodil	narciso m	decumbent	rastrero
dahlia	dalia f	decussate	decusado
daily feed	comida f diaria	deed	título m calificativo de propiedad
dairy	lechería f		
dairy products	productos m lácteos	deep plow, to	arar profundamente
dairyman	lechero m	deep rooting	de enraizamiento profundo
daisy	margarita f	deep-rooted	arraigado
Dallis grass	hierba f Dallis	deepen, to	profundizar
dam	represa f	deferred grazing	pastoreo m diferido
damage	daño m	deficiency (disease)	carencia f
damage, to	dañar	deficiency disease	enfermedad f carencial
damp	húmedo	deficiency of rain	falta f de lluvia
damper	registro m	deficiency symptom	síntoma m de carencia
damper	ventanilla f	deficiency symptoms	síntomas m carenciales
damping off	caída f de almácigo	deficient in lime	pobre en cal
damping off	mal m de los semilleros	deficit	déficit m
damping off	mal m de semillero	deflocculate, to	deflocular
dandelion	diente m de león	defoliate, to	deshojar
dark	oscuro m	defoliate, to	deshojarse
darken, to	obscurecer	defoliating machine	máquina f deshojadora
darken, to	oscurecerse	defoliation	defoliación f
darkening	obturación f	defoliator	deshojador m
data	datos m	deforestation	desmontadura f
date (fruit)	dátil m	deformed	deforme
date grove	palmeral m	degenerate, to	degenerar
date palm	palma f datilera	degeneration	degeneración f
day	día m	degraded	degradado
daylight	luz f del día	degree	grado m
daylight	luz f diurna	degree of saturation	grado m de saturación

ENGLISH - SPANISH EQUIVALENTS

ENGLISH	SPANISH	ENGLISH	SPANISH
dehiscent fruit	fruto m deshicente	detergent	detergente m
dehorn, to	descornar	deteriorate, to	deteriorarse
dehydrate	secar	deterioration	deterioro m
dehydrate, to	deshidratar	developing countries	países m en vía de desarrollo
dehydrate, to	secar	deviation	desviación f
dehydration	deshidratación f	dew retting	enriaje m por los elementos
dehydration plant	secadero m de verduras	diagnosis	diagnosis m
delay	retardación f	dial	esfera f
delay	retraso m	diaphragm pump	bomba f de membrana
deletion	supresión f	diarrhea	diarrea f
delivery	entrega f	dibasic	dibásico
deltoid	deltoide	dibble	escardillo m
demand, to	requerir	dibble	plantador m
demineralization	desmineralización f	dicalcium phosphate	bisuperfosfato m cálcico
demonstrate, to	demostrar	die, to	morir
demonstration	demostración f	die-back	acronecrosis m
demonstration farm	finca f de demostración	die-back	gangrena f regresiva
denitrify, to	desnitrificar	diet	dieta f
dense	denso	differential	diferencial f
density	densidad f	differentiation	diferenciación
dent	abolladura f	differing	diferente
dentate	dentado	dig up, to	arrancar
department store	almacenes m	dig, to	cavar
department store	tienda f por departamento	digestible	digerible
depletion	agotamiento m	digestible nutrient	nutrimento m digerible
deposit, to	depositar	digestion	digestión f
deposited, to be	depositarse	digitate	digitada
depreciation	depreciación f	digitate	palmeado compuesto
depression	depresión f del terreno	dike	dique m
depression	depresión f	dill	aneldo m, abesón m
depth	profundidad f	dill	eneldo m
depth of drainage	profundidad f del drenaje	dilution	dilución f
depth of soil	profundidad f del suelo	dilutor	diluidor m
descending	descendente	dinitrophenol	dinitrofenol m
descent	descendencia f	dioecious	dioico
desert	desierto m	dip	baño m garrapaticida
deserted	abandonado m	dip, to	sumergir
desiccate, to	desecar	diploid	diploide
desiccation	desecación f	diplont	generación f diploide
design	diseño m	dipping vat	baño m de inmersión
design of experiments	disposición f experimental	directions for use	modo m de empleo
design, to	diseñar	disbud, to	desbotonar
dessiccator	desecador	disbud, to	desyemar
detach, to	desprender	disbudding	desbrote m
detassel, to	despanojar		

ENGLISH - SPANISH EQUIVALENTS

ENGLISH	SPANISH	ENGLISH	SPANISH
disc coulter	reja f circular	dotted	punteado
disc harrow	grada f de discos	double	doble
discolored	descolorido	double cross	híbrido m doble
disease	enfermedad f	double flower	flor f doble
disease control	control m de enfermedades	double nose (bulb)	nariz f doble
disease resistance	resistencia f a las enfermedades	double superphosphate	bisuperfosfato m
		double-working	injerto m intermedio
disease symptom	síntoma m de enfermedad	downpour	chaparrón m
diseased	enfermo	downy mildew	mildiú m moho m
disinfectant	desinfectante m	draft (air)	corriente f de aire
disinfection	desinfección f	drag, to	arrastrar
disk	disco m	drain cock	grifo m de vaciado
disk harrow	rastra f de discos	drain pipe	tubo m de drenaje
disk plow	arado m de discos	drain valve	válvula de desagüe
disking	disqueo m	drain, to	avenar
dissemination	diseminación f	drain, to	desaguar
dissolve, to	disolver	drain, to	drenar
distal	distal	drainage	desagüe
distemper	moquillo m	drainage	drenaje m
distillate	destilado m	drainage basin	cuenca f de desagüe
distribute, to	distribuir	drainage ditch	cuneta f
distribution	distribución f	drainage ditch	zanja f de desagüe
distribution channel	canal m de distribución	drawer	gaveta f
distributor	distribuidor m	dredge, to	dragar
disulfide	bisulfuro m	dressing percent	porcentaje de partes utilizables de un animal
ditch	zanja f		
ditchdigger	zanjadora f	dried	seco
diurnal	diurno	drier	secadora f
diversified	diversificado	drill	taladro m
diversified farming	agricultura f diversificada	drill (fertilizer)	abonadora f mecánica
diversion ditch	zanja f de desvío	drill (seeder)	sembradora f de surcos
divide, to (bot)	multiplicar por división	drill coulter	reja f de sembradora
division of labor	división f del trabajo	drill hoe	marcador m
dock, to	atracar	drill, to	taladrar
dodder	cúscuta f	drizzle	llovizna f
dolomite	dolomita f	drizzle, to	rociar
dominance	dominación f	drone	zángano m
dominance	dominancia f	drop	gota f
dominant	dominante	drop formation	formación f de gotas
dormancy	estado m latente	drop in temperature	enfriamiento m
dormancy	reposo m invernal	dropping of buds	caída f de yemas
dormant bud	yema f dormida	drosophila	drosófila f
dormant period	período m de reposo	drought	sequía f
dosage	dosificación	drug	medicamento m
dotted	moteado	drupe, stone fruit	fruto m de hueso

ENGLISH - SPANISH EQUIVALENTS

ENGLISH	SPANISH	ENGLISH	SPANISH
dry	secar		**- E -**
dry cell battery	pila f		
dry farming	agricultura f de secano	ear	oreja f
dry land	secano m	ear (of corn)	mazorca f
dry matter	materia f seca	ear tag	etiqueta f de oreja
dry out, to	resecar	early	tempranero
dry rot	podredumbre f seca	early	temprano
dry rot	pudricíon f seca	early (precocious)	precoz
dry up, to	requemarse	early blight	marchitez f temprana
dry well	pozo m absorbente	early variety	variedad f temprana
dry, to	secar	earthmover	trailla f mecánica
dryer	secadora f	earthquake	terremoto m
drying	secado m	earthworm	gusano m de tierra
drying	secamiento m	earthworm	lombriz f de tierra
drying-floor	suelo m secadero	earthy	térreo
dryness	sequedad f	earwig	tijereta f
duck	pato m	east	este
duct	conducto m	ebullition	ebullición f
duodenum	duodeno m	echo	eco m
duplicate genes	genes m duplicados	ecologist	ecólogo m
durability	durabilidad f	ecology	ecología f
duration of illumination	duración f de exposición	economic	económico m
duration of storage	duración de la conservación	economic factors	factores m económicos
dust	polvo m	economic threshold	umbral m económico
dust cloud	nube m de polvo	economics	economía f
dust-pan	palita f	economist	economista f
dust, to	espolvorear	economy	economía f
dust, to	polvorear	edaphic	edáfico m
dust, to	pulverizar	edible	comestible
dust, to (apply)	pulverizar	eelworm	anguílula f
duster	espolvoreadora f	eelworm	nematodo m
duster	pulverizadora f	effect	efecto m
dusting preparation	producto m en polvo	effective	eficaz
dusting preparation	producto m en polvo	effective precipitation	lluvia f efectiva
dusty	polvoroso	effervesce, to	espumar
Dutch elm disease	enfermedad f holandesa del olmo	efficient	eficiente
		egg	huevo m
dwarf	enano m	egg laying	oviponición f
dwarf variety	variedad f enana	egg white	albúmina f
dwarfing	enanismo m	egg white	clara f de huevo
dwarfing rootstock	patrón m enanizante	egg yolk	yema f
dwarfism	nanismo	eggplant	berengena f
dwelling	vivienda f	elasticity	elasticidad f
dye	tinte f	elder	sabuco m
dynamometer	dinamómetro	electric	eléctrico

ENGLISH - SPANISH EQUIVALENTS

ENGLISH	SPANISH	ENGLISH	SPANISH
electric fence	cerca f eléctrica	entire (bot)	indiviso
electrical soil heating	calentamiento m eléctrico del suelo	entomologist	entomólogo m
		entomology	entomología f
electricity	electricidad f	environment	ambiente m
electrode	electrodo m	environment	medio m ambiente
electron microscope	microscopio m electrónico	enzymatic	enzimático
electronic leaf	hoja f electrónica	enzyme	enzima f
element	elemento m	epidemic	epidemia f
elevator	elevador m	epidemiology	epidemiología f
elevator (grain)	almacén m de granos	epidermis	epidermis f
elliptical	elíptico	epigeous	epígea
elm	olmo m	epiphyllum	epifilo m
elongation	extensión f	epistasis	espistasis m
elutriation	elutriación f	equator	ecuador m
emasculation	emasculación f	equinox	equinoccio m
embryo	embrión m	equipment	equipo m
embryo, latent	embrión m latente	eradicate, to	extirpar
embryo, rudimentary	embrión m rudimentario	eradication	extinción f
embryos	embriones m	erect	erecto
emergence	emergencia f	ergot	ergotismo m
emery paper	papel m de esmeril	Erlenmeyer flask	frasco m Erlenmeyer
emery powder	polvo m de esmeril	erode, to	erosionarse
emery stone	piedra f de esmeril	erosion	erosión f
employee	empleado m	erosion control	lucha f contra la erosión
employer	patrón m	esophagus	esófago m
empty, to	vaciar	espalier	árbol m en espaldera
emulsifiable	emulsionable	espartograss	esparto m
emulsifier	agente m emulsionante	essential oils	aceites m esenciales
emulsion	emulsión f	establish, to	establecer
encephalitis	encefalitis f	estate	predio m
end	fin m	estimate	estimación f
end, to	terminarse	estimate, to	calcular
endive	escarola f	etiolation	ahilamiento m
endless belt	sinfín m	etiolation	descoloración f
endocarp	endocarpio m	euploid	euploide m
endosperm	endosperma f	European corn borer	taladrador europeo del maíz
endosperm	endospermo m	European Economic Community	Comunidad f Económica Europea (CEE)
energy	energía f	evaporate, to	evaporar
engine	motor m	evaporation	evaporación f
engineer	ingeniero m	evaporator	evaporador m
English pea	guisante m verde	evapotranspiration	evapotranspiración f
English walnut	nogal m inglés	evergreen	de hojas f perennes
enrich, to	enriquecer	everlasting flower	siempreviva f
ensilage, to	ensilar	ewe	oveja f
enterprise	empresa f		

ENGLISH - SPANISH EQUIVALENTS

ENGLISH	SPANISH	ENGLISH	SPANISH
excelsior	zacate m de empaque	fan	abanico m
excess	exceso m	fan	ventilador m
excrement	excremento m	fancy (produce grade)	seleccionado
exit	salida f	farm account	cuenta f agrícola
exotic	exótico	farm accounting	contabilidad f agrícola
expansion tank	tanque m de expansión	farm animals	ganado m de labor
expenses	gastos m	farm appraisal	avalúo m
expensive	caro	farm buildings	dependencias f de la finca
experiment	experimento m	farm credit	crédito m agrícola
experiment	prueba f	farm hand	bracero m
experimental area	zona f experimental	farm hand	obrero m agrícola
experimental field	campo m experimental	farm house	casa f hacienda
experimental plot	lote m de experimentos	farm income	ingresos m agrícolas
experimental plots	campo m experimental	farm job	labor m agrícola
export	exportación f	farm machinery	maquinaria f agrícola
export, to	exportar	farm management	manejo m de la finca
exportation	exportación f	farm management	manejo m gerencial de la finca
exporter	exportador m	farm pond	charca f
expulsion	expulsión f	farm prices	precios m al productor
extension service	servicio m de extensión	farm taxation	impuestos m agrícolas
extensive	extensivo	farm type	tipo m de finca
extensive crops	cultivos m extensivos	farmer	agricultor m
extermination	exterminio m	farmer	campesino m
external parasite	ectoparásito m	farmer	finquero m
extract	extracto m	farming	agricultura f
extract, to	extraer	farming	agropecuario
extraction	extracción f	farrow, to	parir
eye	ojo m	fasciation	fasciación f
eye spot	mancha f ojival	fat	gordo
		fat	grasa f
		fatigue	fatiga f
		fatten, to	cebar
- F -		fattening	ceba m
		fatty acid	ácido m graso
"4-H" club	club m 4-H	faucet	canilla f
F.O.B.	precio m sobre vagón	faucet	grifo m
fabric	tela f	faucet	llave f
factors of production	factores m de producción	feather	pluma f
faded	marchito	feces	heces f
fading	decoloración	feed	alimento m
fall (of fruits, leaves, etc)	caída f	feed pipe	tubo m de alimentación
fallow	barbecho	feed pump	bomba f de alimentación
fallow, to	estar en barbecho	feed stuffs	alimentos m
family labor	mano f de obra familiar	feed, to	alimentar

ENGLISH - SPANISH EQUIVALENTS

ENGLISH	SPANISH	ENGLISH	SPANISH
feeder	ganado m de engorde	field	campo m, fil m
feeding	alimentación f	field bean	haba f
feeding trough	comedero m	field capacity	capacidad f de campaña
feedlot	pastadero m	field capacity	capacidad f de campo
feldspar	feldespato m	field crop	cultivo m extensivo
fell, to (tree)	talar	field mouse	ratón m campesino
felling	corta f	field pea	guisante m forrajero
female	hembra f	field resistance	resistencia f a campo
female	sexo m femenino	fig	higo m
fence	alambrado m	filament (bot)	filamento m
fence	cerca f	filbert	avellana f
fence, to	cercar	filbert (plant)	avellano m
fenced or trellised with wire	alambrado	file	lima f
fennel	hinojo m	file, to	limar
ferment, to	fermentar	filiform	filiforme
fermentation	fermentación f	fill in, to (gaps in a row)	rellenar
fermentation process	proceso m de fermentación	fill, to	llenar
fern	helecho m	filled	relleno
ferrous sulphate	sulfato m de hierro	film	película f
fertile	fértil	filter	filtro m
fertile plain	vega f	filter paper	papel m de filtro
fertility	fertilidad f	filter paper	papel m filtro
fertility gradient	gradiente m de fertilidad	filter strip	faja f filtrante
fertilization	fecundación f	filter, to	filtrar
fertilization	fertilización f	finance	finanza f
fertilize, to (ie, egg or ovule)	fecundar	finance, to	financiar
fertilize, to (with fertilizer)	abonar	fine dust	polvillo m
fertilizer	abono m	fine grained	de grano m fino
fertilizer	fertilizante m	fineness	fineza f
fertilizer distribution	distribución f de abonos	finger millet	mijo m africano
fertilizer drill	abonadora f mecánica	finger nail	uña f
fertilizer mixture	mezcla f de fertilizantes	finish, to	terminar
fertilizer proportioner	dosimetro m	fir	abeto m
fertilizer recommendation	consejo m de abonado	fire	fuego m
fertilizer requirement	requerimiento m de abono	firkin	cuñete m
fertilizer spreader	distribuidor m de abonos	firmness	dureza f
fertilizing	abonado m	fish meal	harina f de pescado
fescue	cañuela f	fish pond	piscina f
fetus	feto m	fish solubles	solubles m de pescado
fever	fiebre f	fission	fisión f
fiber	fibra f	fit	ajuste m
fiberglass	fibra f de vidrio	fit, to	sentar
fibrous	fibroso	fix, to	reparar
fibrous root	raíz f fibrosa	fix, to (i.e. nitrogen)	fijarse
		fixation	fijación f

ENGLISH - SPANISH EQUIVALENTS

ENGLISH	SPANISH	ENGLISH	SPANISH
fixed capital	capital m inmueble	flower pot	envase m
fixed costs	costos m fijos	flower pot	tiesto m
flame gun	lanza-llamas f	flower shop	tienda f de flores
flat (horticultural)	cajonera f	flower stalk	pedúnculo m
flat (level)	llano	flower vase	jarrón m para flores
flat rate	tanto m alzado	flower vase	vaso m para flores
flatten, to	aplanar	flower, to	florecer
flavor	sabor m	flower, to	florecerse
flax	lino m	flowering	floración f
flea	pulga f	flowerpot	maceta f
flea beatle	pulguilla f	flowers of sulphur	azufre m en flor
flecking	abigarrado m	flue barn	granero m de ventilación automática
fleece	lana f		
	vellón m vellocino m	flume	canal f de madera
flesh (meat)	carne f	flush (of growth)	renuevo m
flesh (not meat)	pulpa f	flushing (of flowers)	floración f
fleshy	carnoso	flushing (of foliage)	foliación f
fleshy leaf	penca f	fly	mosca f
flexible	flexible	fly, to	volar
flood	inundación f	fodder	forraje m
flood control	defensa f contra las inundaciones	fodder	pienso m
		foecal matter	materia f fecal
flood irrigation	riego m por inundación	fog	niebla f
flood plain	terreno m de aluvión	fog machine	nebulizador m
flooding	anegación f	foliage	follaje m
flooding	inundación f	foliage plant	planta f de hojas
floral arrangement	ramillete m de flores	folic acid	ácido m fólico
florence flask	frasco m Florence	follicle	folículo m
floriculture	floricultura f	food	alimento m
floriculturist	floricultor m	food	comida f
floriferous	de abundante floración	food crops	cultivos m de plantas alimenticias
floriferous	florido		
florist	florista m & f	food energy	energía f alimenticia
floristry	arte m floral	foot	pie m
flour	harina f	foot and mouth disease	fiebre f aftosa
flourescent lamp	lámpara f fluorescente	foot rot	pie m podrido
flourine	flúor m	footpath	senda f
flourmill	molino m de harina	forage	forraje m
flower	flor f	forage crop	cosecha f forrajera
flower bearing	floreciente	forbs	hierbajos m
flower bed	cuadro m de flores	force, to	forzar
flower bud	yema f floral	forced fruit	fruta f tempranera
flower formation	formación f de las flores	forcing	forzado m
flower garden	jardín m de flores	forecast	pronóstico m
flower iniciation	iniciación f floral	forecasting	pronosticación f

ENGLISH - SPANISH EQUIVALENTS

ENGLISH	SPANISH	ENGLISH	SPANISH
foreman	capataz m, mayordomo m	fruit (bot)	fruto m
forest	bosque m	fruit (culinary)	fruta f
forest floor	suelo m forestal	fruit flesh	mesocarpio m
forest litter	barrujo m	fruit formation	fructificación f
forest management	maneja f del bosque	fruit grower	fruticultor m
forester	silvicultor m	fruit peeler	perero m
forge	fragua f	fruit thinning	aclarar frutos
fork (agricultural)	horquilla f	fruit tree	árbol m frutal
fork lift	elevador m de horquilla	fry, to	freír
forklift	elevador m de paletas	fryer (hen)	pollo m para freír
forklift	montecargos m	fuchsia	adelaida f
formaldehyde	formaldehído m	fuel	combustible m
formicide	formicida f	fuel oil	petróleo m combustible
formula	fórmula f	full	lleno
formulation	formulación f	full	pleno m
forsythia	forsitia f	fumigant	fumigante m
foundation	fundamento m	fumigate with sulphur	azufrar
foundation stock	material m básico	fumigate, to	fumigar
fowl	ave m	functional design	diseño m funcional
fowl cholera	cólera f aviar	funeral wreath	corona f mortuoria
fowl pest	peste m aviar	fungicidal	fungicido
fowl pox	viruela f aviar	fungicide	fungicida f
fox grape	parriaz f	fungus	hongo m
foxglove	digital f	fungus (mushroom)	hongo m
foxtail	rabito m peludo	funnel	embudo m
foxtail millet	panizo m blanco	furnish, to	suministrar
fragrance	fragancia f	furrow	surco m
fragrant	oloroso	furrow irrigation	riego m por surcos
frame	esqueleto m	furrow, to	surcar
framework	armazón m	fusarium wilt	fusariosis f
freckle	peca f	fuse	fusible m
freesia	fresia f	Future Farmers of America (FFA)	futuros agricultores de América
freeway	autopista f	future trading	ventas f para entregar
freeze drying	liofilización f	futures market	mercado m a término
freeze, to	congelar	fuzziness	vellosidad f
freezer	congeladora f	F1 generation	primera generación f filial
fresh	fresco	F2 generation	segunda generación f filial
fresh water	agua f dulce		
fresh water swamp	terreno m pantanoso de agua dulce		

- G -

friable	friable		
fritillaria	Corona f imperial	gaillardia	gallardia f
front	frente m	gall	abogalla f
frost hardy	resistente a la helada	gall	agalla f
frozen	congelado m	gall midge	mosquito m de agalla

48

ENGLISH - SPANISH EQUIVALENTS

ENGLISH	SPANISH	ENGLISH	SPANISH
gall wasp	avispa f de agalla	gladiolus	gladiolo m
galvanize, to	galvanizar	gland	glándula f
gamete	gameto m	glandular	glanduloso
gamma radiation	radiación f gamma	glandular hair	pelo m glandular
gamopetalous	gamopétalo	glass fiber	fibra f de vidrio
gamosepalous	gamosépalo	glass wool	lana f de vidrio
garden	jardín m	glasshouse	invernadero m
garden center	tienda f de semillas	glaze, to	acristalar
garden design	diseño m de jardín	glazing bar	barra f para poner vidrios
garden hose	manga f	globe artichoke	alcachofa f
garden hose	manguera f	globe thistle	cardo m
garden pea	guisante m verde	globe thistle	yesquero m
garden trowel	trasplantador m	globe valve	válvula f derecha
garden, to	trabajar el jardìn	glory of the snow	gloria f de la nieve
gardener	jardinero m	gloxinia	gloxinia f
gardener	plantista m	glume	gluma f
garlic	ajo m	gnat	jején m
gas burner	quemador m de gas	go to seed, to	espigar
gas damage	daño m de gas	golden currant	grosellero m dorado
gasket	empaque m	goldenrod	solidago m
gas mask	máscara f de gas	goldenrod	vara m de oro
gas poisoning	asfixia f	gooseberry	grosella f espinosa
gate (irrigation)	compuerta f	gopher	tuza f
gelatin	gelatina f	gourd	calabacín m
gene	gen m	gourd	calabaza f
generative	generativo	gourd	zapallo m
generator	generador m	grade	categoría f
generic name	nombre m generífico	grader	máquina f calibradora
genotype	genotipo m	grader	máquina f clasificadora
gentian	genciana f	grading	clasificación f
genus	género m	grading regulation	reglas f pl de normalización
geological	geológico	grading room	cuarto m de clasificación
geranium	geranio m	grading room	lugar m de clasificación
germ	germen m	graft	injerto m
germinate, to	germinar	graft hybrid	híbrido m de injerto
germinating coffee bean	abejoncito m	graft union	soldadura f
germination	germinación f	graft union	unión f del injerto
gherkin	pepinillo m	graft, approach	injerto m por aproximación
gherkin	pepino m	graft, bark	injerto m de corteza
gibberellic acid	ácido m giberélico	graft, bridge	puente m de injerto
gill (mushroom)	laminilla f	graft, cleft	injerto m de hendidura
gin, to	despepitar	graft, cleft	injerto m de para
ginkgo	ginkgo m	graft, crown	injerto m de corona
girdle, to	anillar	graft, inarch	injerto por aproximación en arco
glabrous	glabro		

ENGLISH - SPANISH EQUIVALENTS

ENGLISH	SPANISH	ENGLISH	SPANISH
graft, nurse root	injerto m de raíz-nodriza	greenhouse plant	planta f de invernadero
graft, root	injerto m de raíz	grey mold	moho m gris
graft, side	injerto m de costado	grey mold	podredumbre f
graft, to	injertar	groove	encaje m
graft, wedge	injerto m de incrustación	groove	ranura f
graft, whip and tongue	injerto m de lengüeta	gross weight	peso m bruto
graft, whip and tongue	injerto m inglés	gross yield	producción f bruta
grafted	trabajado	gross yield	rendimiento m bruto
grafting	injertación f	ground cherry	tomatillo m falso
grafting knife	abridero m	ground ivy	hiedra f terrestre
grafting knife	cuchillo m de injertar	ground limestone	carbonato m cálcico
grafting knife	injertador m	ground water	agua f subterránea
grafting wax	betún m de injertar	ground (wire)	toma f de tierra
grafting wax	betún m de injertar	groundsel	zuzón m, hierba f caballar
grain	grano m	grow together, to	cicatrizar
grain size	tamaño m del grano	grow, to	cultivar
granular	granuloso	grow, to	producir
granulate	granulado m	grow, to	sembrar
granulate, to	granular	grow, to (ie the plant grows)	crecer
grape	uva f	grower	campesino
grape hyacinth	jacinto m racimoso	grower	cultivador
grape hyacinth	muscari m	grower	cultivador m comercial
grape juice	jugo m de uva	grower	productor
grape juice	zumo m de uva	growing method	método m de siembra
grapefruit	toronja f	growing period	período m de crecimiento
grass	gramínea f	growing point	ápice m
grass	hierba f	growing technique	técnica f del cultivo
grass (as in lawn)	cesped m	growth	crecimiento m
grasshopper	saltamontes m	growth chamber	fitotrón m
grating	grilla f	growth chamber	invernadero m climático
gravel	grava f	growth habit	hábito m de crecimiento
gravel	gravilla f	growth inhibition	refreno m del crecimiento
gravel soil	suelo m de grava	growth inhibitor	retardante m de crecimiento
gray mold	moho m gris	growth reduction	retardación f del crecimiento
gray mold	podredumbre f		
grease gun	grasera f	growth regulator	regulador m de crecimiento
grease, to	engrasar	growth retardant	inhibidor m
green manure	abono m verde	growth retardant	retardante m
green manure crop	cultivo m de abono en verde	growth stimulation	estimulación f del crecimiento
green revolution	revolución f verde	growth, active	estado m activo de crecimiento
greenhouse	invernadero m		
greenhouse bench	mesa f para plantas	grub	oruga f
greenhouse crop	cultivo m de invernadero	guano	guano m
greenhouse culture	cultivo m en invernadero	guaranteed price	precio m garantizado

ENGLISH - SPANISH EQUIVALENTS

ENGLISH	SPANISH
gummosis	gomosis f
gutter	canal m
gypsophila	gisofila f
gypsum	yeso m

- H -

ENGLISH	SPANISH
habit	hábito m
habit (of plant)	porte m
habitat	habitación f
habitat	habitat m
hail	granizo m
hail, to	granizar
hailstorm	granizada f
hair	pelo m
hairiness	pilosidad f
hairy	piloso
hairy	velloso
hairy vetch	veza f velluda
hall	sala f
halo	halo m
halo blight (of bean)	enfermedad f de manchas de la grasa
halter	jaquimón m
ham	jamón m
hammer	martillo m
hammer, to (nail)	poner un clavo
hammer mill	trituradora f de martillos
hammer-mill	molino m de martillos
hamper	cesto m de mimbre
hand	mano m
hand seeder	sembrador m de mano
handle	mango m
handle, to	manejar
handling	manipuleo m
hand truck	troquita f
haploid	haploide
haplont	generación f haploide
hard coated	de cáscara f dura
hard hat	casco m
hard water	agua f dura
harden off, to	endurecer
hardening	enduramiento m

ENGLISH	SPANISH
hardpan	capa f dura
hardware	ferretería f
hardwood cutting	estaca f leñosa
hardy	resistente al frío
hardy plants	plantas capaces de sobrevivir el invierno
harrow	escarificador m
harrow	grada f
harrow	rastra f
harrow tooth	diente m de grada
harrow, to	gradar
harvest	cosecha f
harvest	safra f
harvest (sugar cane)	safra f
harvest, to	cosechar
harvester	segadora f
hatch, to	empollarse
hatch, to	salir del huevo
hatchet	hacha f
hatching	acción f de empollar
hay	heno m
hay chopper	picadora f de heno
haybaler	enfardadora f de heno
hayloft	henil m
haymaker	heneador m
haymaking	henificación f
haze	tufo m
hazelnut	avellano m
haziness	bruma f
head	cabeza f
head (of tree)	copa f
head smut	carbón m de la inflorescencia
head, to	descabezar
heading stage	espigando
head training	entrenamiento m de cabeza
health	salud m
health	sanidad f
healthy	sano
heap	parva f
heart rot	podredumbre f del corazón
heart shaped, cordate	acorazonado
heartwood	duramen m
heat loss	pérdida de calefacción
heat treatment	termo-terapia f

ENGLISH - SPANISH EQUIVALENTS

ENGLISH	SPANISH	ENGLISH	SPANISH
heat treatment	tratamiento m por calor	heterosis	heterosis f
heat treatment	tratamiento m térmico	heterosis	vigor m híbrido
heat, to	calentar	heterotypic division	división f heterotípica
heath	érica f	heterozygosis	heterocigosis f
heating cable	cable m de calefacción	heterozygote	heterozigoto m
heating plant	instalación f de calefacción	hibernate, to	hibernar
heating technician	técnico m de la calefacción	hibernate, to	invernar
heavy	pesado	hibiscus	hibisco m
heavy pruning	poda f severa	hide	cuero m
heavy rain	lluvia f torrencial	high	alto
heavy soil	suelo m pesado	high pressure area	anticiclón m
hectare	hectárea f	high pressure boiler	caldera f de alta presión
hedge	seto m	high pressure mercury vapor lamp	lámpara f de vapor de mercurio de alta presión
hedge	seto m vivo	higher plants	plantas f pl superiores
hedge shears	tijeras f de jardinero	highway	carretera f
hedge shears	tijeras f pl de jardinero	hill	loma f
hedge shears	tijeras f pl para setos vivos	hill	recalzar
heel (of cutting)	talón m	hill reaction	reacción f de Hill
heel cutting	pata f de caballo	hiller	aporcadora f
heifer	novilla f	hilling (plants)	recalce m
height	altura f	hillside	ladera f
height of withers	alzada f del caballo	hilly	alomado
heliotrope	heliotropo m	hilum	hilo m
hemlock	abeto m	hilum	ombligo m
hemorrhage	hemorragia f	hire, to	emplear
hemp	cáñamo m	hired hand	obrero m agrícola
hen	gallina f	hirsute	hirsuto
henhouse	gallinero m	hirsute	velloso
hepatica	hepática f	histology	histología f
herb	hierba f	hitch, to	acoplar
herb	yerba f	hoarfrost	helada f blanca
herbaceous	herbáceo	hoe	azada f
herbaceous perennials	plantas f pl vivaces	hoe	binadora f
herbage	herbaje m	hoe, to	azadonar
herbarium	herbario m	hoe, to	escardar
herbicide	herbicida m	hog	cerdo m
herd	manada f	hog cholera	cólera m porcino
herd book	registro m genealógico	hoist	aparejo m elevador
heredity	herencia f	hoist, to	alzar
heritability	heredabilidad f	hole	hoyo m
hermaphrodite	hermafrodita m & f	hollow	hondonada f
hermaphroditism	hermafroditismo m	hollow	hueco
heroin	heroína f	holly	acebo m
hesperidium	hesperidio m	holly	agrifolio m
heterogamy	heterogamia f		

ENGLISH - SPANISH EQUIVALENTS

ENGLISH	SPANISH	ENGLISH	SPANISH
hollyhock	malva f	host indexing	prueba f del huésped
hollyhock *(Althaea rosea)*	alcea f	host plant	planta f huésped
home economics	ciencias f domésticas	host-pathogen relationship	relación f huésped-patógeno
homogenization	homogeneización	host-plant	planta f huésped
homogenize, to	homogeneizar	hot	caliente
homologue	homólogo m	hot	caluroso
homozygote	homozigoto m	hot air heater	quemador m de aire caliente
honesty plant	lunaria f	hot dip galvanized	galvanizado en caliente
honey	miel f	hot water boiler	caldera f de agua caliente
honey locust	acacia f de tres espinas	hot water treatment	hidrotermoterapia f
honeydew	secreción dulce or azucarada	hot water treatment	tratamiento m con agua caliente
honeysuckle	madreselva f	hotbed	cama f caliente
hood	aparato por el que se levan los olores o gases	hothouse	invernadero m
hoof	casco m	hothouse	invernadero m calentado
hoof	pezuña f	hour	hora f
hoof and horn meal	harina f de cuerno y pezuña	hourly rate	salario m según tiempo
hopper	tolva f	house	casa f
hopseed *(Dodonea viscosa)*	ocotillo m	house plant	planta f ornamental
horizon	horizonte m	household	casero (a)
hormone	hormona f	household refuse	basuras f pl de ciudad
horn	cuerno m	hull	cáscara f
horn meal	harina f de cuerno	hulled seed	semilla f descascarada
hornbeam	ojaranzo m	huller	descascaradora f
hornet	sesia f apiforme	hunger	hambre m
horse	caballo m	humic acid	ácido m húmico
horse bean	haba f de burro	humid	húmedo
horse chestnut	castaño m de Indias	humidity	humedad f
horse manure	estiércol m de caballo	hump	joroba f
horse radish	rábano m rusticano	humus	humus m
horse radish	rábano m picante	humus content	contenido m de humus
horsepower	caballos m de fuerza	hurdle	cañizo m
horticultural	hortícola	hurdle	zarzo m
horticultural advisor	asesor m hortícola	husk	chala f
horticultural school	escuela f de horticultura	hyacinth	jacinto m
horticulture	horticultura f	hyacinth bean	frijo m caballero
horticulturist	horticultor m	hybrid	híbrido m
horticulturist (woman)	horticultora f	hybrid vigor	heterosis f
hose	manguera f	hybrid vigor	vigor m híbrido
hose	tubo m	hybridization	hibridación f
hose	manga f de agua	hybridization	hibridización f
hosebib	grifo m	hybridize, to	hibridar
hosebib	llave f	hydrangea	hortensia f
host	hospedero m		
host	huésped m		

ENGLISH - SPANISH EQUIVALENTS

ENGLISH	SPANISH	ENGLISH	SPANISH
hydrated	hidratado	illuminated	iluminado
hydraulic	hidráulico	illumination period	duración f de la iluminación
hydraulic lift	alzador m hidráulico	imbibition	imbibición f
hydraulic lift	elevador m hidráulico	immature	inmaduro
hydrazide	hidrácida	immersed	inmerso
hydrazine	hidracina f	immune	inmune
hydric	hídrico	immunity	inmunidad f
hydrocarbon	hidrocarburo m	immunization	inmunización f
hydrochloric acid	ácido m clorhídrico	immunize	inmunizar
hydrocooling	enfriamiento m del agua	immunosorbent technique	técnica f de inmunosorbencia
hydrogen	hidrógeno m		
hydrogen ion concentration	concentración de los iones de hidrógeno	impact resistance	resistente al choque
		imperial grass	hierba f imperial
hydrology	hidrología f	impermeability	impermeabilidad f
hydrolysis	hidrólisis f	impermeable	impermeable
hydrometer	hidrómetro m	implant, to	implantar
hydromorphic	hidromorfo	import	importación f
hydroponics	hidroponía f	import, to	importar
hydroponics	hidropónicos m pl	importer	importador m
hydrotropism	hidrotropismo m	impoverish	empobrecer
hydroxide	hidróxido m	impoverishment (of soil)	empobrecimiento
hygrometer	higrómetro m	improve, to	mejorar
hygrometry	higrometría f	improvement	mejora f
hygroscopic	higroscópico m	improvement	mejoramiento m
hygrothermograph	higrotermógrafo m	improvement of soil structure	mejoría f estructural del suelo
hymenopteron	himenóptero m		
hypertrophy	hipertrofia f	impurity	impureza f
hypha	hifa f	inactivation	inactivación f
hypocotyl	hipocotilo m	inarch, to	succionar
hypogenous	hipógea	inarching	apuntalamiento m
hypogynous	hipógino	inarching	injerto m de arco
hypsometer	hipsómetro m	inbred variety cross	híbrido m línea variedad
hyssop	hisopo m	inbreeding	endocría f
		inbreeding	endogamía f
		inbreeding	endogamía
- I -		incandescent lamp	lámpara f de incandescencia
		incense	incienso m
ice	hielo m	incense cedar	libocedro m
ice cream	helado m	incidence	incidencia f
ice plant	hierba f de hielo	incision	incisión f
Iceland poppy	adormidera f	inclement weather	intemperie f
ignition	encendido m	inclination	inclinación f
ileum	ilión m	income	ingresos m
illuminate, to	iluminar	income statement	declaración f de ingresos

ENGLISH - SPANISH EQUIVALENTS

ENGLISH	SPANISH	ENGLISH	SPANISH
incompatibility	incompatibilidad f	information	información f
incompatible	incompatible	information network	red f de información
increase	alza f	infrared	infra-rojo
increase	incremento m	infraspecific	infraespecífico
increase	aumento m	infundibular	infundibuliforme
increase, to	aumentar	ingestion	ingestión f
increase, to	incrementar	ingredient	ingrediente m
incubation	incubación f	inheritable	heredable
incubation period	período m de incubación	inheritance	herencia f
incubator	incubadora f	inhibitor	inhibidor m
indebtedness	endeudamiento m	initiation	iniciación f
indehiscence	indehiscencia f	inject, to	inyectar
indehiscent	indehiscente	injection	inyección f
indented	amuescado	injurious impurity	impureza f perjudicial
index	índice m	inlay graft	injerto m de incrustación
indexing	indización f	inlet	entrada f
indicator	indicador m	inner bark	corteza
indicator plant	planta f indicadora	innertube	neumático m
indigenous	indígena	inoculation	inoculación f
indigo	añil m	inoculum	inóculo m
indirect costs	costos m indirectos	inorganic	inorgánico
indolebutyric acid	ácido m indolbutírico	inorganic matter	materia f inorgánica
induction	inducción f	input	insumo m
indusium	indusio m	insect	insecto m
industrial crop	cultivo m industrial	insect control	lucha f contra los insectos
industrialization	industrialización f	insect damage	daño m de insectos
industrialize, to	industrializar	insect trap	trampa f para insectos
industry	industria f	insect vector	insecto m vector de la enfermedad
inedible	incomible, incomestible		
inert matter	impureza f anodina	insecticide	insecticida f
infect, to	infectar	insectivore	insectívoro m
infected	infectado	insecurity of tenure	inseguridad f de tenencia
infection	infección f	inseminate, to	fecundar
infectious	infeccioso	insemination	fecundación f
infectivity	infectividad f	insert, to	insertar
inferior (bot)	ínfero	insertion	inserción f
inferior (bot)	hipógino	insipid	insípido
infertile	estéril	insipid	soso
infest, to	infestar	insolation	insolación f
infestation	ataque m	inspection	inspección f
infestation	infestación f	inspection belt	cinta f de control
inflatable house	invernadero m neumático	inspection for disease	inspección f fitosanitaria
inflorescence	inflorescencia f	inspection service	servicio m de inspección
influence	influencia f	inspector	inspector m
influence flowering, to	influir en la floración	instar	instar m

ENGLISH - SPANISH EQUIVALENTS

ENGLISH	SPANISH	ENGLISH	SPANISH
institute	instituto m	ion	ion m
instruction	instrucción f	ionic	iónico
instruction panel	tablero m	ionizing radiation	radiación f ionizante
insulating film	hoja f aislante	ipecac	ipecacuana f
insulating material	material m aislante	iris	iris m
insulation	aislamiento m	iron	hierro m
insurance	seguro m	iron (clothes)	plancha f
intensification	intensificación f	iron deficiency	carencia f en hierro
intensity	intensidad f	irradiance	iluminación f energética
intensity of lighting	fuerza f de iluminación	irradiate, to	irradiar
interaction	interacción f	irradiation	irradiación f
interception	intercepción f	irregular	irregular
interchange	intercambio m	irrigatable	irrigable
interchangeable	intercambiable	irrigate, to	irrigar
intercropping	cultivo m intercalado	irrigate, to	regar
intercropping	intercalamiento m	irrigation	irrigación f
interference	interferencia f	irrigation	riego m
intermediate stock	tronco m intermedio	irrigation controller	programador m de riego
internal breakdown	descomposición f interna	irrigation ditch	regata f
internal parasite	endoparásito m	irrigation water	agua f de riego
internal secretion	secreción f interna	isoenzymatic	isoenzimático
internal transport	transporte m interior	isoenzyme	isoenzima f
international center	centro m internacional	isogenic	isogénico
internode	entrenudo m	isolate, to	aislar
internode	internudo m	isolation	aislamiento m
interruption in growth	interrupción f del crecimiento	isothermal	isoterma f
interstate	interestatal	isotope	isótopo m
interstock	intermediario m	isoyelic	isoyela
interstock	patrón m intermedio	ivy	hiedra f
interval	intervalo m	ivy	yedra f
interveinal mosaic	mosaico m internerval	ivy leafed geranium	geranio m hiedra
intervention	intervención f	ixora	ixora f
intestine	intestino m		
introduction	introducción f		
invade	invadir		
invasion	invasión f	**- J -**	
inversion	inversión f		
invertase	invertasa f	jam	mermelada f
invertebrate	invertebrado	japanese azalea	azalea f japonesa
invest, to	invertir	japanese beetle	escarabajo m japonés
investment	inversión f	japanese cherry	ciruelo m japonés
involucrate	involucrado	japanese quince	membrillero m japonés
involucre	envoltura f	japanese wineberry	zarza f japonesa
involucre	involucro m	jassid	cicadela f
iodine	yodo m	jay	grajo m

ENGLISH - SPANISH EQUIVALENTS

ENGLISH	SPANISH	ENGLISH	SPANISH
jelly (gelatin)	gelatina f	knife coulter	cuchilla f del arado
Jerusalem artichoke	tupinambo m	knife, grafting	navaja f para injerto
johnsongrass	grama f johnson	knife picking	cuchillo m de pizcar
joint costs	costos m unidos	knock down, to (fruit)	varear
joint costs	costos m conjuntos	knot	lazo m
joint ownership	propiedad f colectiva	knotgrass	pasto m chato
jonquil	narciso m arracimado	knottiness	nudosidad f
journal	revista f	knotty	nudoso
judge, to	juzgar	kohl rabi	colirrábano m
juice	jugo m	kudzu	kudzú m
juicy	jugoso		
juicy	sucoso		
jujube	yuyuba f		
June drop	caída f intempesiva	**- L -**	
jungle	selva f		
juniper	enebro m		
juniper	nebrina f	label	etiqueta f
jute	yute m	labiate	bilabial
juvenile form	forma f juvenil	labiate	labiada f
juvenile period	juventud f	labile	lábil
		labor	mano f de obra
		labor	trabajo m
		labor cost	coste m de la mano de obra
- K -		labor force	mano f de obra utilizada
		labor intensive	de trabajo m intensivo
		labor productivity	productividad f del trabajo
kale	col f enana	labor records	registro m del trabajo
keel (botanical)	quilla f	labor requirements	necesidades f de mano de obra
kelp	ceniza f de algas		
kenaf	kenaf m	labor saving	economía f de trabajo
kentia palm	kentia f	laburnum	laburno m
kernal	pepita f	laburnum	lluvia f de oro
kernel	grano m	lace wing	neuróptero m
kerria	querria f	lactation	lactación f
ketone	cetona f	lady's slipper	zapatillo m de Venus
key	llave f	ladybird	vaquita f de San Antón
kid	cabrito m	ladybird beetle	crisomélido m
kidney bean	frijol m	lake	lago m
kidney bean	frizole m	lamb	cordero m/f
kikuyugrass	hierba f kikuyu	lambing season	paridera f
kitchen	cocina f	lamella (mushroom)	laminilla f
kitchen garden	huerta f familiar	laminated beam	viga f laminada
knapsack mistblower	atomizador m de espalda	land	tierra f
knife	cuchillo m	land capability	aptitud f de la tierra
knife (folding)	navaja f	land classification	clasificación de terrenos

57

ENGLISH - SPANISH EQUIVALENTS

ENGLISH	SPANISH	ENGLISH	SPANISH
land development	fomento m de tierras	lawn	césped m
land owner	propietario m	lawn mower	segadora f de hierba
land reclamation	rehabilitación f de tierras	lawn rake	astrillo m
land reform	reforma f agraria	lawn sprinkler	regador m de prado
land register	catastro m	layer	capa f
land rent	arrendamiento m	layer (propagation)	acodo m
land survey	reconocimiento m topográfico	layer, to (propagation)	acodar
		layering	acodo m
land taxation	impuesto m territorial	layering, air	acodado m aéreo
land tenure	régimen m de tenencia de tierras	layering, compound	acodado m compuesto
		layering, mound	acodado m en montículo
land use	aprovechamiento m de tierra	layering, serpentine	acodado m serpentario
land use pattern	régimen de aprovechamiento de la tierra	layering, simple	acodado m simple
		layering, tip	acodado m de punta
		layering, trench	acodado m en trinchera
land use planning	planeamiento del aprovechamiento de la tierra	layers, in	en capas
		layout	diseño m
land value	valor de la tierra	layout	trazo m
landlord	propietario m	leach, to	lixiviar
landscape	paisaje m	leach, to (soil)	deslavar
landslide	derrumbe m	leach, to (soil)	deslavazar
larch	alerce m	leaching	lixiviación f
large intestine	intestino m grueso	lead arsenate	aseniato m de plomo
larkspur	espuela f de caballero	leader (tree)	tallo m principal
larva	larva f	leaf	hoja f
larvicidal	larvicida	leaf analysis	análisis m foliar
larvicide	larvicida f	leaf analysis	diagnóstico m foliar
larynx	laringe f	leaf axil	axila f de la hoja
lasting	durable	leaf base	base f de hoja
late blight	añublo m tardío	leaf blade	lámina f de hoja
late blight	tizón m tardío	leaf blight	marchitez f de la hoja
late maturing variety	variedad de madurez tardía	leaf bud	yema f foliar
lateral branch	rama f lateral	leaf curl	abarquillado m de las hojas
lateral root	raíz f lateral	leaf cutting ant	hormiga f cortadora
lateral shoot	chupón lateral	leaf damage	deterioro m de las hojas
latex	látex m	leaf margin	borde m de la hoja
lath	listón m de madera	leaf miner	mosca f minadora
latin square	cuadrado m latino	leaf mold	moho m de la hoja
latitude	latitud m	leaf roller	arrollador m de la hoja
lattice design	plan m experimental reticular	leaf roller	tortrix m
		leaf rolling	enrollamiento m de hojas
lavatory	inodoro m	leaf rust	roya f foliar
lavatory	letrina f	leaf scar	cicatriz f de la hoja
lavender	espliego m	leaf shape	forma f de las hojas
lavender	lavándula f	leaf spot	mancha f de la hoja

ENGLISH - SPANISH EQUIVALENTS

ENGLISH	SPANISH	ENGLISH	SPANISH
leaf spot	viruela f	lengthening of daylength	alargamiento m del día
leaf spot (symptom)	punteado m	lenticel	lentejilla f
leaf stripper	deshojador m	lenticel	lentícula f, lenticela f
leaf surface	superficie f de la hoja		
leaf surface	superficie f de la hoja	lentil	lenteja f
leaf tip	ápice m de la hoja	lesion	lesión f
leaf-mold	mantillo m de hojas	lesion nematode	nemátado m de los prados
leaf-spine	espina f foliar	lespedeza	lespedeza f
leafhopper	cicálida f	lettuce	lechuga f
leafhopper	saltahoja f	lettuce, head	lechuga f repollada
leafless	deshojado	levee	dique m
leafless	nudicaulo	level	llano
leaflet	hojuela f	level	nivel m
leafy	foliado	level, to	enrasar
leafy	frondoso	level, to	igualar
leafy vegetables	hortilizas f verdes	level, to	nivelar
leak	gotera f	levelling	nivelación f
leak, to	salirse	lever	palanca f
leakage	pérdida f	liabilities	capital m pasivo
lean (thin)	flaco	liabilities	pasivos m
lean, to	inclinarse	liatris	liatris f
lean-to greenhouse	invernadero m adosado	liatris	serratula f
lease	arriendo m	liberalization	liberalización
lease contract	contrato m de arrendamiento	lice	piojos m
		lichen	líquen m
leaseholder	arrendatario m	licorice	regaliz m
leather	cuero m	life cycle	ciclo m vital
leather	piel f	lifter	arrancadora f de plantas
leathery	correoso	lifter (i.e. bulbs, potatoes)	arrancadora f
leathery (botanical)	coriáceo	light	luz f
leaves	hojas f	light absorption	absorción f de la luz
leek	puerro m	light deficiency	falta f de luz
leg (animal)	pata f	light deficient	pobre de luz
leg (human)	pierna f	light distribution	distribución f de luz
legume	legumbre f	light entry	caída f de luz
legumes	leguminosas f	light fitting	aparato m de iluminación
lemon	limón	light intensity	intensidad f luminosa
lemon tree	limonero m	light supply	surtido m de luz
lemongrass	yerbaluisa f	light transmission	transmisión f luminosa
lender	prestamista m	light trap	trampa f de luz
length of day	día m natural	lightening	relámpago m
length of day	duración f de la luz del día	lighting	iluminación f
length of growing season	duración f de la temporada de cultivo	lightning arrestor	pararrayos m
		lightweight	ligero
lengthening	alargamiento m	lignin	lignina f

ENGLISH - SPANISH EQUIVALENTS

ENGLISH	SPANISH	ENGLISH	SPANISH
ligulate (ray) flower	flor f ligulada	litmus	tornasol m
lilac	lila f	litter	litera f
lily	azucena f	litter (animal)	cama f
lily	lirio m	live weight	peso m vivo
lily of the Nile	lirio m del Nilo	livestock	ganado m
lily of the valley	lirio m del valle	living room	sala f
lily, calla	liriocalla f	lixiviate, to	lixiviar
lime	cal f	load	carga f
lime (fruit)	lima f	loader	cargadora f
lime (fruit)	limón m	loading bay	puente m de carga
lime content	contenido m en cal	loam	suelo m franco
lime marl	marga f calcárea	loan	préstamo m
lime status	contenido m en calcio	lobe (botanical)	lóbulo m
lime sulphur	caldo m sulfocálcico	lobelia	lobelia f
lime tree	tilo m	lock	cerradura f
lime, to	encalar	locknut	tuerca f
lime-sulfur	cal-azufre m	locust	chapulín m
limestone	piedra f calcárea	lodging	vuelco m de un cultivo
limestone	piedra f caliza	lodging (plants)	vuelco m
limestone	piedra f de cal	lodicule	lodícula f
liming	encalado m	loess	loess m
liming material	enmienda f calcárea	log	trozo m
linden	tila f	loin	lomo m
line	línea f	long range	de largo alcance
line breeding	endogamia f	long shoot (plant)	brote m largo
linear	lineal	long-day plant	planta f de día largo
linen	lino m	long-day treatment	tratamiento m de días largos
linkage	enlace m		
linseed meal	harina f de linaza	London rocket	ruqueta f de Londres
linseed oil	aceite m de linaza	long-horned beetle	longicornio m
lint	fibre m de algodón	longevity	longevidad f
lip	labio m	longitude	longitud f
lipolysis	lipólisis	longitudinal growth	desarollo m longitudinal
liquid	líquido m	looper caterpillar	cruga f geómetra
liquid assets	bienes m líquidos	loose	suelto
liquid disinfectant	líquido m desinfectante	loose smut	carbón m desnudo
liquid fertilizer	fertilizante m líquido	loosen up, to	mullir
liquid fuel	combustible m líquido	lop, to	podar
liquid manure	purín m	loquat	níspero del Japón
liquidity	liquidez f	loss	pérdida
liquification	licuación f	loss of light	pérdida f de luz
liquorice	alcazuz m	lot	lote m
lister	arado m sembrador lister	lot	parcela f
lister	surcadora f	lot	solar m
literature	literatura f	lotus	nelumbio m

ENGLISH - SPANISH EQUIVALENTS

ENGLISH	SPANISH	ENGLISH	SPANISH
louse	piojo m	man-day	hombre-día m
love-in-a-mist	neguilla f	man-hour	peonada f de una hora
low	bajo m	manganese	manganeso m
low pressure area	región f ciclonal	manganese deficiency	carencia f en manganeso
low temperature breakdown	descomposición f interna de las frutas	manhole	agujero m de hombre
low-volume sprayer	atomizador m	Manila hemp (Musa textilis)	abacá m
lowland	tierra f baja	manual labor	mano f de obra
lowland rice	arroz m de riego constante	manual labor	trabajo m manual
lucerne	alfalfa f	manure	estiércol m
Lunaria	Lunaria f	manure (chicken)	gallinaza f
lupin	altramuz m	manure (steer)	estiércol m de vaca
lupin	lupino m	manure spreader	esparcidor de estiércol
lux-meter	luxámetro m	map, to	cartografiar
lyophilic	liofílico m	maple (Acer spp.)	arce m
lyophilization	liofilización f	marginal costs	costos m marginales
lysimeter	lisímetro m	marginal costing	costa f de producción parcial
		marguerite	margarita f
		marigold	damasquina f
		marigold	maravilla f
		marjoram	mejorana f
- M -		marjoram	sampsuco m
		marker	marcador m
maggot	oruga f	market garden	explotación f hortícola
magnesia	magnesia f	market planning	planificación f del mercado
magnesium	magnesio m	market price	precio m del mercado
magnesium deficiency	carencia f en magnesia	market report	información f del mercado
magnesium sulfate	sal f de higuera	market stabilization	establización f del mercado
magnesium sulfate	sulfato m de magnesia	market structure	estructura f del mercado
magnifying glass	lente m de aumento	marl	marga f
magnolia	magnolia f	marly soil	suelo m margoso
mahonia	mahonia f	marmalade	mermelada f
maidenhair fern	culantrillo m de poza	marsh plant	planta f de pantano
maidenhair fern (Adiantum sp.)	adianto m	marshy soil	suelo m pantanoso
main axis(bot)	eje m principal	mask	máscara
main branch	rama m principal lateral	master of science	ingeniero m
main bud	yema f principal	mattock	zapapico m
main drain	colector m	mature, to	madurar
main root	raíz f principal	max-min thermometer	termómetro m maxi-mini
main stem	tallo m principal	maximum price	precio m máximo
male sterile	androestéril	maximum price	precio m máximo
maleic hydrazine	hidrazida f maleica f	maximum temperature	temperatura f máxima
malformation	malformación	meadow nematode	anguílula f de raíz
mallow	malva f	mealy	harinoso
		mealy bug	pulgón m lanífero

ENGLISH - SPANISH EQUIVALENTS

ENGLISH	SPANISH	ENGLISH	SPANISH
mean price	precio m medio	mite	ácaro m
measure, to	medir	mix, to	mezclar
measurement	medida f	mixed bud	lamburda f
measuring tape	cinta f de medir	mixed bud	yema f mixta
mechanization	mecanización f	mixer	mezcladora f
medicinal herbs	plantas f medicinales	mock orange	jeringuilla f
Mediterranean fruitfly	mosca f mediterránea de las frutas	modification	modificación f
		moist	húmedo
medium	medio m	moisten, to	humectar
medium-late	semitardío	moisture content	contenido m en agua
melon	melón m	moisture deficiency	carencia f de humedad
melon, honey dew	melón m chino	moisture retaining	hidrófilo
membrane	membrana f	moisture tension	tensión de humedad
membranous	membranoso	moldboard	vertedera f
mercury	mercurio m	mole	topo m
mercury compounds	compuestos m mercurios	mole cricket	grillotalpa m
meristem	meristemo m	molecular weight	peso m molecular
mesophyll	mesófilo m	molybdenum	molibdeno m
mesquite	yaque m	monkey flower	mimulo m
metabolism	metabolismo m	monkshood	acónito m
metamorphosis	metamorfosis f	monkshood	napelo m
methyl bromide	bromuro m de metilo	monobasic	monobásico
Michaelmas Daisy	aster m	monoculture	monocultivo m
microbes	microbios m	monoecious	monóico
microclimate	microclima m	monopetalous	monopétalo
microscopic	microscópico	morning glory	ipomea f,
midrib	nervio m central		enredadera de campanillas f, dondiego de día m, dompedro m
mignonette	reseda f		
mildew	mildeu m, mildiu m		
mimosa	mimosa f	mortar	mortero m
mine	mina f	mortgage	hipoteca f
mine, to	minar	mosaic	mosaico m
mineral	mineral m	moss	musgo m
mineralization	mineralización f	moth	polilla f
minerals	minerales m	mother bulb	bulbo m madre
minimum price	precio m mínimo	mother cell	célula f madre
minimum temperature	temperatura f mínima	mother plant	planta f madre
mint	hierbabuena f	mother plant	planta f progenitora
mist	neblina f	motherstock	planta f madre
mist (for propagation)	nebulización f	motion study	estudio m de los movimientos
mist propagation	multiplicación f con niebla artificial		
		mottled	moreado
mist propagation	propagación f en niebla	mouldboard	vertedera f
mistblower	atomizador m	mountain ash	serbal m
mistletoe	muérdago m	mouse	ratón m

ENGLISH - SPANISH EQUIVALENTS

ENGLISH	SPANISH	ENGLISH	SPANISH
mow the grass	cortar el césped	natural enemy	enemigo m natural
mud	lodo m	natural gas	gas m natural
muddy	limoso	natural resources	recursos m naturales
muddy	lodoso	naturalize, to	degenerarse
muddy spot	atascadero m	nature	naturaleza f
mulberry	mora f	navel	ombligo m
mulch	cobertura f	navel orange	naranja f de ombligo
mulcher	mócher m	navy bean	haba f
mulcher	moledora f	necrosis	necrosis f
mulcher-transplanter	desenrolladora f situadora de película plástica	necrotic	necrosado
		nectar	néctar m
mulching	acolchamiento m de suelos	nectar gland	glándula f nectarífera
multilocular	plurilocular	nectarine	abridor m
multiple regression	regresión f múltiple	nectarine	nectarina f
multispan greenhouse	invernadero m multicuerpo	nectary	nectario m
mummies (fruit)	frutas secas f	needle (bot)	aguja f
mummy disease	enfermedad f de la momificación	needle-shaped	acicular
		neglect	descuido m
muriate of potash	cloruro m potásico	neglect, to	descuidar
mushroom	champiñón m, hongo m	neighborhood	vecindario m
mushroom compost	estiércol m usado para el cultivo del champiñón	nematicide	nematicida f
		nematode	nematodo m
must	mosto m	nerve	nervio m
mutagenic	mutageno	nerves	nervaderas f
mutant	mutante m	net	red f
mutation	mutación	net blotch	mancha f reticulada
mutation breeding	mejoramiento m por mutación	net income	ingresos m netos
		net weight	peso m neto
mycelium	micelio m	nettle	ortiga f
myrtle	mirto m	neutral	neutro
		neutralization	neutralización f
		new value	valor m en nuevo
		New Zealand flax	formio m
	- N -	New Zealand spinach	espinaca f de Nueva Zelandia
		Newcastle disease	neumoencefalitis m aviar
nail	clavo m	niacin	niacina f
nail, to	clavar	nickel	níquel m
napiergrass	hierba f elefante	nicotiana	tobaco m
napthylene acetic acid	ácido m naftalenacético	nicotine	nicotina f
naranjilla	naranjilla f	nicotinic acid	ácido m nicotínico
narcissus	narciso m	night frost	hielo m nocturno
narcotic	narcótico m	night interruption	interrupción f de la noche
narrow leaved	acicular	night soil	excrementos m humanos
nasturtium	capuchina f	nightfall	anochecer m
natalgrass	hierba f de Natal		

ENGLISH - SPANISH EQUIVALENTS

ENGLISH	SPANISH	ENGLISH	SPANISH
nitrate	nitrato m	nutritive	nutritivo
nitrate of lime	nitrato m de cal	nutritive value	valor m nutritivo
nitrate of potash	nitrato m de potasa		
nitric	nítrico		
nitrification	nitrificación f		
nitrify, to	nitrificar		
nitrogen	nitrógeno m		- O -
nitrogen balance	equilibrio m de nitrógeno		
nitrogen deficiency	carencia f en nitrógeno	oak	encina f
nitrogen fertilizers	nitrogenados m	oak	roble m
nitrogen fixation	fijación f del nitrógeno	oak grove	encinal m
nitrogenous	nitrogenado	oats	avena f
nitrogenous fertilizer	abono m nitrogenado	oats, wild	avena f silvestre
nitrous	nitroso	obedient plant	planta f de bisagra
no-tillage	no laboreo	obesity	obesidad f
noctuid	noctuela f	oblong	oblongo
node	nudo m	obovate	trasovado
nodulation	nodulación f	obsolescence	obsolescencia f
nomenclature	nomenclatura f	obstruction	obstrucción f
non-recurrent parent	padre m no recurrente	occurrence	existencia f
non-returnables	embalaje m perdido	ocher	ocre m
Norfolk Island Pine	araucaria f	off-flavor	gusto m diferente
noxious	nocivo	offals	residuos m de matadera
noxious	perjudicial	offset	deportado m
nozzle	boquerel m	offset	hijuelo m
nozzle	boquilla f	offset (bulb)	bulbo m lateral
nucellar	nucelar	offset (bulb)	bulbillo m
nucleic	nucleico	oil	aceite m
nucleolus	nucleólo m	oil burner	quemador m de aceite
nucleotide	nucleótido m	oil crops	cultivos m oleaginosos
nucleus	núcleo m	oil palm	palma f de aceite
nurse crop	cultivo m protector	oilcake	torta f oleaginosa
nurse graft	injerto m nodrizo	oilseeds	semillas f oleaginosas
nurse, to	amamantar	oily	oleaginoso m
nursery	vivero m	okra	okra f
nursery bed	semillero m		quimbombó m
			quingombó m
nursery stock	productos m del vivero	oleander	oleandro m
nut	nuez f	oleander (Nerium oleander)	adelfa f
nutgrass	cebolleta f	olive	aceituna f
nutmeg	nuez f moscada	olive grower	olivicultor m
nutrient	elemento m nutritivo	olive tree	olivo m
nutrient solution	solución f nutritiva	olive-green	verde oliva
nutrition	nutrición f	one-celled	unicelular
nutritional requirement	requisito m de nutrición	onion	cebolla f
nutritious	nutritivo		

ENGLISH - SPANISH EQUIVALENTS

ENGLISH	SPANISH	ENGLISH	SPANISH
onion harvester	cosechadora f de cebollas	orthotropism	ortotropismo m
onion maggot	mosca f de las cebollas	osmosis	ósmosis f
onion set	cebollita f para plantar	osmotic	osmótico
ontogeny	ontogenia f	ounce	onza f
oosphere	oosfera f	outbreak	brote m
opening of flowers	abertura f	outdoor crop	cultivo m al aire libre
operate, to	manejar	outlet	desembocadura f
operating costs	costes m de funcionamiento	outlet	salida f
operating statement	cuenta f de la explotación	outlook	perspectiva f
operation	manejo m	oval	oval m
operator	operario m	oval	ovalado
opium	opio m	ovary	ovario m
opportunity cost	costos m de oportunidad	ovate	oviforme
opposite (bot)	opuesto	oven	horno m
opuntia	higuera f chumba	over-ripe	sobre-maduro
orange	naranja f	overcropping	cultivo m abusivo
orange tree	naranjo m	overfeed, to	sobrealimentar
orchard	huerta f	overgraze, to	sobrecargar
orchard	huerto m frutal	overgrazing	pastoreo m abusivo
orchardgrass	pata f de gallo	overgrowth	sobrecrecimiento m
orchid	orquídea f	overhead	gastos m generales fijos
order of work	sucesión f de los trabajos	overripe	pasado
organelle	organelo m	overstocking	sobrecarga f de ganado
organic	orgánico		por unidad de
organic matter	materia f orgánica		superficie
organic matter	substancia f orgánica	overweight	peso m excesivo
organism	organismo m	overwinter, to	invernar
organization	organización f	overwintered	invernante
organochlorine	organoclorado	ovicidal	ovicido
organochlorine pesticide	pesticida f organoclorada	ovipositor	oviscapto m
organogenesis	organofénesis f	ovule	óvulo m
organoleptic	organoléptico	own capital	capital m propio
organophosphorus	organofosforado	owner	dueño m
organophosphorus pesticide	pesticida f organofosforada	ox	buey m
orient	oriente m	oxalis	acerderilla f
orient, to	orientar	oxidation	oxidación f
oriental poppy	adormidera f oriental	oxygen	oxígeno m
orientation	orientación f	oyster shell scale	cochinilla f ostriforme
origin	origen m	oyster shells	conchas f de ostra
original costs	costos de instalación	oystershell scale	serpeta f del manzano
original seed	semilla f original		
original value	valor m de adquisición		
ornamental garden	jardín m de adorno		
ornamental plant	planta f ornamental		
orthotropic	ortotrópico		

ENGLISH - SPANISH EQUIVALENTS

ENGLISH	SPANISH	ENGLISH	SPANISH
	- P -	papilla	papila f
		pappus	papo m
pack, to	embalar	pappus	vilano m
pack, to	empacar	papyrus	papiro m
pack, to	empaquetar	paraffin wax	parafina f
packer	empaquetador m	parallel	paralelo
packing	embalado m	parallel veined	de nervadura paralela
packing	embalaje m	paralysis	parálisis f
packing	empaque m	paralyze, to	paralizar
packing cloth	tela f de embalar	parasite	parásito m
packing shed	almacén m de embalaje	parasitic	parasítico
packing station	sala f de embalaje	parasitic plant	planta f parasítica
padded	acojinado	parasitism	parasitación f
padding	acolchamiento m	parasitism	parasitismo m
paddock	potrero m	parasitoid	parasitoide m
paddy (rice)	palay m	parasitology	parasitología f
pail	balde m	parcel of land	parcela f
paint	pintura f	parcel out, to	parcelar
paint, to	pintar	parchment (coffee)	pergamino m
paintbrush	pincel m	parenchyma	parénquima f
palatability	palatabilidad f	parent rock	roca f madre
palatability	sabor m	parietal	parietal
palisade tissue	tejido m de empalizada	park	parque m
pallet	paleta f	parsley	perejil m
pallet truck	transportador m de paletas	parsnip	pastinaca f
palmate	palminervado	parted (bot)	partido
palmatifid	palmatifido	parthenocarpy	partenocarpia f
palmette training	palmeta f	parthenogenesis	partenogénesis m
palpitation	palpitación f	partner	socio m
pampas grass	ginerlo m	partnership	sociedad f
pampas grass	hierba f de las pampas	partnership firm	sociedad f colectiva
pamphlet	folleto m	passion flower	parcha f
pandanus	pandano m	passion flower	pasiflora f
pane	vidrio m	passion flower	pasionaria f
pane width	anchura f de vidrio	passionfruit	granadilla f, parcha f
panel	panel m	passionfruit	chinola f
pangolagrass	garrachuelo m	paste	pasta f
panicle	panícula f	pasteurization	pasteurización f
panicle	panoja f	pasteurize, to	pasterizar, pasteurizar
paniculate	paniculado	pasteurizer	pasterizadora f,
pansy	pensamiento m		pasteurizadora f
papain	papaína f	pasture	pastura f
papaya	papaya f	pasture, to	pastar
paphiopedilum	zapatillo m de Venus	pasture, to	pastorear
papilionaceous	papilionáceo	patch	mancha f

ENGLISH - SPANISH EQUIVALENTS

ENGLISH	SPANISH	ENGLISH	SPANISH
patch	parche m	peel, to	pelar
patch budding	injerto m de parche	peeled	pelado
patch budding	injerto m de pieza	pelargonium	pelargonio m
patent, plant	patente m de plantas	pellet	pelotilla f
patent, to	patentar	pelleted	peletizado
path	sendero m	pendulous	colgante
pathogen	patógeno m	pendulous	pendiente
pathogenic	patógeno	pennywort	organillo m
pathogenicity	patogenicidad f	pentachlorophenol	pentaclorofenol m
pathologist	patólogo m	peony	peonía f
pathology, plant	patología f vegetal	peperomia	peperomia f
pathotype	patotipo m	pepper	ají m
pattern of damage	imagen f del daño	pepper	pimienta f
paulownia	paulonia f	peppermint	menta f
pay	pago m	percolate, to	infiltrar
pay day	día m de pago	percolation	infiltración f
payee	tenedor m, portador m	perennial	perenne
pea	guisante m	perennial	vivaz
peach	durazno m	perennial irrigation	riego m permanente
peach	melocotón m	perfoliate	perfoliado
peach (clingstone)	violeto m	performance	actuación f
peach tree	melocotonero m	perfumery	perfumería f
peak load	punta f de trabajo	pergola	pérgola f
peanut	cacahuete m	perianth	periantia m
peanut	maní m	perianth	perigonio m
peanut meal	harina f de maní	pericarp	pericarpio m
pear	pera f	periclinal chimera	quimera f periclinal
pear tree	peral m	periodicity	periodicidad f
peasant farming	explotación f familiar rudimentaria	perishable	perecedero
		perishable goods	productos m perecederos
peat	turba f	peristalsis	peristaltismo m
peat bog	turbal m	perithicium	peritecio m
peat moss	esfagno m, musgo de pantano m	peritoneum	peritoneo m
		periwinkle	pervinca f
peat soil, muck soil	tierra f turba	periwinkle	vinca f
pebble	guija f, guijarro m	perlite	perlita f
pecan	pacana f	permanent pasture	pastura f permanente
pecan nut	pacana f, nuez lisa f	permeability	permeabilidad f
pectin	pectina f	peroxidase	peroxidasa f
pedicel	pedicelo m	perpetual flowering	remontante
pedigree	linaje m	persimmon	níspola f
pedology	pedología f	persimmon	palosanto m
peduncle	pedúnculo m	persimmon	placaminero m
peduncle	tallo m de la flor	persistence	persistencia f
peel	piel f	persistent (bot)	permanente

ENGLISH - SPANISH EQUIVALENTS

ENGLISH	SPANISH	ENGLISH	SPANISH
personnel	empleados m	phytopathologist	fitopatología f
Peruvian lily	peregrina f de Lima	pick	pico m
pest	plaga f	picker (machine)	pizcadora f
pest control	combate m contra las plagas	pick, to	coger
		pick, to	cosechar
pest incidence	incidencia f de las plagas	pick-up (truck)	camioneta f
pesticide	pesticida m	pick-up (truck)	vagoneta f
pesticide	producto m fitosanitario	pick-up baler	recogedora-enfardadora f
petal	pétalo m	picker	recogedora f
petiole	peciolo m	picking	recolección f
petri dish	disco m de Petri	picking (ie. harvesting)	cosecha f
petty spurge	euforbia f	picking basket	cesta f de recolección
petunia	petunia f	picking bucket	saco m de recolección
peyote	peyote m	picking platform	plataforma f recogedora
pH	pH	picking season	época de recolección
pH scale	escala f pH	pickles	conservas f en vinagre
pharynx	faringe f	piece of land	extensión f de tierra
phase	fase f	piece work rate	salario m a destajo
phenotype	fenotipo m	pig	cerdo m
phloem	floema f	pig manure	estiércol m de puerco
phlox	flox m	pigeon	paloma f
phormium	formio m	pigeon pea	guandú m
phosphate	fosfato m	pigment	pigmento m
phosphate rock	fosfato m natural	pigmentation	pigmentación f
phosphate rock	fosforita f	pigsty	chiquero m
phosphatic fertilizers	abonos m fosfatatos	pigweed	bledo m rojo
phosphorescence	fosforescencia f		hierba f de marrano
phosphorus	fósforo m	pilose	velloso
photocell	fotocélula f	pimento	pimentón m
photoelectric	fotoeléctrico	pin	pasador m
photoelectric cell	célula fotoeléctrica	pinch, to	despuntar
photoperiodicity	fotoperiodicidad f	pinch, to	pellizcar
photoperiodicity	fotoperiodismo m	pinching	pellizco m
photospectometer	fotoespectrómetro m	pinching	pinzamiento m
photosphere	fotoesfera f	pine	piña f
photosynthesis	fotosíntesis m	pine	pino m
phyllode (of succulent)	paleta f	pine cone	piña f
phyllotaxis	disposición f de las hojas	pine needle	pinocha f
phylloxera	filoxera f	pine nut	piñón m
physioclimatology	fisioclimatología f	pineapple	piña f
physiological disorder	trastorno m fisiológico	pink (flower)	clavel m coronado
physiological race	raza f fisiológica	pinnate	pinado
physiology	fisiología f	pinnately lobed	pinadolubulado
phystostegia	planta f de bisagra	pinnatifid	pinatifido
phytocide	fitocida m	pinniform	peniforme

ENGLISH - SPANISH EQUIVALENTS

ENGLISH	SPANISH	ENGLISH	SPANISH
pint	pinta f	plant density	intensidad f de plantación
pioneer species	especie f colonizadora	plant disease	enfermedad f de las plantas
pipe	tubo m	plant food	alimento m para plantas
pipe heating	calefacción f por tubos	plant kingdom	reino m vegetal
pipes	tubería f	plant louse	áfido m
pipette	pipeta f	plant louse	chinchita f de las plantas
pistachio (Pistacia vera)	alfóncigo m	plant material	plantulas f
pistil	pistilo m	plant pathologist	fitopatólogo m
pistillate	pistilado	plant physiologist	fitofisiólogo m
piston	pistón m	plant production	fitotecnia f
piston pump	bomba f de pistón	plant production	producción f vegetal
pit	fosa f	plant sample	muestra f de material vegetal
pit	huesa f		
pit (fruit)	cascaraña f	plant spacing	distancia f entre plantas
pitch	pez f	plant taxonomy	taxonomía f vegetal
pitch (roof slope)	pendiente	plant, to	plantar
pitcher plant	nepente m	plant, to	sembrar
pitchfork	horca f	plantain	plátano m
pitchfork	horcón m	plantation	hacienda f
pitchfork	horquilla f	plantation	plantacíon f
pith	tuétano m	planter (man)	plantador m
pith (bot)	médula f	planter (woman)	plantadora f
pith ray (bot)	rayo m medular	planting	siembra f
pitomba	pitomba f	planting hole	hueco m
pitting	deshuesamiento m	planting scheme	plan m de cultivo
pittosporum	pitósporo m	planting season	época de siembra
plagiotropic	plagiotrópico	plantlet	plantilla f
plagiotropism	plagiotropismo m	plantlet	plántula f
plague	plaga f	plasmolysis	plasmólisis f
plains	llanos m	plastic	plastidio m
plaintain lily	finquia f	plastic	plástico m
plan	plan m	plastic foam	espuma f de plástico
plan, to	planificar	plastic pot	maceta f de plástico
plane table	plancheta f	plastic tie	banda f de plástico
plane tree	plátano	plastid	plasto m
plank	tabla f	platform	plataforma f
planning	planificación f	platinum	platino m
plant	planta f	pledge	prenda f
plant (esp. large herbaceous)	mata f	pliers	alicates m
plant (factory)	fábrica f	plot	lote m
plant association	comunidad f de plantas	plot	parcela f
plant border	arriate m marginal	plough	arado m
plant breeder	experto m en fitomejoramiento	plough in, to	enterrar con arado
		plough out, to	arrancar con arado
plant breeding	fitogenética f	plough share	reja f

ENGLISH - SPANISH EQUIVALENTS

ENGLISH	SPANISH	ENGLISH	SPANISH
plough, to	arar	polyamide	poliamida f
plow	arado m	polyandrous	poliandro
plow again, to	sobrearar	polycarpic	policárpico
plow under, to	enterrar con el arado	polyembryony	poliembrionía f
plow under, to	incorporar	polyester	poliéster m
plow up, to	arrancar con el arado	polyethylene	polietileno m
plow, to	arar	polymer	polimeré m
plowing	aradura f	polymer	polímero m
plowing	labranza f	polymorphism	polimorfismo m
plowman	arador m	polypetalous	polipétalo
plowshare	reja f del arado	polyploid	poliploide m
plowsole	piso m del arado	polyploidy	poliploidia f
plug	tapón m	polypodium	polipodia m
plugged	tapado	polypropylene	polipropileno m
plum	ciruela f	polysaccharide	polisacárido m
plum tree	cirolero m	polysepalous	polisépalo
plum tree	ciruelo m	polystyrene	polistireno m
plumbago	teleza f	polyvalent	polivalente
plumule	plumilla f	polyvinyl chloride	cloruro m de polivinilo
plumule	plúmula	pomace	bagazo m
pod	vaina f	pome	fruta f de pepita
pod (of cacao)	majorca f, mazorca f	pomegranate fruit	granada f
podzol	podzol m	pomegranate tree	granado m
podzol	suelo m podsol	pomologist	fruticultor m
poinsettia	flor f de navidad	pomology	fruticultura f
poinsettia	paño m de Holanda	pomology	pomología f
poinsettia	pastora f	pond	charco m
poinsettia	poinsetia f	pond	estanque m
poison	veneno m	pool	piscina f, alberca f
poison plant	planta f venenosa	poplar	álamo m
poison, to	envenenar	poppy	adormidera f
poisoning	envenenamiento m	population	población f
poisonous	venenoso	pore	poro m
polarity	polaridad f	pore space	porosidad f
pole	palo m	pore space	volumen m de poros
pole	pértiga f	pork	carne m de cerdo
policy	política f	porosity	porosidad f
pollard	moyuelo m	porous	permeable
pollen	polen m	porous	poroso
pollen grain	grano m de polen	porridge	papilla f
pollinate, to	polenizar	post	poste m
pollination	polinización f	post-climateric	post climatérico
pollinator	polinizador m	post-emergence application	aplicación f después de la emergencia
pollution	ensuciamiento m, polución f, contaminacíon f		

ENGLISH - SPANISH EQUIVALENTS

ENGLISH	SPANISH	ENGLISH	SPANISH
post office box	apartado m postal	power-take-off	toma f de fuerza
post-sowing application	aplicación f después de la siembra	pox	viruela f
postharvest	postcosecha	prairie	pradera f
post-hole digger	cavadora f de hoyos	prairie dog	perro m de las praderas
pot	maceta f	pre-emergence application	aplicación f antes de la emergencia
pot	pote m	pre-germinate, to	pregerminar
pot plant	planta f de tiesto	pre-heat, to	precalentar
pot shards	pedazos m de macetas	pre-heater	precalentador m
pot, clay	maceta f de barro	pre-packing	preembalaje m
pot, peat	macetas f de fibra de turba	pre-soak, to	remojar
pot, to	plantar en macetas	pre-sowing application	applicación f antes de la siembra
potash	potasa f	preceding crop	cultivo m precedente
potash fertilizer	abono m potásico	precipitate	precipitado m
potash salt	sal f de potasa	precipitation	precipitación f
potassium	potasio m	precision seeder	sembrador m de precisión
potassium content	contenido m en potasio	preclimacteric	preclimatérico
potassium deficiency	carencia f de potasio	precocity	precocidad f
potassium fixation	fijación f de potasio	precook, to	precocer
potato	papa f or patata f	precooking	precocción f
potato digger	cosechadora f de patatas	precooling	prerrefrigeración f
potato digger	excavadora f de papas	predator	depredador m
potato field	papal m	predator	predator m
potato planter	sembradora f de papas	prediction	predicción f
potato scab	sarna f de la papa	pregnancy	preñada f
potherb	hortaliza f de hoja	pregnant	embarazado
potting soil	tierra f para maceta	prematurely ripe	maduro prematuro
poultry	aves f de corral	preparation	preparación f
poultry farm	granja f avícola	prepare, to	preparar
poultry manure	gallinaza f	preplanting	presiembra f
poultry production	producción f avícola	preservation	conservación f
poultry raiser	avicultor m	preservative	producto m de protección
pound	libra f	preservatives	medios m de conservación
pound, to	golpear	preserve	conserva f de fruta
pour into, to	regar	preserve, to	conservar
powdered milk	leche f en polvo	preserve, to	preservar
powdery mildew	mildiu m	preserved fruit	conservas f de frutas
powdery mildew	oídio m	preserving industry	industria f conservera
powdery mildew	tizón m polvoriento	press	prensa f
power	fuerza f	press, to	prensar
power saw	sierra f mecánica	pressure	presión f
power take-off	toma f de fuerza	pressure gauge	manómetro m
power tool	herramienta f mecánica	prestressed concrete	hormigón m pretensado
power, to	accionar	pretreatment	pretratamiento m
power-driven	motorizado		

ENGLISH - SPANISH EQUIVALENTS

ENGLISH	SPANISH	ENGLISH	SPANISH
price	precio m	prop	rodrigón m
price control	control m de precios	prop root	raíz f áerea de sostén
price control	regulación f de precios	propagate, to	multiplicar
price index	índice m de precios	propagate, to	propagar
price list	lista f de precios	propagating bin	cajonera f
price supports	subvención f a los precios	propagating house	invernadero m de multiplicación
prick out, to	picar	propagation	multiplicación
prickle	copina f	propagation	propagación f
prickly pear cactus	nopal m	propagation greenhouse	invernadero m de multiplicación
prime costs	costos m primarios	propagator	propagador
prime, to (pump)	cebar	propane	propano m
primordium	primordio m	property	propiedad f
primrose	prímula f	proplastic	proplástico m
principles of farm management	teoría de la explotación agrícola	proportion	proporción f
privet	ligustro m	proportioner	dosímetro m
probability	probabilidad f	prostrate	postrado
proceeds	producto m	prostrate	procumbente
process	procedimiento	protandry	protandria f
process, to	elaborar	protect, to	proteger
processing	elaboración f	protected from frost	protegido de la helada
processing	transformación f	protection	protección f
processing industry	industria f de procesamiento	protein	proteína f
processing plant	fábrica f elaboradora	protein concentrate	concentrado m protéico
procumbent	echado	prothallium	prótalo m
procumbent	procumbente	protogynous	proterógino
produce	productos m	protogyny	protoginia f
produce, to	producir	protoplasm	protoplasma m
producer	productor m	prototype	prototipo m
production	producción f	protozoa	protozoarios m
production means	medio m de producción	protozoan	protozoario
productive	productivo	protuberance	protuberancia f
productivity	productividad f	proved sire	toro m probado
profile	perfil m	provision market	mercado m de abasto
profile	sección f vertical de un suelo	proximal	proximal
		prune	ciruela f pasa
profitable	lucrativo	prune, to	cortar
progeny	descendencia f	prune, to	podar
progeny	progenie f	pruning	poda f
progesterone	progesterona f	pruning cut	herida f
program	programa m	pruning knife	podadera f
project	proyecto m	pruning saw	sierra f podadera
proliferous	prolífero	pruning season	podazón f
promoter	promotor m	pruning shears	tijera f de podar

ENGLISH - SPANISH EQUIVALENTS

ENGLISH	SPANISH	ENGLISH	SPANISH
pruning shears	tijera f podadera	purlin	jabalcón m
prunings	leña f proveniente de la poda	purpose	propósito m
		purslane	verdolaga f
pseudo fruit	fruto m aparente	put a lid on, to	tapar
pseudostem	pseudotallo m	putrefaction	putrefacción f
pseudostem	seudotallo m	putrefy, to	putreficarse
psorosis	sorosis f	putrid	descompuesto, pútrido
psylla	psilas f	putty	mástic m
psyllid	psila f	pycnidium	picnidio m
pteridophyte	pteridófita f	pylorus	piloro m
pteridophyte	teridófita f	pyracantha	piracanta m
PTO	toma f de fuerza, pitio m	pyrethrum	pelitre m
PTO driven sprayer	pulverizador m sobre toma de fuerza	pyrethrum	piretro m
		pyriform	piriforme
pubescent	pubescente		
puckered	abollamiento		
puddle	charco m		
puddling	encharcamiento m		- Q -
pull, to	tirar		
pullet	polla f	quackgrass	grama f del norte
pulley	polea f	quadrant level	teodolito m
pulp	pulpa f	quail	codorniz f
pulse	pulso m	quality	calidad f
pulverize, to	polvificar	quality control	control m de calidad
pulverize, to	pulverizar	quality grading	clasificación f por calidad
pumice	piedra f pómez	quality loss	pérdida f de calidad
pump	bomba f	quality norm	norma f de calidad
pump, to	bombear	quarantine	cuarentena f
pumping station	estación f de bombeo	quarter horse	caballo m americano
pumpkin (Carribbean)	auyama f	queen bee	abeja f reina
pumpkin	calabaza f, zapallo m	quick coupling pipe	tubo m de acoplamiento
pupa	crisálida f	quick freezing	congelación f rápida
pupa	ninfa f	quicklime	cal f calcinada
pupa	pupa f	quicklime	cal f viva
pupate, to	crisalidarse	quincunx	quincunce m also disposición f quincuncial
purchasing power	poder m adquisitivo		
pure culture	cultivo m puro	quinine	quina f
pure culture	cultura f pura	quinine	quinina f
pure line	línea f pura	quotient	cociente m
purebred	de raza f pura		
purebred	puro		
puree	puré m		
purification	purificación f		
purify, to	purificar		
purity	pureza f		

ENGLISH - SPANISH EQUIVALENTS

ENGLISH	SPANISH	ENGLISH	SPANISH
- R -		ratoon, to	retoñar
		rattan	ratán m
rabbit	conejo m	rattlesnake	víbora
race	raza f	raw materials	materias f primas
raceme	racimo m	ray	rayo m
racemose	racimoso	ray floret	flor f radial
rachis	raquis m	reaction	reacción f
radiant heat	calor m radiante	reagent	reactivo m
radiating surface	superficie f radiante	receptacle	receptáculo m
radiation	radiación f	recessive	recesivo
radiator	radiador m	rectangle	rectángulo m
radicle	radícula f	red cabbage	repollo m morado
radicular	radiculoso	red hot poker	
radioactive fall out	precipitación f radioactiva	(Kniphofia spp.)	atizador al rojo vivo m
radioactivity	radioactividad f	red hot poker plant	tritoma f
radioisotope	radioisótopo m	red mite	araña f roja
radiosensitivity	radiosensibilidad f	reduce, to	reducir
radish	rábano m	reducing valve	válvula f reductora
raffia	rafia f	reduction	reducción f
rafter	cabrio m	reduction division	división f reductora
rag	trapo m	reed	junco m
rain gauge	pluvíometro m	reefer	rífer m
rain, to	llover	reel	devanadera f
rainfall	lluvia f	reference price	precio m de referencia
raison	pasa f	refill, to	rellenar
rake	rastrillo m	reflection	reflexión f
rake in, to	rastrillar	reflector	reflector m
rambutan	rambután m	reforestation	reforestación f
ramie (fiber)	ramina f	refractive	refringente
ramie (plant)	ramio m	refractometer, hand held	refractómetro m manual
ramification	ramificación f	refractometry	refractometría f
ramified	ramificado	regeneration	regeneración f
rampant	rastrero	regime	régimen
random sample	muestra f seleccionada al azar	regression	regresión f
		regreen, to	reverdecer
rangpur lime	rangpur m	regrow, to	rebrotar
ranunculus	ranúnculo m	reinforce, to	reforzar
raphia palm	rafia f	reinforced	reforzado
raspberry	frambuesa f	reinforcement	refuerzo m
rasp	rallador m	reject (processing)	destrío m
rasp	rallo m	rejuvenation	rejuvenecimiento m
rat	rata f	relative humidity	humedad f relativa
rate	dosificación f	relay	ralé m
rate	tasa f	remedy	remedio m
rate of germination	vigor m germinativo	removable	desmontable

ENGLISH - SPANISH EQUIVALENTS

ENGLISH	SPANISH	ENGLISH	SPANISH
removal	remoción f	ripening room	cámara f de maduración
renewed growth	retoño m	river clay	arcilla f aluvial
reniform	reniforme	rock	roca f
repellent	repelente m	rock garden	rocalla f
replace plants, to	rellenar	rock phosphate	fosfato m natural
replacement part	repuesto m	rockery	jardín m rocoso
replacement value	valor m de sustitución	rodent	roedor m
replant, to	replantar	roll, to	rodar
replanting	replantación f	roller	rodillo m
replication	replicación f	roller	rollo m
repot, to	mudar de tiesto	roller conveyer	transportador m por rodillos
requirement	requerimiento m	roof	techo m
research	investigación f	roofing felt	cartón m embreado
research station	estación f experimental	root	raíz f
researcher	investigador m	root activity	actividad f radicular
reseeding	resiembra f	root ball	cepellón champa
residual value	valor m residual	root bud	yema f radicular
residue	residuo m	root cap	cofia f
resin	resina f	root cap	pilorriza f
resistance	resistencia f	root cutting	estaca f de raíz
resistant	resistente	root hair	pelo m radical
respiration	respiración f	root hairs	pelos m radicales
response	respuesta f	root lesion nematode	nematodos m de los prados
rest	reposo m	root pattern	imagen f radicular
retailer	detallista m	root penetration	penetración f de las raíces
retard, to	retrasar	root rot	podredumbre f radical
retarded bulbs	bulbos m retardados	root sucker	brote m radicular
return valve	válvula f de retorno	root system	sistema m radicular
reversible plough	arado m reversible	root, to	arraigar
rhizogenesis	rizogénesis	root, to	barbar
rhizoid	rizoide m	root, to	echar raíces
rhizome	rizoma m	rooting	enraizamiento m
rhombic	romboidal	rooting	radicación f
rhubarb	ruibarbo m	rootlet	raiceja f
ribbed	estriado	roots	raíces f
riboflavin	riboflavina f	rootstock	patrón m
ridge	caballete m	rope	cuerda f
ridge culture	cultivo m en lomos	rose	rosa f
ridger	arado m para aporcar	rose bush	rosal m
rinse, to	enjuagar	roselle	rosella f
rip, to (soil)	remover	rosemary	romero m
ripe	maduro	rosetting	formación de rosetas
ripen, to	madurar	rot	putrefacción f
ripeness	madurez	rot, to	descomponer
ripeness	sazón f	rot, to	pudrir

ENGLISH - SPANISH EQUIVALENTS

ENGLISH	SPANISH	ENGLISH	SPANISH
rotary cultivator	cultivador m rotativo	saguaro	saguaro m
rotary mower	segadora f rotativa	sale value	valor m en venta
rotary sprinkler	aspersor m rotativo	saleable	suministrable
rotavator	avellanador m	saline	salado
rotenone	rotenona f	saline	salino
rotten	podrido	salinity	salinidad f
rough	áspero	salinizacion	salinización f
row	fila f	saliva	saliva f
row	hilera f	salsify	salsifí m
row	línea f	salt	sal f
row planting	plantación en hileras	salt content	contenido m en sal
row spacing	distancia f entre líneas	salt lick	salegar f
rugose	arrugado	saltiness	salsedumbre f
run, to (machine)	andar	saltpeter	salitre m
runner	estolón m	samara	sámara f
runner	latiguillo m	sample	muestra f
runner	serpa f	sample, to	tomar muestras
rupture	ruptura f	sand	arena f
rush	junco m	sand drift	montón m de arena
russeting	aspereza f de los frutos	sand dune	duna f de arena
rust	herrumbre f	sand hill	loma f de arena
rust	roya f	sandalwood	sándalo m
rust (metal)	óxido m	sandy	arenoso
rust, to	oxidar	sandy clay	suelo m arcillo-arenoso
rusty	con roya f	sandy soil	suelo m arenoso
rusty	herrumbroso	sanitary	sanitario m
rusty	roñoso	sanitation	sanidad f
rusty (metal)	oxidado	sap	jugo m
rutabaga	colinabo m	sap	savia f
ryegrass	ballico m	sapodilla	níspero m
		sapodilla	zapote m
		saprophyte	saprófito
		saprophytic	saprofítico
		sapwood	albura f
		sapwood	sámago m

Handwritten annotations: rubber — goma, objeto de hule, goma o caucho; rubber scrubber — estropajo - esponja y lija

-S-

ENGLISH	SPANISH	ENGLISH	SPANISH
sack	saco	sash	ventana f
saddle graft	injerto m a caballo	saturate, to	saturar
safety margin	plazo m de seguridad	saturation	saturación f
safety valve	válvula f de seguridad	saturation point	punto m de saturación
safflower	alazor m	sausage	salchicha f
sage	salvia f	savanna	sabana f
sagebrush	artemisa f	savoy cabbage	col f rizada
sagittate	sagitado	saw	sierra f
sagittate	sagital	saw fly	tentredinido m,
sago palm	sagú m		mosca de sierra f

ENGLISH - SPANISH EQUIVALENTS

ENGLISH	SPANISH	ENGLISH	SPANISH
saw, to	serruchar	screw worm	gusano m tornillo
sawdust	aserrín m	screwdriver	destornillador m, desarmador m
sawhorse	caballete m, burro m	scrubber	scrubber m
sawmill	aserradero m	scutellum	escutelo m
scab	escabro m	scythe	guadaña f
scab	roña f	scythe, to	guadañar
scabiosa	escabiosa f	sea-weed	alga f
scald	recalamiento	seal, to	precintar
scale (insect)	cochinilla f	season	temporada f
scale (weight)	balanza f	season, to	condimentar
scallion	ajo m porro	season, to	sazonar
scape	vara f	seasonal labor	mano m de obra estacional
scar	cicatriz f	seasonal labor	trabajo m estacional
scarce	escaso m	secateur	tijeras f de podar
scarcity	escasez m	second crop	cultivo m consecutivo
scarification	escarificación f	secretion	secreción f
scarified seed	semilla f escarificada	sectorial chimera	quimera f sectorial
scarlet	escarlata	security (econ)	garantía f
scarlet runner bean	patol m	sedative	sedativo m
scatter, to	diseminar	sediment	sedimento m
scatter, to	distribuir	sedimentary rock	roca f sedimentaria
scented	oloroso	sedimentation	sedimentación f
scented	perfumado	sedum	hierba f callera
scented geranium	geranio m aromático	seed	grana f
scentless	inodoro	seed	semilla f
schedule	horario m	seed (small)	pepita f
school lunch	comida f escolar	seed bed	semillero m
scion	injerto m	seed certification	certificación f de semillas
scion	púa f	seed cleaner	limpiadora f de semillas
scion	púa f de injerto	seed cleaner	limpiasemillas f
scion	vástago m	seed coat	tegumento m
sclerotia	esclerocios m	seed disinfectant	desinfectante m para semillas
scoop, to (hyacinth)	ahuecar	seed drill	sembradora f
scorch	quemadura f	seed growing	cultivo m de semillas
scorch, to	agostar	seed leaf	cotiledón m
scour erosion	erosión f por abrasión	seed plant	planta f de semilla
scours	disentería f	seed pod	cápsula de la semilla
scraper	niveladora f	seed potato	papa f de siembra
screen	tela f metálica	seed registration	registro m de semillas
screen	zaranda f	seed sample	muestra f de semillas
screen, to	proteger	seed stalk	pedúnculo m
screen (sprinkler)	cedazo m	seed testing	control m de semillas
screw	tornillo m	seed trade	comercio m de semillas
screw pine	pandano m		
screw, to	atornillar		

estropajo
lavadora de gases

ENGLISH - SPANISH EQUIVALENTS

ENGLISH	SPANISH	ENGLISH	SPANISH
seed tray	caja f de semillero	serology	serología f
seed treatment	tratamiento m de las semillas	serrate	aserrado
		service charges	gastos m de gestión
seed, to	sembrar	serving	porción f
seed-dealer	proveedor m de semillas	sesame	ajonjolí m
seedbed	semillero m	sesame	sésamo m
seeder	sembradora f	sessile	sentado
seeding machine	sembradora f	sessile	sésil
seedling	plantilla f	settle, to	asentarse
seedling	plántula f	settle, to (soil)	asentar
seedstalk	tallo m fructífero	settlement	colonización f
segregation	segregación f	sew, to	coser
seismography	sismografía f	sewage	aguas f negras
select, to	seleccionar	sewage sludge	lodo m de ciudades
selection	selección f	sewer	cloaca f
selective	selectivo	sex	sexo m
selective cutting	corta f de mejoramiento	sex pheromone	sex-feromona f
self-fertile	autoestéril	sexual	gamíco
self-fertilization	autofecundación f	sexual propagation	multiplicación f sexual
self-fertilization	autofertilización f	sexual reproduction	reproducción f sexual
self-incompatability	autoincompatibilidad f	shade	sombra f
self-pollination	autofecundación f	shade house	sombráculo m
self-pollination	autopolinización f		sombreadero m
self-service	autoservicio m	shade, to	abrigar
self-sterile	autosteril	shade, to	dar sombra f
selfing	autofecundación f	shadehouse	sombreadero m
selfing	autofertilización f	shading	sombreado m
sell, to	vender	shadiness	abundancia f de sombras
selling price	precio m de venta	shady	umbrático
semen	semen m	shady	umbrío
semi-arid	semiárido	shaft	eje m
semi-automatic	semi automático	shaker	agitador m
semi-darkness	penumbra f	shaker (tree)	máquina f de sacudir
semi-early	semiprecoz	shallot	chalote m
semitropical	semitropical	shallow	poco profundo
senescence	senectud f	shallow	superficial
sensitive plant	planta sensitiva f	shallow rooted	raíces f superficiales
sensitivity	sensibilidad f	shank (plow)	timón m de arado
sepal	sépalo m	share cropping	aparcería f
separate, to	separar	share holder	aparcero m
separation	separación f	sharecropper	aparcero m
separator, cream	descremadora f	sharp	afilada
septum	septo m	sharpen, to	afilar
sequoia	secoya f	shasta daisy	artemisa f
sericulture	sericultura f	shattering	desgrane m

ENGLISH - SPANISH EQUIVALENTS

ENGLISH	SPANISH	ENGLISH	SPANISH
shaving	viruta f	shrivel, to	encorgerse
shears	tijeras f	shrub	arbusto m
sheath	vaina f	shrubby	arbustivo
shed, to (animals)	pelechar	sib, to	aparear entre hermanos
shedding (plants)	defoliación f	sick	enfermo
sheep	ovino m, oveja f	sickle	hoz f
sheep dip	baño m garrapaticida	side delivery rake	rastrillo m de descarga lateral
sheep manure	estiércol m de aveja		
sheep raising	crianza f ovina	side dressing	abonado m lateral en cobertera
sheet erosion	erosión f laminar		
shell	cáscara f	side grafting	injerto m lateral
shell lime	cal f de conchas	side shoot	tallo m lateral
shell, to	desgranar	sidehill plow	arado m de vertedera giratoria
shell, to	desvainar		
sheller	descascaradora f	sieve	tamiz m
shelling	desgrane m	sieve	zaranda f
shelter belt	faja f protectora	sieve tube	tubo m criboso
shepherd's purse	panique sillo m	sieve, to	tamizar
shield budding	injerto m de escudete	sifter	cribadora f
shield budding	injerto m de ojo	sigatoka disease	sigatoka f
shieldlike	en forma de escudo	significance	significado m
shifting cultivation	agricultura f migratoria	silage	ensilaje m
ship, to	enviar	silica	silicio m
shoot	brote m	silicone	silicona f
shoot	retoño m	siliqua	silicua f
shoot	vástago	silo	ensiladora f
shoot, to	brotar	silo	silo m
shoot, to	nacer	silt	cieno m
shooting (plant)	brotamiento m	silt	limo m
shop (repair)	taller m	silt up, to	embarrar
short (circuit)	corto m circuito	silt, to	formar aluviones f
short day plant	planta f de día corto	silvery	plateado
short day treatment	tratamiento m de día corto	simple	simple, sencillo
short shoot	dardo m	single phase (current)	monofásico m
shoulder (animal)	brazuelo m	sink	fregadero m
shovel	pala f	sinuate	ondulado
shovel, to	palear	sinuate	sinuoso
show symptoms, to	acusar síntomas	sinus (botanical)	seno m
shower	ducha f	sire	padre m
shower, to	duchar	sisal	sisal m
shredder	desmenuzadora f	site	sitio m
shrink, to	encogerse	size	calibre m
shrink, to (soil)	contraer	size	tamaño m
shrinkage	contracción f	size, to	calibrar
shrinkage film	película f de contracción	skeletonize, to	hacer esquelético

ENGLISH - SPANISH EQUIVALENTS

ENGLISH	SPANISH	ENGLISH	SPANISH
skimmed milk	leche f descremada	soak	romojo m
skin	piel f	soak in, to	filtrarse en
skin	cuero m	soak up, to	absorber
skin (fruit)	cáscara f	soak, to	humedecer
skin disease	enfermedad f de la piel	soak, to	remojar
skin, to	pelar	soaker hose	tubo m flexible perforado
skunk	mapurito m	sod	césped m
sky blue	azul celeste	sod	tepe m or tierra f herbosa
slaked lime	cal f apagada	soda ash	ceniza f de soda
slaked lime	cal f muerta	sodium	sodio m
slaughter	matanza f	sodium chlorate	clorato m de sodio
slaughter, to	matar	sodium nitrate	nitrato m sódico
slaughterhouse	matadero m	soft	blando
slender	grácil	soft	suave
slide	diapositiva f	soft rot	podredumbre f húmeda
slide rule	regla f de cálculo	soft scale insect	cochinilla f
slip	hijo m	soft water	agua f suave
slippage	deslizamiento m	soft, tender	suave
slippery	resbaloso	soil	suelo m
slope	declive m	soil aeration	aireación f del suelo
slope	pendiente m	soil analysis	análisis m de suelo
slope	talud m	soil analysis report	boletín m de análisis
slow down, to	retardar	soil auger	barreno m de suelo
slow up, to	retardar	soil auger	barreno m para suelos
slug	babosa f	soil classification	clasificación f de suelos
slug	caracol m	soil condition	características f del suelo
small fruit (berry)	baya f	soil conditioner	acondicionador m de suelos
small intestine	intestino m delgado	soil conservation	conservación f de suelos
small leaf	hojita f	soil depletion	agotamiento m del suelo
small truck farmer	hortelano m	soil disease	enfermedad f del suelo
smell	olor m	soil disinfection	desinfección f del suelo
smell, to	oler	soil dressings	enmiendas f
smokehouse	ahumadero m	soil exhaustion	fatiga f del suelo
smooth (bot)	liso m	soil fertility	fertilidad f de los suelos
smut	carbón m	soil heating	calentamiento m del suelo
snail	caracol m	soil improvement	mejoramiento m del suelo
snake	serpiente f, víbora f	soil injector	enyector m para el suelo
snapdragon	antirrino m	soil layer	capa f del suelo
snapdragon	boca f de dragón or dragoncillo m, conejito m	soil management	manejo m del suelo
		soil map	mapa f edafológico
snow	nieve f	soil map	mapa m del suelo
snowball	bola f de nieve	soil mining	empobrecimiento m del suelo
snowdrop	galanto m de nieve		
snowdrop	rompenieve m	soil mixture	mezcla f de tierra
snowy	nevado	soil profile	perfil m del suelo

ENGLISH - SPANISH EQUIVALENTS

ENGLISH	SPANISH	ENGLISH	SPANISH
soil sample	muestra f del suelo	sow broadcast, to	sembrar al voleo
soil sanitation	sanidad f del suelo	sow, to	sembrar
soil science	edafología f	sowbug	cochinilla f de humedad
soil sterilization	desinfección f del suelo	sowing	siembra f
soil sterilization	esterilización f del suelo	sowing season	época f de siembra
soil structure deterioration	deterioración f de la estructura	sowing-date	fecha f de siembra
		soybean	soja f
soil surface	superficie f del suelo	soybean	soya f
soil survey	cartografía f del suelo	space	espacio m
soil survey	reconocimiento m edafológico	space requirement	espacio m que necesita una planta o animal
soil treatment	tratamiento m del suelo	spacing	distancia f en el surco
soil type	tipo m del suelo	spacing	espaciado m
soil types	tipos m de suelos	spacing	espaciamiento m
soil water	agua f del suelo	spade	guataca f
soil-borne virus	virus m transmisible por el suelo	spade	laya f
		spade	pala f
soil-building crop	cultivo m reconstructor del terreno	spade	palendra f
soil-restoring crop	cultivo m renovador del suelo	spade	zapa f
		spadix	garrancha f
soilless culture	cultivo m sin suelo	spadix	mazorca f
soilless culture	cultivo m sin tierra	spanish moss	barba f española
solanaceous	solanáceo	spare parts	repuestos m
solanine	solanina f	sparkplug	bujía f
solder	soldadura f	sparrow	gorrión m
solder, to	soldar	spathe	vaina f
soldered joint	soldadura f	spatulate	espatulado
solenoid valve	válvula f solenoide	spawn, to (mushrooms)	sembrar
solstice	solsticio m	spearmint	menta f crespa
soluble	soluble	species	especie f
soluble salts	sales f solubles	specific gravity	gravedad f específica
solution	solución f	speck	pinta f, manchita f
solution, diluted	solución f diluida	spectrophotometric identification	identificación f espectrofotométrica
sooty mold	fumagina f		
sooty mold	negrón m	spectrum	espectro m
sorghum	sorgo m	sperm	esperma f
sort, to	clasificar	sphagnum moss	musgo m, esfagnáceo
sour cherry	cereza f ácida	sphagnum peat moss	esfagno m
sour orange	zamboa f, naranja f agria	spider web	telaraña f
sour, acidic	agrio	sphincter	esfínter m
source of infection	foco m de infección	spice	especia f
soursop fruit	guanábana f	spike	espiga f
soursop tree	guanábano m	spikelet	espiguilla f
sow (pig)	puerca f, cerda f, marrana f	spin, to	girar
		spinach	espinaca f

ENGLISH - SPANISH EQUIVALENTS

ENGLISH	SPANISH	ENGLISH	SPANISH
spindly	raquítico	sprinkler irrigation	riego m por aspersión
spine	espina f	sprout, to	brotar
spinning	hilado	sprout, to	pimpollear
splice graft	injerto m de empalme	sprout, to (seed)	germinar
split-plot	parcela f subdividida	sprouting inhibitor	inhibidor m de brotación
spoil, to	deteriorarse	spruce	abeto m
spore	espora f	spruce	picea f
sport	mutación f	spur	espolón m
spot	mancha f	spur	garrón m
spot grazing	pastoreo m irregular	spur	pico m
spot price	precio m al contado	spurge	nogueruela f
spotted	punteado	squall	turbonada f
spotted	salpicado	square	cuadro m
spray boom	rampa f de pulverización	squares (cotton)	brácteas f
spray damage	deterioro m ocasionado por plaguicidas	squash	calabaza f
		squash or pumpkin	ayote m
spray gun	lanza f de pulverización	squash, summer	calabacita f
spray gun	pistola f pulverizadora	squash, winter	calabaza f
spray liquid	líquido m	squatter	colono m usurpador
spray nozzle	boquilla f del pulverizador	squeeze, to	apelmazar
spray nozzle	espumadera f	St. John's wort	hierba f San Juan
spray pump	bomba f aspersora	St. John's wort	hipérico m
spray, to	asperjar	stable	establo
spray, to	echar	stable (horses)	caballeriza f
spray, to	pulverizar	stack	gavilla f
spray, to	rociar	stack silo	silo m pila
sprayer	asperjadora f	stack, to	apilar
sprayer	pulverizador m	stage	fase f
sprayer	rociador m	staghorn fern	platicerio m
spraying	pulverización f	stain	mancha f
spread, to	esparcir	stain, to	manchar
spreader	esparcidora	stake	estaca f
spreader, wetting agent	adherente m	stake	rodriga f
spreader-sticker	adherente-espacidor m	stake	tutor m
spring (auto)	ballesta f	staking	tutorado m
spring (i.e. watch)	resorte m	stalk	cepa f
spring (season)	primavera f	stalk	pezón m
spring (water)	fuente f	stalk	tallo m
spring tooth harrow	cultivador m de dientes flexibles	stall	establo m
		stallion	caballo m semental
spring water	agua f manantial	stamen	estambre m
spring wheat	trigo m de primavera	staminate	estaminado
sprinkle, to	regar	staminate	masculino
sprinkle, to	rociar	stanchion	cornadiza f
sprinkler	rociador m	stand	rodal m

ENGLISH - SPANISH EQUIVALENTS

ENGLISH	SPANISH	ENGLISH	SPANISH
standard deviation	desviación f normal	sterilize, to	esterilizar
standard error	desviación f media	sterilizer	esterilizador m
standard error	error m medio	stewed fruit	compota f
standard of living	norma f de vida	stick	palo m
standardization	normalización f	stick sulphur	azufre m en barras
standardization	estandardización f	sticking	atoramiento
standardize, to	normalizar	stigma	estigma m
staple	grapa f	stile	portillo m de escalones
staple	producto m principal	sting	picadura f
staple, to	grapar, engrapar	stinging hair	pelo m urticante
stapler	grapadora f	stinging nettle	ortiga f
star of Bethlehem	leche f de gallina	stipule	estipula f
starch	almidón m	stirring rod	varita f
starch	fécula f	stitch	punto m
starchy roots	raíces f feculentas	stitch, to	coser
starling	estornino m	stock (Matthiola spp.)	alhelí m
star thistle	cardo m estrella	stock (grafting)	patrón m
starter	arranque m del motor	stock plant	planta f madre
starter culture	cultivo m matriz	stock taking	inventarización f
starting material	material m inicial	stolon	estolon m
static load	carga f estática	stoma	estoma f
statistic	estadística f	stomach	estómago m
statistical analysis	analisis m estadistica	stomach poison	veneno m estomacal
steam	vapor m	stone	piedra f
steam bath	baño m de vapor	stone (fruit)	cuesco, hueso m
steam boiler	caldera f de vapor	stony	pedregoso
steam pipe	tubo m para vapor	stop flowering, to	dejar de florecer
steam pressure	presión de vapor	stop, to	parar
steam trap	separador m de agua	storable until Christmas	navideño
steam, to	esterilizar al vapor	storage	almacenaje m
steaming (soil)	desinfección f del suelo por vapor	storage	almacenamiento m
steep	empinado m	storage	conservación f en el almacén
steer	novillo m castrado	storage costs	costos m de almacenamiento
steer, to	guiar	storage disease	enfermedad f de almacenamiento
steering mechanism	tren m del volante	storage temperature	temperatura f de conservación
stem	tallo m	store, to	almacenar
stem	vástago m	storehouse	almacén m
stem borer	barrenador m del tallo	storm damage	daños m causados por la tempestad
stem clasping	amplexicaulo	stove	estufa f
stem cutting	estaca f del tallo	stover	chala f
step ladder	escalera f	strain	raza f
step terrace	terraza f de escalón		
sterile	estéril		
sterility	esterilidad f		

83

ENGLISH - SPANISH EQUIVALENTS

ENGLISH	SPANISH	ENGLISH	SPANISH
strain (breeding)	línea f	stylet	estilete m
strainer	coladora f	subgenus	subgénero m
strainer	filtro m	subirrigation	riego m subterráneo
strap shaped	ligulado	subject to flooding	inundable
stratification	estratificación f	sublimate	sublimado m
stratified	estratificado	submerge, to	sumergir
stratify, to	estratificar	subsidiary effect	efecto f secundario
straw	paja f	subsidize, to	subvencionar
straw baler	prensador m de paja	subsidy	subsidio m
straw bedding	paja f de cama	subsoil	subsuelo m
straw-bale	fardo m de paja	subsoil, to	subsolar
strawberry	fresa f	subsoil, to	arar profundaménte
strawberry plant	planta f de fresa	subsoiler	arado m de subsuelo
streak	raya f, vena f, faja f, reta f	subsoiler	subsueladora f
		subsoiling	aradura f del subsuelo
stream	arroyo m	subsoiling	subsolada f
stream	río m	subspecies	subespecie f
strength	fuerza f	substance	sustancia f
stretch, to	estirar	substrate	substrato m
stretch, to	prolongar	substrate	sustrato m
stretch, to (wire)	tender	subterranean	subterráneo
striated	rayado	subtillage	cultivo m subsuperficial
string	cuerda f	subtropical	subtropical
string bean	habichuela f	succulent	suculento m
string bean	vainita f	succulent plant	planta suculenta f
stringless (bean)	sin hilo	sucker	chupón m
stringy	fibroso	sucker	hijuelo m
strip, to (thorns)	despintar	sucker	pimpollo m
strip cropping	cultivo en fajas	sucker	retoño m
strip-crop	sembrar en fajas para evitar la erosión	sucker, root	vástago m
		sucker, shoot	chupón m
stripe	lista f	sucker, to	serpollar
stripe	raya f	suckling pig	lechón m
stripe rust	roya f lineal	sucrose	sacarosa f
striped	rayado	suction tube	tubo m de admisión
strong	fuerte	sudangrass	sorgo m Sudanensis
structure	estructura f	suet	grasa f
strut	puntal m	suit (spray)	traje m protector
stubble	rastrojo m	sugar	azúcar m
stubble mulch	cubierta f protectora de rastrojo	sugar crop	zafra f
		sugar mill	ingenio m
stud farm	haras f, acaballadero m	sugar pea	guisante m azucarado
stump	tocón m	sugarbeet	remolacha f de azúcar
stump	tronco m	sulfate	sulfato m
stunting	achaparramiento m	sulphate	sulfato m
style	estilo m		

ENGLISH - SPANISH EQUIVALENTS

ENGLISH	SPANISH
sulphate of ammonia	sulfato m amónico
sulphate of copper	sulfato m de cobre
sulphate of potash	sulfato m de potasa
sulphate of potash-magnesia	sulfato m doble de potasio y magnesio
sulphite	sulfito m
sulphur	azufre m
sumac	zumaque m
sumergir	submerge, to
summer oil	aceite m blanco
summit	cumbre f
sun	sol m
sunflower	girasol m
sunken	hundido
sunny	soleado
sunscorch	quemadura f del sol
sunshine	luz f del sol
sunstroke	golpe m de sol
superficial	superficial
superior (bot)	superior
supermarket	supermercado m
superphosphate	superfosfato m
supplemental lighting	iluminación f accesoria
supplementary drainage	drenaje m supletorio
supplementary lighting	iluminación f accesoria
supplies	provisiones f
supply	abasto m
supply	oferta f
supply, to	proveer
supply, to	suministrar
supplying	abastecimiento m
support prices	precios m de sustención
surface	superficie f
surface drain	zanja f
surface irrigation	riego m superficial
surface waters	aguas f superficiales
surfactant	surfactante m
surplus	exceso m
surplus	sobrante m
survey	encuesta f
survey	reconocimiento m
survey, to (land)	apear
surveying	agrimensura f
surveyor	agrimensor m

ENGLISH	SPANISH
survival	supervivencia f, sobrevivencia f
survive, to	sobrevivir
susceptibility	susceptibilidad f
susceptible	propenso m
susceptible to frost	sensible al frío
sustained yield	rendimiento m sostenido
suture	sutura f
swallow, to	tragar
swallowing	deglutición f
swamp	pantano m
swampy	pantanoso
swarm of bees	enjambre m
sweeper (machine)	barredora f
sweet basil (Ocimum basilicum)	albahaca f
sweet corn	maíz m dulce
sweet gum	liquidámbar m
sweet gum	ocozol m
sweet pea	guisante m de olor
sweet potato	batata f
sweet william	minutisa f, manutisa f, clavel del Japón m
swell, to	hinchar
swell, to (buds)	hincharse
swelling	abultamiento m
swelling	hinchazón f
swiss chard	acelga f
switch	interruptor m
swollen	hinchado
sword shaped	ensiforme
sycamore	sicómoro m
symbiosis	simbiosis f
symbiotic	simbiótico
sympetalous	simpétalo
symptom	síntoma m
symptomatology	sintomatología f
syncarp	sincarpo m
syndrome	síndrome m
synergistic	sinergético
synonymy	sinonimia f
synthesize, to	sintetizar
syrup	jarabe m
system	sistema m
systematics	sistemática f

ENGLISH - SPANISH EQUIVALENTS

ENGLISH	SPANISH	ENGLISH	SPANISH
		tensiometer	tensiometro m
		tension (voltage)	tensión f
	- T -	tension (voltage)	voltage m
		tension rod	varilla f de tensión
		tepal	tépalo m
tablespoonful	cucharada f	terminal	terminal
taken (graft)	pegado	terminal	terminal m
taking up (nutrient)	asimilación f	terminal bud	yema f terminal
talc	talco m	terminal flower	flor f terminal
tamarind	tamarindo m	termite	termes m, comején m,
tamarisk	tamarisco m		termita f térmite m
tangerine	mandarina f	ternate	terno
tangerine	tangerina f	terrace	terraza f
tank	tanque m, aljibe m	tetrapetalous	tetrapétalo
	deposito m	tetraploid	tetraploide
tap root	raíz f penetrante	texture	textura f
tap water	agua f corriente	thallophyte	talófita f
tap-rooted	pivotante	thallophytic	talofítico
tape measure	cinta f de medir	thallus	talo m
tapioca	tapioca f	thaw, to	deshelar
tapping (rubber)	pica f	therapy	terapia f
target price	precio m indicativo	thermocouple	par m térmico
taro	taro m	thermocouple	termocupla f
tarragon	estragón m	thermocouple, to	termopar m, also
task	tarea f		par térmico m
taste	sabor m		pila termoeléctrica f
taxonomy	taxonomía f	thermograph	termógrafo m
tea	té m	thermometer	termómetro m
teak	teca f	thermoperiod	termoperíodo m
team work	trabajo m de equipo	thermostat	termóstato m
tear strength	resistencia f al desgarro	thiamine	tiamina f
teaspoonful	cucharadita f	thick	grueso
technique	técnica f	thickener	agente m de condensación
technological	tecnológico	thigmotaxis	tigmotaxia f
teff	tef m	thigmotropism	tigmotropismo m
tegument	tegumento m	thin, to	aclarar, desahijar
temperate	templado	thin, to	entresacar
temporary	temporal	thinner	raleador m
tenant	arrendatario m	thinner (chemical)	raleo m químico
tendency	tendencia f	thinning	aclareo m, desahije m
tender	suave	thistle	cardo m
tenderness	ternura f	thorn	oxiacanta f
tendril	pleguete m	thorned	espinoso
tendril	zarcillo m	thorny	pinchudo
tensile strength	esfuerzo m de tracción	three way valve	válvula f de tres vías

ENGLISH - SPANISH EQUIVALENTS

ENGLISH	SPANISH	ENGLISH	SPANISH
thresher	trillador m	topsoil	capa f vegetal
threshed	trillado	topwork, to	sobreinjertar
threshing machine	trilladora f	topworked	sobreinjertado
thrip	piojillo m	topworking	injerto m de copa
thrips	trips m, tisanóptaro m	topworking	injerto m de reconstrucción
throat	garganta f	topworking	reinjerto m
thyme	salsero m	topworking	sobreinjerto m
thyme	senserina f	tortrix moth	tortrix m
thyme	tomillo m	toxicity	toxicidad f
tick	garrapata f	toxicology	toxicología f
tie, to	amarrar	trace	traza f
tie, to	atar	trace element	microelemento m
tiger lily	azucena f tigrina	trace element	oligoelemento m
tigridia	flor del tigre	tracer	indicador m
till, to (soil)	cultivar	tracer	marcador m
tillage	labranza f	tracer	trazador m
tiller, to	ahijar	trachea	tráquea f
tilth	condición f de la tierra	tracheid	traqueida f
tissue	tejido m	traction	tracción f
tissue culture	cultivo m de tejido	tractor	tractor m
tissue paper	papel m de seda	tractor mounted sprayer	pulverizador m para acoplar al tractor
titration	titulación f	trade value	valor m comercial
toilet (portable)	excusado m	transect	transecto m
tolerance	tolerancia f	transformation	transformación f
tolerant	tolerante	transformer	transformador m
tomato	tomate m	translocation	translocación f
tomato paste	pasta f de tomates	translucent	transluciente
tomato paste	puré m de tomates	transmission	transmisión f
tomentose	afieltrado	transpiration	transpiración f
tomentose	tomentoso	transpire, to	transpirar
tomentum	tomento m	transplant, to	trasplantar
ton	tonelada f	transplantation	trasplantación f
tool	herramienta f, fierro m	transplanter	repicadora f
tool bar	porta útiles f	transplanter	sembradora f de plantulas, transplantador m
top dressing	abono m de cobertura	trap	trampa f
top graft	injerto m en cabeza	traveller's tree	ravenala f
top soil	capa f arable	tray	caja f, tabla f
top soil	capa f vegetal	treatment	tratamiento m
top work, to	reinjertar	tree	árbol
top, to	despuntar	tree form	forma f del árbol
topiary	topiaria f	tree peony	peonía f arbórea
topography	topografía f	tree stump	tocón
topping	tapeadora f	tree with central leader	árbol con eje central
topsoil	capa f arable		
topsoil	capa f fértil		

ENGLISH - SPANISH EQUIVALENTS

ENGLISH	SPANISH	ENGLISH	SPANISH
tree with modified central leader	árbol con guía modificada	tunic (bulb)	túnica f
trellis	soporte m	tunnel	túnel m
trellised vine	parra f	turf	césped m
trench	zanja f	turgid	turgente
trench around base of plant to hold water	alcorque m	turgidity	turgencia f
trench, to	zanjar	turgidity	turgescencia f
trenching plow	arado m abrezanjas	turnbuckle	tensor m
trial	prueba f	turn off, to (electrical)	apagar
triangular	triangular	turn on, to (electrical)	prender
tribasic	tribásico	turnip	nabo m
trichome	tricoma f	turpentine	trementina f
trickle irrigation	riego m de gotas	twig	rama f
trifoliate	trifoliado	twine	cuerda f
trifoliate orange	naranjo m trifoliado	twining	voluble
trim, to	recortar	type	tipo m
tripetalous	tripétalo m		
triploid	triploide		
triploidy	triploidía f		
tripod	trípode m		
tristeza	tristeza f de los cítricos		
tropism	tropismo m	**- U -**	
true-to-type	de pura raza f		
true-to-type	genuino		
truffle	trufa f	ultraviolet	ultravioleta
trunk	tronco m	umbel	parasol m
truss (construction)	cabrio m	umbel	umbela f
try, to	tratar	undamaged	sano
try, to (as in taste)	probar	under mist	bajo nebulización
tub plant	planta f de cuba	underfeeding	subalimentación f
tube	tubo m	underground	subterráneo
tuber	tubérculo m	unfruitful	infructífero
tubercles	tubérculos m	unfruitfulness	infructuosidad f
tuberose	azucena f	unheated	sin calefacción
tuberous	tuberoso	unicellular	unicelular
tuberous begonia	begonia f tuberosa	unilocular	unilocular
tuberous plant	planta f tuberosa	union	unión f
tuberous roots	raíces f tuberosas	unirrigated land	secano m
tubing	tubería f	unirrigated land	sequero m
tubular	tubiforme	unisexual	unisexual
tulip	tulipán m	unit	unidad f
tumor	tumor m	unit costs	costos m de producción
tung	tung m	unmarketable	invendible
tung oil	aceite de palo o tung	unripe	inmaduro
		untreated	sin tratar
		urea	urea f

ENGLISH - SPANISH EQUIVALENTS

ENGLISH	SPANISH	ENGLISH	SPANISH
urea formaldehyde	urea-formol m	veination	nervadura f
ureal	ureal	veination	venación f
urediospore	uredospora f	veneer graft	injerto m de chapa
urine	orina f	ventilation	ventilación f
urn-shaped	vasiforme	ventilate, to	airear, orear, oxigenar
use	uso m	ventilate, to	ventilar
usefull life	vida f útil	ventilator	ventilador m
utilization	utilización f	verbena	verbena f, hierba sagrada f
		vermiculite	vermiculita f
		vernalization	vernalización f
		vernation	vernación f
- V -		veronica	verónica f
		versatile	versátil
		vesicle	vesícula f
		vessel (bot)	vaso m
vacuole	vacuola f	vetch	vicia f
vacuum	vacío m	vetiver	vetiver m
vacuum cooling	refrigeración f al vacío	viability	viabilidad f
valve	válvula f	viable	viable
valve, float	válvula f flotante	vibrate, to	vibrar
vanillin	vainilla f	vibrator	vibrador m
vapam (metham)	vapam (N-metil ditiocarbamato de sodio)	vigorous	vigoroso
		vigorous rootstock	patrón m de vigor
vapor barrier	barrera f antivapor	vine	trepadora f
vaporization	vaporación f	vinegar	vinagre m
vaporous	gaseoso	vineyard	viña f, viñedo m
variability	variabilidad f	violet	violáceo
variable costs	costos m variables	violet	violeta f
variance	variancia f variación f	virology	virología f
variegated	abigarrado	virulence	virulencia f
varietal purity	pureza f de la variedad	virus disease	enfermedad f virósica
variety	variedad f	virus disease	virosis f
variety trial	ensayo m de variedades	virus-attack	ataque m de virus
vascular bundle	haz f vascular	viscosity	viscosidad
vascular disease	enfermedad f vascular	viscous	viscoso
vascular tissue	tejido m vascular	visible radiation	radiación f visible
vasiform	vasiforme	vitamin	vitamina f
vector	vector m	viticulture	viticultura f
vegetable	hortaliza f	viticulturist	vinicultor m
vegetable greens	verduras f	volatile	volátil
vegetable growing	olericultura f	volatilize, to	volatilizarse
vegetate, to	vegetar	volume	volumen m
vegetation	vegetación f		
vein	vena f		

ENGLISH - SPANISH EQUIVALENTS

ENGLISH	SPANISH	ENGLISH	SPANISH
- W -		weather	tiempo m
		weather station	puesto m meteorológico
		weather, to	descomponerse
wages	paga f, sueldo m, jornal m, salario m	wedge	cuña f
		wedge, grafting tool	hendidor
wall	muro m	weed	hierba f
wall	pared f	weed	mala hierba f, cizaña f
walnut	nogal m	weed	maleza f
warm-water treatment	tratamiento m con agua templada	weed control	control m de malezas
		weed, to	desherbar
wash, to	lavar	weed, to	desmalezar
wash, to	limpiar	weed, to	escardar
waste	desperdicio m	weeder	arrancador m de malezas
waste land	tierra f incultivable	weeping tree	arból m llorón
water conservation	conservación f de agua	weevil	gorgojo m
water consumption	consumo m de agua	weevil	picudo m
water level	plano m de agua	weight	peso m
water lily	nenúfar m	weight loss	pérdida f de peso
water lily	ninfea f	weld, to	soldar, gueldear
water movement	movimiento m de agua	well	pozo m
water pressure	presión f de agua	wet soil	suelo m húmedo
water purification	purificación f de agua	wet, to	mojar
water seal	cerrado m hidráulico	wettable	humedecible
water shortage	escásez f de agua	wetter (spreader)	mojante f
water sprout	chupón m	wetting	humectante
water storage capacity	capacidad f de retención	wheat	trigo m
water storage capacity	capacidad f de retención de agua	wheelbarrow	carretilla f
water table	capa f freática	whip and tongue graft	injerto m de fusta y lengua
water, to	mojar	whip and tongue grafting	injerto m inglés
water, to	regar	whip graft	injerto m de fusta
water-soluble	hidrosoluble	white rust	roya f blanca
watercress	berro m	whitefly	mosca f blanca
watering	riego m	whitewash, to	blanquear
watering can	regadera f	wholesale market	mercado m al por mayor
waterlily	ninfea f	wholesale trade	comercio m al por mayor
waterlogging	anegamiento m	wholesaler	mayorista mf
waterlogging	saturación f en agua	whorl	verticilo m
watermelon	sandía f	whorled	verticilado
waterproof	impermeable	wild	silvestre, salvaje, bravío
watery, juicy	acuoso		
wavelength	longitud f de onda	wild carrot	zanahoria f silvestre
wavy	ondulado	willow	sauce m
wax, grafting	cera f para injertos	wilt, to	marchitarse
weak rootstock	patrón m débil	wilting point	punto m de marchitamiento
wear and tear	envejecimiento m técnico	wind, prevailing	vientos m reinantes

ENGLISH - SPANISH EQUIVALENTS

ENGLISH	SPANISH	ENGLISH	SPANISH
windbreak	cortaviento m	wreath	corona f de flores
windbreak	paravientos m	wrinkle, to	arrugarse
windbreak	protección f contra el viento	write off, to	amortizar
windbreak	rompeviento m		
window	ventana f		
wind machine	máquina f de aire		**- X -**
windrow, to	hacer hileras		
windrower	hileradora f		
winery	guanería f		
wing	ala f	xylem	vaso m leñoso
winged	alado	xylem	xilema f
winter	invierno m		
winter dormancy	reposo m invernal		
wintergreen	pirola f		
wintering	invernación f		**- Y -**
wire cutters	cizallas f		
wire netting	malla f de gallinero		
wire netting	tela f métalica	yarrow	milenrama f, milhojas f
wireworm	doradillo m	yarrow	perla f
wisteria	glicina f, vistaria f	yellow jasmine	gelsemio m
witch hazel	hamamelina f	yellow mombin	
witch hazel	hamamelis m	(Spondias mombin)	abal m
witches broom disease	escoba f de bruja	yellowing	amarilleo m
wither, to	marchitarse	yew	tejo m
withered	ajado, marchito,	yield	rendimiento m
	mustio, desecado	yield increment	incremento m de la
witloof chicory	achicoria f de Bruselas		producción
wood	madera f	ylang-ylang	ilang-ilang m
wood preservation	conservación f de madera	ylang-ylang	ylang-ylang m
wood shaving	viruta f de madera		
wood sorrel	vinagrillo m		
wooden strip	rejilla f de madera		
woods	bosque m		**- Z -**
woody	leñoso		
woody plants	plantas f leñosas	zinc	zinc m
wool	lana f	zinnia	zinia f, cinnia f
work plan	plan m de trabajo	zonal geranium	geranio m zonal
work, to	trabajar	zonal pelargonium	geranio m
worker	obrero m		
worker bee	abeja f obrera		
workplace	lugar m de trabajo		
worm	gusano m		
worsen, to	empeorar		
wound	herida f		
wounds	heridas f		

PART THREE
TERCERA PARTE

SPANISH – ENGLISH
ESPAÑOL – INGLÉS

SPANISH - ENGLISH EQUIVALENTS

SPANISH	ENGLISH	SPANISH	ENGLISH

- A -

SPANISH	ENGLISH
abacá m	Manila hemp *(Musa textilis)*
abal m	yellow mombin *(Spondias mombin)*
abandonado m	deserted
abarquillado m de las hojas	curly top
abarquillado m de las hojas	leaf curl
abarquillamiento m	curling
abastecimiento m	supplying
abasto m	supply
abatir	to knock or cut down
abedul m	birch
abeja f	bee
abeja f mecánica	artificial bee
abeja f obrera	worker bee
abeja f reina	queen bee
abejoncito m	germinating coffee bean
abejorro m	bumble bee or garden chafer
abejón m	bumble bee
abejorro m	garden chafer
abenico m	fan
abertura f	opening of flowers
abesón m	dill
abeto m	fir
abeto m	hemlock
abeto m	spruce
abigarrado	variegated
abigarrado m	flecking
abiú m	caimo *(Pouteria caimito)*
abogalla f	gall
abolladura f	dent
abollamiento	puckered
abonado m	fertilizing
abonado m lateral en cobertera	side dressing
abonadora f mecánica	fertilizer drill
abonar	fertilize, to (with fertilizer)
abono m	fertilizer
abono m completo	complete fertilizer
abono m compuesto	compound fertilizer
abono m de cobertura	top dressing
abono m nitrogenado	nitrogenous fertilizer
abono m potásico	potash fertilizer

SPANISH	ENGLISH
abono m verde	green manure
abonos m fosfatatos	phosphatic fertilizers
abortamiento m	blast
aborto m	abortion
abridero m	grafting knife
abridor m	nectarine
abrigar	shade, to
absceso m	abscess
absentista f	absentee owner
absorber	absorb
absorber	soak up, to
absorción f de la luz	light absorption
absorción f	absorption
abultamiento m	swelling
acaballadera m	stud farm
acacia f de tres espinas	honey locust
ácaro	bryobia
ácaro	mite
accesorio m	attachment
accionar	power, to
acción de contacto	contact action
acción f capilar	capillary action
acción f de batimiento	churning action
acción f de empollar	hatching
acebo m	holly
aceite m	oil
aceite m blanco	summer oil
aceite m de hígado de bacalao	cod liver oil
aceite m de linaza	linseed oil
aceite m de palo	tung oil
aceites m esenciales	essential oils
aceituna f	olive
acelerador m	accelerator
acelga f	swiss chard
acerderilla f	oxalis
acetato m	acetate
acicular	narrow leaved
acicular	needle-shaped
ácido m	acid
ácido m ascórbico	ascorbic acid
ácido m clorhídrico	hydrochloric acid
ácido m fólico	folic acid
ácido m giberélico	gibberellic acid
ácido m graso	fatty acid

SPANISH - ENGLISH EQUIVALENTS

SPANISH	ENGLISH	SPANISH	ENGLISH
ácido m húmico	humic acid	adelaida f	fuchsia
ácido m indolbutírico	indolebutyric acid	adelanto m	advancement, pay advance
ácido m naftalenacético	Napthylene acetic acid	adelfa f	oleander *(Nerium oleander)*
ácido m nicotínico	nicotinic acid	adherente m	spreader, wetting agent
acidificar	acidify	adherente-espacidor m	spreader-sticker
aclarar	to thin	adhesivo m	adhesive
aclarar frutos	fruit thinning	adianto m	maidenhair fern
aclareo m	thinning		*(Adiantum sp.)*
aclimatación f	acclimation	aditamento m	accessory
aclimatizar	acclimitize	adjunto m	attached
acodado m aéreo	layering, air	adormidera f	iceland poppy
acodado m compuesto	layering, compound	adormidera f	poppy
acodado m de punta	layering, tip	adormidera f oriental	oriental poppy
acodado m en montículo	layering, mound	adsorbe	adsorb
acodado m en trinchera	layering, trench	adsorción	adsorption
acodado m serpentario	layering, serpentine	adventicio	adventitious
acodado m simple	layering, simple	aemiárido	semi-arid
acodar	layer, to (propagation)	aereación	aeration
acodo m	layer (propagation)	aéreo	aerial
acodo m	layering	aerología f	aerology
acodo m aéreo	air-layering	aerosol	aerosol
acodo m al aire	air layering	aeróbico	aerobic
acojinado	padded	aeróbio	aerobic
acolchamiento m	padding	aficida f	aphicide
acolchamiento m de suelos	mulching	áfido	aphid
acondicionador m de suelos	soil conditioner	áfido m verde de manzana	apple aphid
acondicionador m del aire	air conditioner	afieltrado	tomentose
acoplar	attach	afilado	sharp
acoplar	hitch, to	afilar	sharpen, to
acorazonado	heart shaped, cordate	afrecho m	bran
acónito m	monkshood	agalla f	gall
acónito m	Aconitum	agalla f de los pomas	crown gall
acreaje m	acreage	agalla m	cyst
acristalar	glaze, to	agámico	asexual
acronecrosis m	die-back	agar m	agar
actividad f radicular	root activity	agave m	agave
actuación f	performance	agavilladora f	binder
acuático	aquatic	agente m de condensación	thickener
acuicultura f	aquaculture	agente m de extensión	county agent
acuoso	watery, juicy	agente m emulsionante	emulsifier
acusar síntomas	show symptoms, to	agerato m	Ageratum
achaparramiento m	stunting	agitador m	agitator
achicoría f	chicory	agitador m	shaker
achicoria f de Bruselas	witloof chicory	agostamiento	burning
achiote m	annatto tree *(Bixa orellana)*	agostar	scorch, to

SPANISH - ENGLISH EQUIVALENTS

SPANISH	ENGLISH	SPANISH	ENGLISH
agostar	to parch, to wither	aislamiento m	insulation
agotamiento m	depletion	aislamiento m	isolation
agotamiento m del suelo	soil depletion	aislar	isolate, to
agraria	agricultural	ajado	withered
agregación f	aggregation	ají m	capsicum
agregado m	aggregate	ají m	pepper
agricultor m	farmer	ajo m	garlic
agricultura	farming	ajo m porro	scallion
agricultura f	agriculture	ajonjolí m	sesame
agricultura f de secano	dry farming	ajuste m	fit
agricultura f diversificada	diversified farming	akí m	akee (Blighia sapida)
agricultura f migratoria	shifting cultivation	a través de	across
agridulce	bittersweet	al voleo	broadcast
agrietamiento m	cracking	ala f	wing
agrifolio m	holly	alado	winged
agrimensor m	surveyor	alagar	to flood
agrimensura f	surveying	alambrado	fenced or trellised with wire
agrio	sour, acidic	alambrado m	fence
agrobiología f	agrobiology	alambrar	to fence or trellis with wire
agropecuario	farming	alambre m de púas	barbed wire
agropiro m crestado	crested wheatgrass	álamo m	poplar, cottonwood
agrónomo m	agronomist	alanina f	alanine
agua f corriente	tap water	alargamiento m	lengthening
agua f de riego	irrigation water	alargamiento m del día	lengthening of daylength
agua f del suelo	soil water	alazor m	safflower
agua f dulce	fresh water	albahaca f	sweet basil (Ocimum basilicum)
agua f dura	hard water		
agua f manantial	spring water	albaricoque m	apricot
agua f suave	soft water	albaricoquero m	apricot tree
agua f subterránea	ground water	alberca f	pool
agua m capilar	capillary water	albura f	sapwood
agua m salobre	brackish water	albúmina f	albumen
aguacate m	avocado	albúmina f	egg white
aguas f negras	sewage	alcachofa f	globe artichoke
aguas f superficiales	surface waters	alcalinidad f	alkalinity
aguileña f	columbine	álcali m	alkali
aguja f	needle (bot)	alcalino	alkaline
agujero m de hombre	manhole	alcanfor m	camphor
ahijar	tiller, to	alcaparra f	caper
ahilamiento m	etiolation	alcaravea f	caraway
ahuecar	scoop, to (hyacinth)	alcazuz m	liquorice
ahumadero m	smokehouse	alcea f	hollyhock (Althaea rosea)
aireación f del suelo	soil aeration	alcorque m	trench around base of plant
airear	aerate, to ventilate	aleación f	alloy
aislado	isolated	alelomorfo f	allelomorph

SPANISH - ENGLISH EQUIVALENTS

SPANISH	ENGLISH	SPANISH	ENGLISH
alelopatía f	allelopathy	alvéolo m	alveole
alerce m	larch	alvéolo m	alveolus
aleurona f	aleurone	alza f	increase
alfalfa f	alfalfa	alzada f del caballo	height of withers
alfalfa f	lucerne	alzador m hidráulico	hydraulic lift
alfalfal m	alfalfa field	alzar	hoist, to
alfalfar	alfalfa field	amamantar	nurse, to
alforfón m	buckwheat	amaranto m	Amaranthus
alfóncigo m	pistachio (Pistacia vera)	amargo	bitter
alga f	sea-weed	amarilis f	amaryllis
algarroba f	carob fruit	amarilleo m	yellowing
algodonal m	cotton field	amarrar	tie, to
algodón m absorbente	absorbent cotton	ambiente m	environment
alhelicillo m	allysum, sweet	aminoácido m	amino acid
alhelí m	stock	amonio m	ammonium
alicates m	pliers	amoníaco m	anhydrous ammonia
alimentación f	feeding	amoníaco	ammonia
alimentar	feed, to	amortiguador m	buffer
alimento m	feed	amortización f	amortization
alimento m	food	amortizar	write off, to
alimento m para animales	animal feed	amplexicaule	stem clasping
alimento m para plantas	plant food	ampolia f	blister
alimentos m	feed stuffs	amuescado	indented
almacenaje m	storage	anacardo m	cashew
almacenamiento m	storage	anaerobio	anaerobic
almacenar	store, to	anafase m	anaphase
almacenes m	department store	anatómico	anatomical
almacén m de granos	elevator (grain)	análisis m de suelo	soil analysis
almacén m	storehouse	análisis m estatistica	statistical analysis
almacén m de embalaje	packing shed	análisis m foliar	leaf analysis
almendra f	almond	análisis m	analysis
almendro m	almond tree	análogo m	analogue
almidón m	starch	anchura f de vidrio	pane width
alomado	hilly	anclar	anchor, to
alopoliploide m	allopolyploid	andar	to run a machine
alpiste m	canary grass	androestéril	male sterile
alternado	alternate	andromonoico m	andromonoecious
altitud m	altitude	andropogón m	bluestem
alto	high	anegación f	flooding
altramuz m	lupin	anegamiento m	waterlogging
altura f	height	anegar	to flood
alud m	avalanche	aneldo m	dill
alumbre m	alum	anemómetro m	anemometer
aluvial	alluvial	aneuploide m	aneuploid
aluvión m	alluvial soil	anémona f	anemone

SPANISH - ENGLISH EQUIVALENTS

SPANISH	ENGLISH	SPANISH	ENGLISH
anfidiploide m	amphidiploid	apelmazar	squeeze, to
angiosperma f	angiosperm	apetecible	appetizing
anguilula f de raíz	meadow nematode	apetito m	appetite
anguílula f	eelworm	ápice m	growing point
anguloso	angular	ápice m de la hoja	leaf tip
anillar	to girdle	apicultor m	beekeeper
anillo m anual	annual ring	apicultura f	beekeeping
anión m	anion	apilar	stack, to
anís m	anise	apio m	celery
ano m	anus	aplanar	flatten, to
anochecer m	nightfall	aplicación f antes de la emergencia	pre-emergence application
anófeles	anopheles		
anón m	Annona sp	aplicación f antes de la siembra	pre-sowing application
antagonismo m	antagonism		
antera f	anther	aplicación f después de la emergencia	post-emergence application
antesis f	anthesis		
anticiclón m	high pressure area	aplicación f después de la siembra	post-sowing application
antineurítico m	antineuritic		
antirrino m	antirrhinum	aplicación f	application
antirrino m	snapdragon	aplicación f total	blanket application
antiséptico m	antiseptic	aplicadora f	applicator
antitoxina f	antitoxin	aplicar	apply
antociano m	anthocyanin	apogamia f	apogamy
antracnosis f	anthracnose	apomixia f	apomixis
ántrax m	anthrax	apomixis f	apomixis
antro m	core (of apple etc.)	aporcadora f	hiller
anturio m	anthurium	apoyar	brace, to
anual	annual	aprovechable	available
añerismo m	alternate bearing	aprovechamiento m de tierra	land use
añil m	indigo		
añublo m tardío	late blight	aptitud f combinatoria	combining ability
apagar	turn off (electrical)	aptitud f de la tierra	land capability
aparato m de iluminación	light fitting	apuntalamiento m	inarching
aparato por el que se levan los olores	hood	aquenio m	achene
		arable, cultivable	arable
aparcería f	share cropping	arado m	plough
aparcero m	share holder	arado m	plow
aparcero m	sharecropper	arado m abrezanjas	trenching plow
aparear entre hermanos	sib, to	arado m de discos	disk plow
aparejo m elevador	hoist	arado m de subsuelo	chisel-subsoiler
apartado m postal	post office box	arado m de subsuelo	subsoiler
apear	survey, to (land)	arado m de vertedera giratoria	sidehill plow
apelmazado	compact		
apelmazamiento m	compactness	arado m para aporcar	ridger
apelmazar	compress, to	arado m reversible	reversible plough
		arado m sembrador lister	lister

SPANISH - ENGLISH EQUIVALENTS

SPANISH	ENGLISH	SPANISH	ENGLISH
arador m	plowman	arrancadora f	lifter (i.e. bulbs, potatoes)
aradura f	plowing	arrancadora f de plantas	lifter
aradura f del subsuelo	subsoiling	arrancar	dig up, to
aradura f en curvas		arrancar con arado	plough out, to
de nivel	contour plowing	arrancar con el arado	plow up
araña f roja	red mite	arranque m del motor	starter
arar	plough, to	arrastrar	drag, to
arar	plow, to	aregar	add, to
arar profundamente	deep plow, to	arrendamiento m	land rent
arar profundamente	subsoiling	arrendatario m	leaseholder
araucaria f	Norfolk Island Pine	arrendatario m	tenant
arándano m agrio	cranberry	arriate m marginal	plant border
árbol	tree	arriendo m	lease
árbol m frutal	fruit tree	arrollador m de la hoja	leaf roller
árbol con eje central	tree with central leader	arroyo m	creek
árbol con guía modificada	tree with modified central lead	arroyo m	stream
árbol de llevas	camshaft	arroz m de riego constante	lowland rice
árbol de paseo	avenue tree	arrugado	rugose
árbol m deciduo	deciduous tree	arrugarse	wrinkle, to
árbol m en espaldera	espalier	árido	dry, arid
árbol m frondoso	broad-leafed tree	artanita f	(Cyclamen spp.)
árbol m llorón	weeping tree	arte m floral	floristry
arbolista f	arboriculturist	artemisa f	sagebrush
arboricultura f	arboriculture	artemisa f	shasta daisy
arbustivo	shrubby	arteria f	artery
arbusto m	bush	arteriola f	arteriole
arbusto m	shrub	artículos m de consumo	consumer goods
arce m	maple (Acer spp.)	artículos m de primera	
arcilla f	clay	necesidad	basic commodities
arcilla f aluvial	river clay	artrópodos	arthropods
arcilloso	clayey	artrópodo m	arthropod
área f	area	ascendente	ascending
arena f	sand	aseniato m de plomo	lead arsenate
arenoso	sandy	asentar	settle, to (soil)
aridez f	aridity	asentar	to level, firm or tamp (soil)
arista f	awn	asentarse	settle, to
arlo m	barberry (Berberis spp.)	aserradero m	sawmill
armario m de pared	closet	aserrado	serrate
armazón m	framework	aserrín m	sawdust
aro m	arum lily	asesor m	advisor
aromático	aromatic	asesor m hortícolo	horticultural advisor
arraigado	deep-rooted	asesoramiento m	advice
arraigar	root, to	asexual	asexual
arrancador m de malezas	weeder	aséptico	aseptic
		asfixia f	gas poisoning

SPANISH - ENGLISH EQUIVALENTS

SPANISH	ENGLISH	SPANISH	ENGLISH
asimilable	available (nutrients)	autopolinización f	self-pollination
asimilación f	taking up (nutrient)	autopoliploide	autopolyploid
asimilar	assimilate, to	autoservicio m	self-service
aspárrago m	asparagus	autosteril	self-sterile
aspereza f de los frutos	russeting	auxina f	auxin
asperjadora f	sprayer	auyama f	pumpkin
asperjar	spray, to	avalúo m	appraisal
áspero	rough	avalúo m	farm appraisal
aspersión a base de aerosol	aerosol spray	ave m	bird
aspersor m rotativo	rotary sprinkler	ave m	fowl
aster m	Michaelmas Daisy, aster	avellana f	filbert
astrillo m	lawn rake	avellanador m	rotavator
atacar, infestar	attack, to	avellanar	to rotavate
atadora f	binder	avellano m	filbert (plant)
ataque m	attack	avellano m	hazelnut
ataque m	infestation	avena f	oats
ataque m de virus	virus-attack	avena f silvestre	wild oats
atar	tie, to	avenar	drain, to
atascadero m	muddy spot	avenica f	fan
atico	aquatic	avería f	breakdown
atizador m al rojo vivo	red hot poker (Kniphofia spp.)	aves f de corral	poultry
		avicultor m	poultry raiser
atmósfera f	atmosphere	avión m	airplane
atomizador m	atomizer	avispa f de agallas	gall wasp
atomizador m	low-volume sprayer	axila f	axil
atomizador m	mistblower	axila f de la hoja	leaf axil
atomizador m de espalda	knapsack mistblower	axilar	axillary
atomizar	atomize, to	ayote m	squash or pumpkin
atoramiento	sticking	azada f	hoe
atornillar	to screw	azadonar	hoe, to
atracar	dock, to	azalea f	azalea
atrayente m	attractant	azalea f japonesa	japanese azalea
aumentar	increase, to	azúcar m	sugar
aumento m	increase	azucena f	lily
autoclave m	autoclave	azucena f	tuberose
autofecundación f	self-pollination	azucena f tigrina	tiger lily
autofecundación f	self-fertilization	azufrar	fumigate with sulphur
autofecundación f	selfing	azufre m	sulphur
autofertilización f	self-fertilization	azufre m en barras	stick sulphur
autofertilización f	selfing	azufre m en flor	flowers of sulphur
autofértil	self-fertile	azul celeste	sky blue
autogama f	autogamous	azulina f	cornflower (Centaurea cyanus)
autoincompatibilidad f	self-incompatability		
automático	automatic		
autopista f	freeway		

SPANISH - ENGLISH EQUIVALENTS

SPANISH	ENGLISH	SPANISH	ENGLISH
		barriga f	belly
- B -		barril m	barrel
babosa f	slug	barrujo m	forest litter
bácon m	bacon	base f de hoja	leaf base
báicon m	bacon	base f del bulbo	basal plate (bulb)
bacteria f	bacteria	básico	alkaline
bacterial	bacterial	basto	crude
bacterias f pl aerobias	aerobic bacterias	basuras f pl de ciudad	household refuse
bactericida f	bactericide	batata f	sweet potato
bactericido	bactericidal	baya f	berry
bacteriología f	bacteriology	baya f	small fruit (berry)
bacteriófago	bacteriophage	begonia f	begonia
bacteriólogo m	bacteriologist	begonia f tuberosa	tuberous begonia
bagazo m	pomace	bellota f	acorn
bajo m	low	berma f	berm
bajo nebulización	under mist	berengena f	eggplant
bala f de paja	bale of straw	berro m	watercress
balanza f	scale (weight)	betún m de injertar	grafting wax
balde m	pail	bibliografía f	bibliography
baleros m	bearings (engine)	biela f	connecting rod
ballesta f	spring (auto)	bienal	biennial
ballico m	ryegrass	bienes m líquidos	liquid assets
balsamina f	balsam	bilabial	labiate
bambú m	bamboo	binadora f	hoe
banana f	banana	bioclimatología f	bioclimatology
banco m	bench	biología f	biology
banco m	bench, greenhouse	biológico m	biological
banda f de plástico	plastic tie	biometría f	biometry
baño m de inmersión	dipping vat	biotina f	biotin
baño m de vapor	steam bath	biotipo m	biotype
baño m garrapaticida	dip	bipinado	bipinnate
baño m garrapaticida	sheep dip	bisexual	bisexual
barba f de la espiga	awn	bisulfuro m	disulfide
barba f española	Spanish moss	bisulfuro m de carbono m	carbon bisulfide
barbar	root, to	bisuperfosfato m	double superphosphate
barbecho	fallow	bisuperfosfato m cálcico	dicalcium phosphate
bardana f	burdock	bivalente m	bivalent
bardana f menor	cocklebur	blando	soft
barra f para poner vidrios	glazing bar	blanquear	whitewash, to
barredora f	sweeper (machine)	blanqueo m	bleaching
barrenador m	borer	bledo m rojo	pigweed
barrenador m del tallo	stem borer	bloque m	block (as in nursery)
barreno m de suelo	soil auger	boca f de dragón	snapdragon
barreno m para suelos	soil auger	bola f de nieve	snowball
barrera f antivapor	vapor barrier	boletín m	extension bulletin

SPANISH - ENGLISH EQUIVALENTS

SPANISH	ENGLISH	SPANISH	ENGLISH
boletín m de análisis	analysis report	bruma f	haziness
boletín m de análisis	soil analysis report	buey m	ox
bomba f de alimentación	feed pump	bujía f	sparkplug
bomba f	pump	bulbiforme	bulbous
bomba f aspersora	spray pump	bulbillo m	offset bulb
bomba f centrífuga	centrifugal pump	bulbo f	bulb (botanical)
bomba f de membrana	diaphragm pump	bulbo m lateral	offset (bulb)
bomba f de pistón	piston pump	bulbo m madre	mother bulb
bombear	pump, to	bulbos m retardados	retarded bulbs
bombilla f	bulb (light)	bureta f	burette
boquerel m	nozzle	burro m	saw horse
boquilla f	nozzle		
boquilla f del pulverizador	spray nozzle		
bórax m	borax		
borde m de la hoja	leaf margin		- C -
boro m	boron		
borraja f	borage		
bosque m	woods	caballeriza f	stable (horses)
bosque m	forest	caballete m	ridge, saw horse
bota f	boot	caballo m	horse
botánica f	botany	caballo m americano	quarter horse
botánico	botanical	caballo m semental	stallion
botón m de plata	Achillea	caballos m de fuerza	horsepower
botritis m	botrytis m	cabeza f	head
bracero m	farm hand	cable m de calefacción	heating cable
bráctea f	bract	cabrio m	rafter
brácteas f	squares (cotton)	cabrio m	truss (construction)
brazuelo m	shoulder (animal)	cabrito m	kid
breca f	brake	cabro m	buck (goat)
bróculi m	broccoli	cacahuete m	peanut
bromo m	brome grass	cacto m	cactus
bromo m secalino	cheat	cachucha f	cap
bromuro m de metilo	methyl bromide	cadáver m de animal	carcass
bronce m	bronze	cadena f	chain
brotamiento m	shooting (plant)	cadena f de frío	cold chain
brotar	bud, to	caduco	deciduous
brotar	shoot, to	caída f	fall (of fruits, leaves, etc)
brotar	sprout, to	caída f de almácigo	damping off
brote m	outbreak	caída f de luz	light entry
brote m	shoot	caída f de yemas	dropping of buds
brote m largo	long shoot	caída f intempesiva	June drop
brote m radicular	root sucker	caja f	tray
broza f	brush (plants)	caja f de cartón	cardboard box
brucelosis m	brucellosis	caja f de fusibles	fuse box
brújula f	compass	caja f de semillero	seed tray

SPANISH - ENGLISH EQUIVALENTS

SPANISH	ENGLISH	SPANISH	ENGLISH
caja f del motor	crankcase	calma f	calm
cajón m	bin	calor m del suelo	bottom heat
cajonera f	cold frame	calor m radiante	radiant heat
cajonera f	flat (horticultural)	caloría f	calorie
cajonera f	propagating bin	calorímetro m	calorimeter
cajonera f fría	cold frame	caluroso	hot
cajuil m	cashew	callejón m	alley
cal f	lime	callo m	callus
cal f apagada	slaked lime	callosidad f	callus
cal f calcinada	quicklime	cama f	bed (garden)
cal f de conchas	shell lime	cama f	litter (animal)
cal f muerta	slaked lime	cama f caliente	hotbed
cal f viva	quicklime	cama f fría	coldframe
cal-azufre m	lime-sulfur	cámara f de combustión	combustion chamber
calabacita f	squash, summer	cámara f de maduración	ripening room
calabacín m	gourd	cambium m	cambium
calabaza f	gourd	camelia f	camellia
calabaza f	pumpkin	camioneta f	pick-up (truck)
calabaza f	squash	campana f de cristal	bell jar
calabaza f	squash, winter	campaniforme	bell shaped
caladio m	caladium	campesino	grower
calcáreo	calcareous	campesino m	farmer
calceolaria f	calceolaria	campo m	country
calcio m	calcium	campo m	field
calcular	estimate, to	campo m experimental	experimental field
caldera f	boiler	campo m experimental	experimental plots
caldera f de agua caliente	hot water boiler	canal f de madera	flume
caldera f de alta presión	high pressure boiler	canal m	canal
caldera f de vapor	steam boiler	canal m	carcass (dressed)
caldo m bordelés	Bordeaux mixture	canal m	gutter
caldo m sulfocálcico	lime sulphur	canal m de aireación	air duct
calefacción f por tubos	pipe heating	canal m de descarga	chute
calentamiento m del suelo	soil heating	canal m de distribución	distribution channel
calentamiento m eléctrico del suelo	electrical soil heating	canasta f	basket
calentar	heat, to	canasta f	cesto m
caléndula f	calendula	cancro m	canker
calibrador m	caliper	canela f	cinnamon
calibrar	calibrate, to	canilla f	faucet
calibrar	size, to	cankro m	canker
calibre m	size	caña f	culm
caliche m	caliche	caña f de bambú	cane of bamboo
calidad f	quality	caña f de las Indias	canna
caliente	hot	cáñamo m	hemp
cáliz m	calyx	cañizo m	hurdle
		cañuela f	fescue

SPANISH - ENGLISH EQUIVALENTS

SPANISH	ENGLISH	SPANISH	ENGLISH
capa aleuronífera	aleurone layer	carencia f de humedad	moisture deficiency
capa f	layer	carencia f de potasio	potassium deficiency
capa f arable	top soil	carencia f en hierro	iron deficiency
capa f del suelo	soil layer	carencia f en magnesio	magnesium deficiency
capa f dura	hardpan	carencia f en manganeso	manganese deficiency
capa f fértil	topsoil	carencia f en nitrógeno	nitrogen deficiency
capa f freática	water table	carga f	load
capa f vegetal	topsoil	carga f de agua	head of water
capacidad f de campaña	field capacity	carga f estática	static load
capacidad f de campo	field capacity	cargador m de balas	bale loader
capacidad f de retención	water storage capacity	cargadora f	loader
capacidad f de retención de agua	water storage capacity	cariópside m	caryopsis
capar	castrate, to	carne f	flesh (meat)
capataz m	foreman	carne f de cerdo	pork
capilaridad f	capillarity	carnoso	fleshy
capital m inmueble	fixed capital	caro	expensive
capital m pasivo	liabilities	caroteno m	carotene (biochem)
capital m propio	own capital	carotina f	carotene (chem)
capón m	capon	carpelo m	carpel
cápsula f	capsule (bot)	carretera f	highway
cápsula f de algodón	boll	carretilla f	wheelbarrow
cápsula de la semilla	seed pod	cartagrafía f aéria	aerial survey
capuchina f	nasturtium	cartografiar	map, to
capullo m	cocoon	cartografía f del suelo	soil survey
caracol m	slug	cartón m	cardboard
caracol m	snail	cartón m embreado	roofing felt
características f del suelo	soil condition	cartón m ondulado	cardboard, corrugated
carácter m	character	casa f	house
carbohidrato m	carbohydrate	casa f hacienda	farm house
carbonato cálcico	calcium carbonate	cáscara f	hull
carbonato m	carbonate	cáscara f	skin (fruit)
carbonato m cálcico	ground limestone	cáscara f	chaff
carbono m	carbon	cáscara f	shell
carbón m	smut	cascaraña f	pit (fruit)
carbón m de la inflorescencia	head smut	casco m	hoof, hard hat
carbón m desnudo	loose smut	casero	household
carbunco m sintomático	blackleg	castaño m	chestnut
carcomido	decayed	castaño m de Indias	horse chestnut
cardo m	cardoon	castrar	castrate, to
cardo m	globe thistle	catastro m	land register
cardo m	thistle	categoría f	grade
cardo m estrella	star thistle	cauce m	bed (river)
carencia f	deficiency (disease)	caupí m	cowpea
		cáustico m	caustic
		cavar	dig, to

SPANISH - ENGLISH EQUIVALENTS

SPANISH	ENGLISH	SPANISH	ENGLISH
cavadora f de hoyos	post-hole digger	cereza f ácida	sour cherry
ceanoto m	ceanothus	cereza f negra	black cherry
ceba m	fattening	cerrado m hidráulico	water seal
cebada f	barley	cerradura f	lock
cebar	fatten, to	certificación f de semillas	seed certification
cebar	prime, to (pump)	césped m	lawn
cebo m	bait	césped m	grass (as in lawn)
ceboleta f	chive	césped m	sod
cebolla f	onion	césped m	turf
cebolleta f	nutgrass	cesta f	basket
cebollita f para plantar	onion set	cesta f de recolección	picking basket
cebollín f	chive	cesto m	basket
cedazo m	screen (sprinkler)	cesto m de mimbre	hamper
cedro m	cedar	cetona f	ketone
célula f	cell	cheque m	berm
célula fotoeléctrica	photoelectric cell	chueca	crooked
célula f madre	mother cell	cianamida f	cyanamide
celulosa f	cellulose	cianimido de calcio m	calcium cyanamid
cemento m	cement	cianotipia f	blueprint
ceniza f	ash	cicadela f	jassid
ceniza f de algas	kelp	cicatriz f	scar
ceniza f de soda	soda ash	cicatriz f de la hoja	leaf scar
censo m	census	cicatrizar	grow together, to
centilitro m	centiliter	cicálida f	leafhopper
centrífuga f	centrifuge	ciclamen f	Cyclamen spp.
centrífugo	centrifugal	ciclamen f	cyclamen
centro m de distribución	clearing house	ciclo m	cycle
centro m internacional	international center	ciclo m vital	life cycle
centrosoma f	centrosome	cidra f	cider
cepa f	stalk	ciego m	caecum
cepellón champa	root ball	ciempiés m	centipede
cepellón m	ball (i.e. root ball)	ciencias f domésticas	home economics
cepillar	brush, to	cieno m	silt
cepillo m	brush	cigüeña f	crank handle
cera f para injertos	wax, grafting	cigüeñal m	crankshaft
cerca f	fence	cigüeñal m	camshaft
cerca f eléctrica	electric fence	cilantro m	coriander
cercar	fence, to	ciliado	ciliate
cerda f	bristle	cilindro m	cylinder
cerda f	sow	cima f	cyme
cerdo m	hog	cincel m	cold chisel
cerdo m	pig	cineraria f	cineraria
cerdo m castrado	barrow	cinnia f	zinnia
cereal m	cereal	cinta f de breca	brake lining
cereza f	cherry	cinta f de control	inspection belt

SPANISH - ENGLISH EQUIVALENTS

SPANISH	ENGLISH	SPANISH	ENGLISH
cinta f de medir	measuring tape	cobertura f	mulch
cinta f de medir	tape measure	cobre m	copper
cinta f de transporte	conveyer belt	cochinilla f	cochineal
circuito m	circuit (electrical)	cochinilla f	scale (insect)
circulación f	circulation	cochinilla f	soft scale insect
circular	circular	cochinilla f de humedad	sowbug
circunvolución f	convolution	cochinilla f ostriforme	oyster shell scale
cirolero m	plum tree	cociente m	quotient
ciruela f	plum	cocina f	kitchen
ciruela f pasa	prune	coco m	coconut
ciruelo m	plum tree	codorniz f	quail
ciruelo m japonés	Japanese cherry	coeficiente m de variación	coefficient of variability
cizallas f	wire cutters	coenzima f	coenzyme
clara f de huevo	egg white	cofia f	root cap
claro	bright	coger	pick, to
clasificación f	grading	cogón m	cogongrass
clasificación f por calidad	quality grading	cohesión f	cohesion
clasificación de terrenos	land classification	col f de Bruselas	Brussels sprouts
clasificación f de suelos	soil classification	col f de China	Chinese cabbage
clasificar	sort, to	col f enana	kale
clavar	nail, to	col f rizada	savoy cabbage
clavel m	carnation	coladora f	strainer
clavel m coronado	pink (flower)	colector m	main drain
clavel m de Japón	sweet william	coleo m	coleus
clavo m	nail	cólera f	cholera
clemátide f	clematis	cólera f aviar	fowl cholera
clima m	climate	cólera m porcino	hog cholera
clima m	clime	colgante	pendulous
climatología f	climatology	coliflor f	cauliflower
climatización f	air conditioning	colina f	choline
cloaca f	sewer	colinabo m	rutabaga
cloche m	clutch	colirrábano m	kohl rabi
clon m	clone	colmena f	beehive
clorato m de sodio	sodium chlorate	coloidal	colloidal
cloro m	chlorine	coloide m	colloid
clorofila f	chlorophyll	colonia f	colony
cloropicrina f	chloropicrin	colonización f	settlement
clorosis f	chlorosis	colono m usurpador	squatter
cloruro m	chloride	color m	color
cloruro m de polivinilo	polyvinyl chloride	colon m	colon
cloruro m potásico	muriate of potash	cólquico m	colchicum
club m 4-H	4-H club	cólquico m de otoño	autumn crocus
cobalto m	cobalt	columna f	column
cobertura f	cover	combate m contra las plagas	pest control
cobertura f	coverage (of a pesticide)	combinada f	combine

SPANISH - ENGLISH EQUIVALENTS

SPANISH	ENGLISH	SPANISH	ENGLISH
combustible m	fuel	conducto m	conduit
combustible m líquido	liquid fuel	conducto m	duct
comedero m	feeding trough	conectivo	connective
comercio m al por mayor	wholesale trade	conejito m	snapdragon
comercio m de semillas	seed trade	conejo m	rabbit
comestible	edible	congelación f rapida	quick freezing
comida f	food	congelado m	frozen
comida f diaria	daily feed	congeladora f	freezer
comida f escolar	school lunch	congelar	freeze, to
comino m	cumin	congestión f	congestion
compana	cloche	cónico	conical
compatibilidad f	compatibility	conífera f	conifer
competencia f	competition	consejo m de abonado	fertilizer recommendation
competir	compete, to	conserva f de fruta	preserve
compost m	compost	conservacionista f	conservationist
compota f	stewed fruit	conservación f	preservation
compresibilidad f	compressibility	conservación f de agua	water conservacion
compresor m	compressor	conservación f de madera	wood preservation
compuerta f	gate (irrigation)	conservación f en atmósfera controlada	controlled atmosphere storage
compuesto	compound (bot.)	conservación f en el almacén	storage
compuesto m	compound	conservación f de suelos	soil conservation
compuesto m arsenical	arsenical compound	conservación f frigorífico	cold storage
compuesto m químico	compound (chemical)	conservación f por el frío	cold storage
compuestos m mercurios	mercury compounds	conservar	preserve, to
comunidad f	community	conservas f de frutas	preserved fruit
comunidad f de plantas	plant association	conservas f en vinagre	pickles
Comunidad f Económica Europea (CEE)	European Economic Community	consistencia f	consistency
con roya f	rusty	construcción	construction
concávo	concave	consumidor m	consumer
concentración f	concentration	consumo m	consumption
concentración de los iones de hidrógen	hydrogen ion concentration	consumo m de agua	water consumption
concentración f parcelaria	fragmented holdings	contabilidad f agrícola	farm accounting
concentrado m	concentrate	contabilidad f sobre la producción	cost accounting
concentrado m protéico	protein concentrate	contaminación	contamination
conchas f de ostra	oyster shells	contaminación f del aire	air pollution
condado m	county	contaminar	contaminate, to
condensación f	condensation	contar	count, to
condensador m	condenser	contenido m	content
condensar	compact, to	contenido m de humus	humus content
condensar	condense, to	contenido m en agua	moisture content
condición f climatológica	climatic conditions	contenido m en cal	lime content
condición f de la tierra	tilth	contenido m en calcio	lime status
condimentar	season, to		

SPANISH - ENGLISH EQUIVALENTS

SPANISH	ENGLISH	SPANISH	ENGLISH
contenido m en potasio	potassium content	corta f	felling
contenido m en sal	salt content	corta f de mejoramiento	selective cutting
contorno m	contour	cortar	prune, to
contracción f	shrinkage	cortar el césped	mow the grass
contracción f	contraction	cortaviento m	windbreak
contraer	shrink, to (soil)	corteza	inner bark
contrasurco	backfurrow	corteza f	bark
contrato m de arrendamiento	lease contract	corto m	short circuit
		corral m	barnyard
control m	control	correa f de transmisión	belt
control m biológico	biological control	correa f transportadora, cinta f de transmisión	belt conveyor
control m climático	climate control		
control m de calidad	quality control	correctivo m	amendment
control m de enfermedades	disease control	corredor m	broker
		correguela f menor	bindweed
control m de malezas	weed control	correlación f	correlation
control m de precios	price control	correoso	leathery
control m de semillas	seed testing	corriente m	electrical current
convexo	convex	corriente f de aire	draft (air)
cooperación f	cooperation	corrosión m	corrosion
cooperativa f	co-op	cosecha f	crop
cooperativa f	cooperative	cosecha f	harvest
coordenadas f	co-ordinates	cosecha f	picking (ie. harvesting)
copa f	crown	cosecha f forrajera	forage crop
copa f	crown (tree)	cosechadora f de algodón	cotton picker
copa f	head (of tree)	cosechadora f de cebollas	onion harvester
copina f	prickle	cosechadora f de patatas	potato digger
copra f	copra	cosechadora-trilladora f	combine
coquicina f	colchicine	cosechar	harvest, to
corazón m	core	cosechar	pick, to
corazón m sangrante	bleeding heart	cosechas f principales	basic crops
corcho m	cork	coser	sew, to
cordero m/f	lamb	coser	stitch, to
cordiforme	cordate	cosmos m	cosmos
cordón	cordon	costa f de producción parcial	marginal costing
coreopsis m	coreopsis		
coriáceo	leathery (botanical)	costo m de instalación	costs of establishment
corimbo m	corymb	costo m de la mano de obra	labor costs
cornadiza f	stanchion		
corola f	corolla	costos de instalación	original costs
corona f	corona	costos m	costs
corona f	crown	costos m de subasta	auction costs
corona f de flores	wreath	costos m de almacenamiento	storage costs
corona f imperial	Fritillaria		
corona f mortuoria	funeral wreath	costos m de funcionamiento	operating costs

SPANISH - ENGLISH EQUIVALENTS

SPANISH	ENGLISH
costos m de producción	unit costs
costos m fijos	fixed costs
costos m indirectos	indirect costs
costos m marginales	marginal costes
costos m unidos	joint costs
costos m variables	variable costs
costo m de producción	cost of production
costos m comparativos	comparative costs
costos m conjuntos	joint costs
costos m de oportunidad	opportunity cost
costos m primarios	prime costs
costoso	costly
costra f	crust
cotiledón m	seed leaf
cotiledón m	cotyledon
crecer	grow, to (ie the plant grows)
crecimiento m	growth
crédito m	credit
crédito m agrario	agricultural credit
crédito m agrícola	farm credit
crédito m bancario	bank loan
crespo	crisp
crespo	curly
cresta f de gallo	cockscomb
criador m	breeder
crianza f ovina	sheep raising
criar	breed, to
cribadora f	sifter
crisalidarse	pupate, to
crisantemo m	chrysanthemum
crisálida f	pupa
crisol m	crucible
crisomelido m	ladybird beetle
cristalizar	crystallize, to
crocus m	crocus
cromatina f	chromatin
cromátida f	chromatid
cromosoma f	chromosome
cromóforo m	chromophore
cruce m	cross
crudo	crude
cruga f geómetra	looper caterpillar
cruzado m	crossbred
cruzamiento m	crossbreeding
cruzar	cross, to

SPANISH	ENGLISH
cuadrado m latino	latin square
cuadrilla f	workcrew
cuadro m	square
cuadro m de flores	flower bed
cuajada f de leche f agria	clabber
cuajado m	curd
cuarentena f	quarantine
cuarto m de clasificación	grading room
cubeta f	bucket
cubierta f protectora de restrojo	stubble mulch
cubreobjeto m	cover slip
cubrir	case, to (mushroom growing)
cucharada f	tablespoonful
cucharadita f	teaspoonful
cuchilla f de injertar	budding knife
cuchilla f del arado	knife coulter
cuchillo m	knife
cuchillo m de injertar	grafting knife
cuchillo m de pizcar	grafting knife
cuello m	collar
cuenca f colectora	catchment area
cuenca f de desagüe	drainage basin
cuenta f agrícola	farm account
cuenta f de la explotación	operating statement
cuerda f	rope
cuerda f	string
cuerda f	twine
cuernecillo m	birdsfoot trefoil
cuerno m	horn
cuero m	hide
cuero m	leather
cuero m	skin
cuervo m	crow
cuesco	stone (fruit)
cueva f	cave
culantrillo m de poza	maidenhair fern
cultivador	grower
cultivador m comercial	grower
cultivador m de dientes flexibles	spring tooth harrow
cultivador m rotativo	rotary cultivator
cultivar	cultivate, to
cultivar	culture, to

SPANISH - ENGLISH EQUIVALENTS

SPANISH	ENGLISH	SPANISH	ENGLISH
cultivar	grow, to	cuñete m	firkin
cultivar	till, to (soil)	cura f	cure
cultivo en fajas	strip cropping	curar	cure, to
cultivo m	crop	curva f de nivel	contour
cultivo m	cultivation	cúscuta f	dodder
cultivo m abusivo	overcropping		
cultivo m al aire libre	outdoor crop		
cultivo m asociado	companion crop		
cultivo m consecutivo	second crop	**- CH -**	
cultivo m de abono en verde	green manure crop	chabacano m	apricot
cultivo m de cobertura	cover crop	chala f	husk
cultivo m de invernadero	greenhouse crop	chala f	stover
cultivo m de semillas	seed growing	chalote m	shallot
cultivo m de tejido	tissue culture	champiñón m	mushroom
cultivo m en invernadero	greenhouse culture	chaparrón m	downpour
cultivo m en lomos	ridge culture	chapulín m	locust
cultivo m extensivo	field crop	charca f	farm pond
cultivo m industrial	industrial crop	charco m	pond
cultivo m intercalado	intercropping	charco m	puddle
cultivo m intermedio	catch crop	chaveta f	cotter pin
cultivo m matríz	starter culture	chicharrones m	cracklings
cultivo m precedente	preceding crop	chicle m	chicle
cultivo m protector	nurse crop	chícharo m	chickpea
cultivo m puro	pure culture	chimenea f	chimney
cultivo m reconstructor del terreno	soil-building crop	chinche f	bug (true bug)
cultivo m renovador del suelo	soil-restoring crop	chinche m tintóreo	cotton stainer
		chinchita f de las plantas	plant louse
cultivo m sin suelo	soilless culture	chiquero m	pigsty
cultivo m sin tierra	soilless culture	chufa f	chufa
cultivo m subsuperficial	subtillage	chuleta f	chop
cultivos m básicos	basic crops	chupón m lateral	lateral shoot
cultivos m comerciales	cash crops	chupón m	water sprout
cultivos m de plantas alimenticias	food crops	chupón m	sucker
cultivos m extensivos	extensive crops		
cultivos m industriales	cash crops		
cultivos m oleaginosos	oil crops		
cultura f	culture		
cultura f iniciadora	culture, starter		
cultura f pura	culture, pure		
cumbre f	summit		
cuneiforme	cuneate		
cuneta f	drainage ditch		
cuña f	wedge		

SPANISH - ENGLISH EQUIVALENTS

SPANISH	ENGLISH	SPANISH	ENGLISH
		dejar de florecer	stop flowering, to
- D -		deltoide	deltoid
		demostración f	demonstration
dalia f	dahlia	demostrar	demonstrate, to
damasquina f	marigold	densidad f	density
dañar	damage, to	densidad f aparente	apparent density
dañarse	breakdown, to	denso	dense
daño m	damage	dentado	dentate
daño m de gas	gas damage	dentado	crenate
daño m de insectos	insect damage	dependencias f de la finca	farm buildings
daños m causados por		deportado m	offset
la tempestad	storm damage	depositar	deposit, to
dar sombra f	shade, to	depositarse	deposited, to be
dardo m	short shoot	depósito m	tanks
datos m	data	depreciación f	depreciation
dátil m	date (fruit)	depredador m	predator
de abundante floración	floriferous	depresión f del terreno	depression
de cáscara f dura	hard coated	depresión f	depression
de enraizamiento profundo	deep rooting	derivado	by-product
de grano m fino	fine grained	derramar	to spill
de hojas f caducas	deciduous	derrumbe m	landslide
de hojas f perennes	evergreen	desaguar	drain, to
de lantal m de hule	rubber apron	desagüe	drainage
de largo alcance	long range	desahijar	to thin
de nervadura paralela	parallel veined	desahije	thinning
de pura raza f	true-to-type	desalcalizar	de-alkalize, to
de raza f pura	purebred	desarollo m longitudinal	longitudinal growth
de trabajo m intensivo	labor intensive	desbotonar	disbud, to
decenio m	decade	desbrote m	disbudding
declaración f de ingresos	income statement	descabezar	head, to
declinación f	declination	descascaradora f	huller
declive m	slope	descascaradora f	sheller
decoloración	fading	descendencia f	descent
decusado	decussate	descendencia f	progeny
defensa f contra las		descendente	descending
inundaciones	flood control	descoloración f	etiolation
deflocular	deflocculate, to	descolorido	discolored
defoliación f	defoliation	descomponer	rot, to
defoliación f	shedding (plants)	descomponerse	decompose, to
deforme	deformed	descomponerse	weather, to
degeneración f	degeneration	descomposición f	decomposition
degenerar	degenerate, to	descomposición f	breakdown (decomposition)
degenerarse	naturalize, to	descomposición f interna	internal breakdown
deglutición f	swallowing		
degradado	degraded		

SPANISH - ENGLISH EQUIVALENTS

SPANISH	ENGLISH	SPANISH	ENGLISH
descomposición f interna de las frutas por temperaturas bajas	low temperature breakdown	desmontable	removable
descompuesto	putrid	desmontadura f	deforestation
descornar	dehorn, to	desnitrificar	denitrify, to
descremadora f	separator, cream	despanojar	detassel, to
descuidar	neglect, to	despepitadora f de algodón	cotton gin
descuido m	neglect	despepitar	to gin (cotton)
desecación f	desiccation	desperdicio m	waste
desacado	withered	despintar	to strip paint
desecador	dessiccator	desprender	detach, to
desecar	desiccate, to	despuntar	pinch, to
desecho m	debris	despuntar	top, to
desembocadura f	outlet	destilado m	distillate
desenrolladora f situadora de película plástica	mulcher-transplanter	destornillador m	screwdriver
deseño m funcional	functional design	destrío m	reject (processing)
desgranar	shell, to	desvainar	shell, to
desgrane m	shattering	desviación f media	standard error
desgrane m	shelling	desviación f	deviation
deshelar	thaw, to	desviación f normal	standard deviation
desherbar	weed, to	desyemar	disbud, to
deshidratar	dehydrate, to	detallista m	retailer
deshidratacíon	dehydration	detergente m	detergent
deshojado	leafless	deterioración f de la estructura	soil structure deterioration
deshojador m	defoliator	deteriorarse	deteriorate, to
deshojador m	leaf stripper	deteriorarse	spoil, to
deshojar	defoliate, to	deterioro m	deterioration
deshojarse	defoliate, to	deterioro m de las hojas	leaf damage
deshuesamiento m	pitting	deterioro m ocasionado por plaguicidas	spray damage
desierto m	desert	deuda f	debt
desinfección f del suelo	soil disinfection	devanadera f	reel
desinfección f del suelo	soil sterilization	déficit m	deficit
desinfección f del suelo por vapor	steaming (soil)	diagnosis m	diagnosis
desinfección f	disinfection	diagnóstico m foliar	leaf analysis
desinfectante m	disinfectant	diapositiva f	slide
desinfectante m para semillas	seed disinfectant	diarrea f	diarrhea
deslavar	leach, to (soil)	día m de pago	pay day
deslavazar	leach, to (soil)	dibásico	dibasic
deslizamiento m	slippage	dicentra f	bleeding heart plant
desmalezar	weed, to	diente m de grada	harrow tooth
desmenuzadora f	chopper	diente m de león	dandelion
desmenuzadora f	shredder	dieta f	diet
desmineralización f	demineralization	diferenciación	differentiation
		diferencial f	differential

SPANISH - ENGLISH EQUIVALENTS

SPANISH	ENGLISH	SPANISH	ENGLISH
diferente	differing	división f del trabajo	division of labor
digerible	digestible	división f heterotípica	heterotypic division
digestión f	digestion	día m	day
digitada	digitate	día m natural	length of day
digital f	foxglove	doble	double
dilución f	dilution	dolomita f	dolomite
diluidor m	dilutor	dominación f	dominance
dinamómetro m	dynamometer	dominancia f	dominance
dinero m efectivo	cash	dominante	dominant
dinitrofenol m	dinitrophenol	dompedro m	morning glory
dióico	dioecious	doradillo m	wireworm
dióxido m de carbono	carbon dioxide	dosel m	canopy
diploide	diploid	dosificación f	dosage
dique m	dike	dosificación f	rate
dique m	levee	dosímetro m	fertilizer proportioner
disco m	disk	dosímetro m	proportioner
disco m de Petri	petri dish	dragar	dredge, to
diseminación f	dissemination	dragoncillo m	snapdragon
diseminar	scatter, to	drenaje m	drainage
disentería f	scours	drenaje m supletorio	supplementary drainage
diseñar	design, to	drenar	drain, to
diseño m	layout, design	drosófila f	drosophila
diseño m de jardin	garden design	ducha f	shower
disolver	dissolve, to	duchar	shower, to
disponible	available (nutrients)	dueño m	owner
disposición f de las hojas	phyllotaxis	duna f de arena	sand dune
disposición f experimental	design of experiments	duodeno m	duodenum
disqueo m	disking	durabilidad f	durability
distal	distal	durable	lasting
distancia f en el surco	spacing	duración de la conservación	duration of storage
distancia f entre líneas	row spacing	duración f de exposición	duration of illumination
distancia f entre plantas	plant spacing	duración f de la iluminación	illumination period
distribución f de luz	light distribution	duración f de utilización	duration of use
distribución f	distribution	duración f de la luz del día	length of day
distribución f de abonos	fertilizer distribution	duración f de la temporada de cultivo	length of growing season
distribucíon f a voleo	broadcast application	duramen m	heartwood
distribuidor m de abonos	fertilizer spreader	durazno m	peach
distribuidor m	distributor	dureza f	firmness
distribuir	distribute, to		
distribuir	scatter, to		
diurno	diurnal		
divalente m	bivalent		
diversificado	diversified		
división f de célula	cell divison		
división f reductora	reduction division		

SPANISH - ENGLISH EQUIVALENTS

SPANISH	ENGLISH	SPANISH	ENGLISH
		embalaje m	baling
		embalaje m	containers
		embalaje m	packing
- E -		embalaje m perdido	non-returnables
		embalar	pack, to
ebullición f	ebullition	embalar en jaula,	crate, to
echado	procumbent	embarazado	pregnant
echar	spray, to	embarrar	silt up, to
echar raíces	root, to	embrague m	clutch (i.e. car)
eco m	echo	embrion m latent	embryo, latent
ecología f	ecology	embrion m rudimentario	embryo, rudimentary
economista f	economist	embriones m	embryos
economía f de trabajo	labor saving	embrión m	embryo
economía f	economics	embudo m	funnel
economía f	economy	embudo m Buchner	buchner funnel
económico m	economic	emergencia f	emergence
ecólogo m	ecologist	empacar	pack, to
ectoparásito m	external parasite	empaque m	packing, gasket
ecuador m	equator	empaquetador m	packer
edafología f	soil science	empaquetar	pack, to
edáfico m	edaphic	empeorar	worsen, to
efecto f secundario	subsidiary effect	empinado m	steep
efecto m	effect	empleado m	employee
eficaz	effective	empleados m	personnel
eficiente	efficient	emplear	hire, to
eje m	axle	empobrecer	impoverish
eje m	shaft	empobrecimiento m	impoverishment (of soil)
eje m delantero	axle, front	empobrecimiento m	
eje m principal	main axis(bot)	del suelo	soil mining
eje m trasero	axle, rear	empollarse	hatch, to
elaboración f	processing	empresa f	enterprise
elaborar	process, to	emulsionable	emulsifiable
elasticidad f	elasticity	emulsión f	emulsion
electricidad f	electricity	en capas	layers, in
electrodo m	electrode	en forma de escudo	shieldlike
elemento m	element	enanismo m	dwarfing
elemento m nutritivo	nutrient	enano m	dwarf
elevador m	elevator	encaje m	groove
elevador m de horquilla	fork lift	encajonar	box, to
elevador m de paletas	forklift	encalado m	liming
elevador m hidráulico	hydraulic lift	encalar	lime, to
eléctrico	electric	encefalitis f	encephalitis
elíptico	elliptical	encendido m	ignition
elutriación f	elutriation	encharcamiento m	puddling
emasculación f	emasculation	encierro m	confinement
embalado m	packing		
embaladora f	baling machine		

115

SPANISH - ENGLISH EQUIVALENTS

SPANISH	ENGLISH	SPANISH	ENGLISH
encina f	oak	enfriar	cool, to
encinal m	oak grove	enganche m	coupling
encogerse	shrink, to	engrapar	to staple
encogerse	shrivel, to	engrasar	to grease
encrespar	curl, to	enjambre m	swarm of bees
encuesta f	survey	enjuagar	rinse, to
endeudamiento m	indebtedness	enlace m	linkage
endocarpio m	endocarp	enlatadora f	cannery
endocría f	inbreeding	enlatar	can, to
endogamia f	inbreeding	enlucido m	coating
endogamia f	line breeding	enmienda f calcárea	liming material
endoparásito m	internal parasite	enmiendas f	soil dressings
endosperma f	endosperm	enraizamiento m	rooting
endospermo m	endosperm	enrasar	level, to
enduramiento m	hardening	enriaje m por los elementos	dew retting
enduracimiento m	hardening	enriquecer	enrich, to
endurecer	harden off, to	enredadora f de campanillas	morning glory
enebro m	juniper		
eneldo m	dill	enrollamiento m de hojas	leaf rolling
enemigo m natural	natural enemy	ensayo m	assay
energía f	energy	ensayo m de variedades	variety trial
energía f alimenticia	food energy	ensiforme	sword shaped
enfardadora f	baling machine	ensiladora f	silo
enfardadora f de heno	haybaler	ensilaje m	silage
enfermedad f	disease	ensilar	ensilage, to
enfermedad f carencial	deficiency disease	ensortijamiento m	curling
enfermedad f de almacenamiento	storage disease	ensuciamiento m	pollution
enfermedad f de la momificación	mummy disease	enterrar con el arado	plough in, to
enfermedad f de la piel	skin disease	enterrar con el arado	plow under, to
enfermedad f de las plantas	plant disease	entomología f	entomology
		entomólogo m	entomologist
enfermedad f de manchas de la grasa	halo blight (of bean)	entrada f	inlet
		entrada f del aire	air supply
enfermedad f del suelo	soil disease	entrecruzamiento m	crossing over
enfermedad f holandesa del olmo	Dutch elm disease	entrega f	delivery
		entrenudo m	internode
enfermedad f vascular	vascular disease	entrenamiento m de cabeza	head training
enfermedad f virósica	virus disease	entresacar	cull, to
enfermedad no parasítica de la manzana	bitter pit	entresacar	thin, to
		envase m	container
enfermo	diseased	envase m	flower pot
enfermo	sick	envejecimiento m	aging
enfriamiento m	drop in temperature	envejecimiento m técnico	wear and tear
enfriamiento m del agua	hydrocooling	envenenamiento m	poisoning

SPANISH - ENGLISH EQUIVALENTS

SPANISH	ENGLISH	SPANISH	ENGLISH
envenenar	poison, to	escarlata	scarlet
enviar	ship, to	escarola f	endive
envoltura f	involucre	escasez f de agua	water shortage
envolturas f	casings	escasez m	scarcity
enyector m para el suelo	soil injector	escaso m	scarce
enzima f	enzyme	esclerocios m	sclerotia
enzimático	enzymatic	escoba f	broom
epidemia f	epidemic	escoba f de bruja	witches broom disease
epidemiología f	epidemiology	escopio m	chisel
epidermis f	epidermis	escuela f de horticultura	horticultural school
epifilo m	epiphyllum	escutelo m	scutellum
epígea	epigeous	esfagno m	sphagnum peat moss
equilibrio m analítico	analytical balance	esfagno m	peat moss
equilibrio m de nitrógeno	nitrogen balance	esfera f	dial
equinoccio m	equinox	esfínter m	sphincter
equipo m	equipo m	esfuerzo m de tracción	tensile strength
época f en que las vacas paren	calving season	esófago m	esophagus
época f de recolleción	picking season	espaciado m	spacing
época f de siembra	planting season	espaciamiento m	spacing
equipo m	equipment	espacio m	space
erecto	erect	espacio m que necesita una planta o animal	space requirement
ergotismo m	ergot	esparcidor de estiércol	manure spreader
érica f	heath	esparcidora	spreader
erosionarse	erode, to	esparcir	spread, to
erosión f	erosion	esparto m	espartograss
erosión f laminar	sheet erosion	espatulado	spatulate
erosión f por abrasión	scour erosion	espárrago m	asparagus
error m medio	standard error	espárrago m ornamental	asparagus fern
escabiosa f	scabiosa	espárrago m ornamental	asparagus, ornamental
escabro m	scab	especia f	spice
escala f pH	pH scale	especie f	species
escalera f	step ladder	especie f colonizadora	pioneer species
escama f	scale (bot)	espectro m	spectrum
escama f de bulbo	bulb scale	esperma f	sperm
escama f de la yema	bud scale	espiga f	spike
escarabajo m	beetle	espigando	heading stage
escarabajo m de la corteza	bark beetle	espigar	go to seed, to
escarabajo m japonés	Japanese beetle	espiguilla f	spikelet
escarabajo m roedor	chafer	espina f	spine
escardar	hoe, to	espina f foliar	leaf-spine
escardar	weed, to	espinaca f	spinach
escardillo m	dibble	espinaca f de Nueva Zelandia	New Zealand Spinach
escarificación f	scarification	espinoso	thorned
escarificador m	harrow		

SPANISH - ENGLISH EQUIVALENTS

SPANISH	ENGLISH	SPANISH	ENGLISH
espistasis m	epistasis	esterilizar al vapor	steam, to
espliego m	lavender (herb)	estéril	barren
espolón m	spur	estéril	infertile
espolvoreadora f	duster	estéril	sterile
espolvorear	dust, to	estiércol de puerco	pig manure
espolvoreo m aéreo	aerial dusting	estiércol m	manure
espora f	spore	estiércol m de aveja	sheep manure
espuela f de caballero	larkspur	estiércol m de caballo	horse manure
espuma f de plástico	plastic foam	estiércol m de vaca	manure (steer)
espumadera f	spray nozzle	estigma m	stigma
espumar	effervesce, to	estilete m	stylet
esqueleto m	frame	estilo m	style
esquilar	clip, to	estimación f	estimate
establecer	establish, to	estimulación f del	
establización f del mercado	market stabilization	crecimiento	growth stimulation
establo m	stable	estipula f	stipule
establo m	barn	estirar	stretch, to
establo m	stall	estolon m	stolon
estaca f	cutting (propagation)	estolón m	runner
estaca f	stake	estoma f	stoma
estaca f de hoja	cutting, leaf	estornino m	starling
estaca f de madera f dura	cutting, hardwood	estómago m	stomach
estaca f de madera f		estragón m	tarragon
semidura	cutting, semi-hardwood	estraña f	aster
estaca f de madera f suave	cutting, softwood	estratificación f	stratification
estaca f de raíz	root cutting	estratificado	stratified
estaca f del tallo	stem cutting	estratificar	stratify, to
estaca f foliáceas	cutting, leafy	estriado	ribbed
estaca f leñosa	hardwood cutting	estructura f	structure
estación f de bombeo	pumping station	estructura f del mercado	market structure
estación f experimental	research station	estrujadora f	grape crusher
estadística f	statistic	estudio m de los	
estado m activo de		movimientos	motion study
crecimiento	growth, active	estufa f	stove
estado m latente	dormancy	etiqueta f	label
estambre m	stamen	etiqueta f de oreja	ear tag
estaminado	staminate	euforbia f	petty spurge
estancia f	cattle ranch	euploide m	euploid
estanque m	pond	evaporación f	evaporation
estar en barbecho	fallow, to	evaporador m	evaporator
este m	east	evaporar	evaporate, to
esterilidad f	sterility	evapotranspiración f	evapotranspiration
esterilización f del suelo	soil sterilization	evolución f del capital	capital turnover
esterilizador m	sterilizer	excavadora f de papas	potato digger
esterilizar	sterilize, to	exceso m	excess

SPANISH - ENGLISH EQUIVALENTS

SPANISH	ENGLISH	SPANISH	ENGLISH
exceso m	surplus	fardo m de paja	bale of straw
excremento m	excrement	faringe f	pharynx
excrementos m humanos	night soil	fasciación f	fasciation
excusado m	portable toilet	fase f	stage
existencia f	occurrence	fase f	phase
exótico	exotic	fatiga f	fatigue
experimento m	experiment	fatiga f del suelo	soil exhaustion
experto m en		fábrica f	plant (factory)
fitomejoramiento	plant breeder	fábrica f elaboradora	processing plant
explanadora f	bulldozer	fecha f de siembra	sowing-date
explotación f agrícola		fécula f	starch
colectiva	communal farming	fecundación f	fertilization
explotación f familiar		fecundación f	insemination
rudimentaria	peasant farming	fecundar	fertilize, to (ie, egg or ovule)
explotación f horticola	market garden	fecundar	inseminate, to
exportación f	exportation	feldespato m	feldspar
exportación f	export	fenotipo m	phenotype
exportador m	exporter	fermentación f	fermentation
exportar	export, to	fermentar	compost, to
expulsión f	expulsion	fermentar	ferment, to
extensión f	elongation	ferretería f	hardware
extensión f de tierra	piece of land	fertilidad f	fertility
extensivo	extensive	fertilidad f de los suelos	soil fertility
exterminio m	extermination	fertilización f	fertilization
extinción f	eradication	fertilización f cruzada	cross-fertilization
extirpar	eradicate, to	fertilizante m	fertilizer
extracción f	extraction	fertilizante m líquido	liquid fetilizer
extracto m	extract	feto m	fetus
extraer	extract, to	fértil	fertile
		fiá f	vineyard
		fibra f	fiber
		fibra f cruda	crude fiber
- F -		fibra f de vidrio	fiberglass
		fibra f de vidrio	glass fiber
		fibre m de algodon	lint
factor m antiescorbútico	antiscorbutic factor	fibroso	fibrous
factor m de proteína		fibroso	stringy
pecuaria	animal protein factor	fiebre f	fever
factores m de producción	factors of production	fiebre f aftosa	foot and mouth disease
factores m económicos	economic factors	fiebre f catarral	blue tongue
faja f	streak	fierro m	tool
faja f de contención	buffer strip	fijación f de potasio	potassium fixation
faja f filtrante	filter strip	fijación f del nitrógeno	nitrogen fixation
faja f protectora	shelter belt	fijación f	fixation
falta f de lluvia	deficiency of rain	fijarse	fix, to (i.e. nitrogen)
falta f de luz	light deficiency		
fanal m	bell jar		

SPANISH - ENGLISH EQUIVALENTS

SPANISH	ENGLISH	SPANISH	ENGLISH
fil m	field	floricultura f	floriculture
fila f	row	florido	floriferous
filamento m	filament (bot)	florista m & f	florist
filiforme	filiform	flox m	phlox
filo m	cutting edge	flúor m	flourine
filoxera f	phylloxera	foco m de infección	source of infection
filtrar	filter, to	foliación f	flushing (of foliage)
filtrarse en	soak in, to	foliado	leafy
filtro m	filter	folículo m	follicle
filtro m	strainer	follaje m	foliage
fin m	end	folleto m	bulletin
financiar	finance, to	folleto m	pamphlet
finanza f	finance	fomento m de tierras	land development
finca f de demostración	demonstration farm	forma f de las hojas	leaf shape
fineza f	fineness	forma f de las hojas	leaf shape
finquero m	farmer	forma f del árbol	tree form
finquia f	plaintain lily	forma f juvenil	juvenile form
fisioclimatología f	physioclimatology	formación de rosetas	rosetting
fisiología f	physiology	formación f de gotas	drop formation
fisión f	fission	formación f de las flores	flower formation
fitocida m	phytocide	formaldehído m	formaldehyde
fitofisiólogo m	plant physiologist	formar aluviones f	silt, to
fitogenética f	plant breeding	formicida f	formicide
fitopatología f	phytopathologist	formio m	New Zealand flax
fitopatólogo m	plant pathologist	formio m	*Phormium* sp.
fitotecnia f	plant production	formón m	chisel
fitotrón m	growth chamber	formulación f	formulation
flaco	lean	forraje m	fodder
flexible	flexible	forraje m	forage
floema f	phloem	forsitia f	forsythia
flor del tigre	tigridia	forzado m	forcing
flor f	blossom	forzar	force, to
flor f	flower	fosa f	pit
flor f cortada	cut flower	fosfato m	phosphate
flor f de navidad	poinsettia	fosfato m natural	rock phosphate
flor f doble	double flower	fosforescencia f	phosphorescence
flor f ligulada	ligulate (ray) flower	fosforita f	phosphate rock
flor f radial	ray floret	fósforo m	phosphorus
flor f terminal	terminal flower	fórmula f	formula
floración f	flowering	fotocalco m	blueprint
floración f	flushing (of flowers)	fotocélula f	photocell
florecer	flower, to	fotoeléctrico	photoelectric
florecerse	flower, to	fotoesfera f	photosphere
floreciente	flower bearing	fotoespectrómetro m	photospectometer
floricultor m	floriculturist	fotoperiodicidad f	photoperiodicity

SPANISH - ENGLISH EQUIVALENTS

SPANISH	ENGLISH	SPANISH	ENGLISH
fotoperiodismo m	photoperiodicity	fumigar	fumigate, to
fotosíntesis m	photosynthesis	fundamento m	foundation
fragancia f	fragrance	fungicida f	fungicide
fragua f	forge	fungicido	fungicidal
frambuesa f	raspberry	fusariosis f	fusarium wilt
frasco m Erlenmeyer	Erlenmeyer flask	fusible m	fuse
frasco m Florence	Florence flask	futuros agricultores	Future Farmers of America
fregadero m	sink	de América	(FFA)
freír	fry, to	galanto m de nieve	snowdrop
frente m	front	gallardia f	gaillardia
fresa f	strawberry	galleta f	biscuit
fresco	fresh	gallina f	hen
fresia f	freesia	gallinaza f	chicken manure
friable	friable	gallinaza f	poultry manure
frijol arroz, poroto arroz	adsake bean	gallinero m	coop
frijol m	kidney bean	gallinero m	henhouse
frijol m de vaca	cowpea	gallo m	cock
frijol m	bean	galpón	barn
frijol m jacinto	hyacinth bean	galvanizado en caliente	hot dip galvanized
frondoso	leafy	galvanizar	galvanize, to
fructificación f	fruit formation	gameto m	gamete
fruta f	fruit (culinary)	gamíco	sexual
fruta f de pepita	pome	gamopétalo	gamopetalous
fruta f tempranera	forced fruit	gamosépalo	gamosepalous
frutas f cítricas	citrus fruit	ganadería f,	animal industry
frutas f conservadas en lata	canned fruit	ganadero m	cattleman
frutas f secas	mummies (fruit)	ganado m	livestock
fruticultor m	fruit grower	ganado m de engorde	feeder
fruticultor m	pomologist	ganado m de labor	farm animals
fruticultura f	pomology	ganado m vacuno	cattle
fruto m	fruit (bot)	gandul m	pigeon pea
fruto m aparente	pseudo fruit	gangrena f regresiva	die-back
fruto m de hueso	drupe, stone fruit	garantía f	security (econ)
fruto m deshicente	dehiscent fruit	garbanzo m	chickpea
fuego m	fire	garganta f	throat
fuelle m	bellows	garrachuelo m	pangolagrass
fuente f	spring (water)	garrancha f	spadix
fuerte	strong	garrapata f	tick
fuerza f	strength	garrón m	spur
fuerza f	power	gas m natural	natural gas
fuerza f de iluminación	intensity of lighting	gaseoso	vaporous
fumagina f	black mold	gastos m	expenses
fumagina f	sooty mold	gastos m de gestión	service charges
fumigante m	fumigant	gastos m generales fijos	overhead

SPANISH - ENGLISH EQUIVALENTS

SPANISH	ENGLISH	SPANISH	ENGLISH
gastos m iniciales de establecimiento	capital cost	gordo	fat
gaveta f	drawer	gorgojo m	weevil
gavilla f	stack	gorrión m	sparrow
gelatina f	gelatin	gota f	drop
gelatina f	jelly (gelatin)	gotera f	leak
gelsemio m	yellow jasmine	grácil	slender
gen m	gene	grada f	harrow
genciana f	gentian	grada f de discos	disc harrow
generación f diploide	diplont	gradar	harrow, to
generación f haploide	haplont	gradiente m de fertilidad	fertility gradient
generador m	generator	grado m	degree
generativo	generative	grado m de humedad	degree of moisture
genes m complementarios	complementary genes	grado m de saturación	degree of saturation
genes m duplicados	duplicate genes	gráfica f	chart
genotipo m	genotype	grajo m	jay
genuino	true-to-type	grama f del Norte	quackgrass
geológico	geological	grama f del Norte	couchgrass
geranio m	geranium	grama f johnson	johnsongrass
geranio m	zonal pelargonium	gramínea f	grass
geranio m aromático	scented geranium	grana f	seed
geranio m hiedra	ivy leafed geranium	granada f	pomegranate fruit
geranio m zonal	zonal geranium	granadilla f	passionfruit
germen m	germ	granado m	pomegranate tree
germinación f	germination	granel	loose
germinar	germinate, to	granero m	barn
germinar	sprout, to (seed)	granero m de ventilación automática	flue barn
género m	genus	granizada f	hailstorm
ginerlo m	pampas grass	granizar	hail, to
ginkgo m	ginkgo	granizo m	hail
girar	spin, to	granja f	barn
girasol m	sunflower	granja f avícola	poultry farm
gisofila f	gypsophila	grano m	grain
glabro	glabrous	grano m	kernel
gladiolo m	gladiolus	grano m de polen	pollen grain
glanduloso	glandular	grano m triturado	crushed grain
glándula f	gland	granulado m	granulate
glándula f nectarífera	nectar gland	granular	granulate, to
glicina f	wisteria	granuloso	granular
gloria f de la nieve	glory of the snow	grapa f	staple
gloxinia f	gloxinia	grapadora f	stapler
gluma f	glume	grapar	staple, to
golpe m de sol	sunstroke	grasa f	fat
golpear	pound, to	grasa f	suet
gomosis f	gummosis	grasera f	grease gun

SPANISH - ENGLISH EQUIVALENTS

SPANISH	ENGLISH	SPANISH	ENGLISH
grava f	gravel		
gravedad f específica	specific gravity	**- H -**	
gravilla f	gravel		
grifo m	faucet	haba f	field bean
grifo m	hosebib	haba f	navy bean
grifo m de vaciado	drain cock	haba f de burro	horse bean
grilla f	grating	habichuela f	bean
grillotalpa m	mole cricket	habichuela f	string bean
grosella f	currant	habichuela f negra	black bean
grosella f espinosa	gooseberry	habitación f	habitat
grosella f negra	black currant	habitat m	habitat
grosellero m dorado	golden currant	hacer esquelético	skeletonize, to
grueso	coarse	hacer hileras	to windrow
grueso	thick	hacha f	axe
grupo m	clump	hacha f	hatchet
guadañar	scythe, to	hacienda f	plantation
guadaña f	scythe	hacienda f ganadera	cattle ranch
guanábana f	soursop fruit	halo m	halo
guanábano m	soursop tree	hamamelina f	witch hazel
guandul m	pigeon pea	hamamelis m	witch hazel
guandú m	pigeon pea	hambre m	hunger
guanería	winery	haploide	haploid
guano m	guano	haras f	stud farm
guardar en cajones	bin, to	harina f	flour
guataca f	spade	harina f de agrios desecados	citrus meal
gueldear	to weld	harina f de algodón	cottonseed meal
guiar	steer, to	harina f de cuerno	horn meal
guija f	pebble	harina f de cuerno y pezuña	hoof and horn meal
guijarro m	pebble	harina f de hojas de alfalfa	alfalfa leaf meal
guineo m	banana	harina f de huesos	bone meal
guisante m	pea	harina f de linaza	linseed meal
guisante m azucarado	sugar pea	harina f de maní	peanut oil
guisante m de olor	sweet pea	harina f de pescado	fish meal
guisante m forrajero	field pea	harina f de sangre	blood meal
guisante m verde	English pea	harinoso	mealy
guisante m verde	garden pea	harpillera f	burlap
gusano m	worm	haz f vascular	vascular bundle
gusano m cortador	armyworm	hábito m de crecimiento	growth habit
gusano m cortador	cutworm	hábito m	habit
gusano m de las yemas	budworm	heces f	feces
gusano m de tierra	earthworm	hectárea f	hectare
gusano m tornillo	screw worm	helada f blanca	hoarfrost
gusto m diferente	off-flavor	helado m	ice cream

SPANISH - ENGLISH EQUIVALENTS

SPANISH	ENGLISH	SPANISH	ENGLISH
helecho m	fern	hidrácida	hydrazide
helicóptero m	helicopter	hidráulico	hydraulic
heliotropo m	heliotrope	hidrocarburo m	hydrocarbon
hembra f	female	hidrología f	hydrology
hemorragia f	hemorrhage	hidromorfo	hydromorphic
hendidor	wedge grafting tool	hidroponía f	hydroponics
heneador m	haymaker	hidropónicos m pl	hydroponics
henificación f	haymaking	hidrosoluble	water-soluble
henil m	hayloft	hidrotermoterapia f	hot water treatment
heno m	hay	hidrotropismo m	hydrotropism
hepática f	hepatica	hidrófilo	moisture retaining
herbáceo	herbaceous	hidrógeno m	hydrogen
herbaje m	herbage	hidrólisis f	hydrolysis
herbario m	herbarium	hidróxido m amónico	ammonia
herbicida m	herbicide	hidrómetro m	hydrometer
heredabilidad f	heritability	hidróxido m	hydroxide
heredable	inheritable	hiedra f	ivy
herencia f	heredity	hiedra f terrestre	ground ivy
herencia f	inheritance	hielo m	ice
herida f	pruning cut	hielo m nocturno	night frost
herida f	wound	hierba f	grass
hermafroditismo m	hermaphroditism	hierba f	herb
hermafrodita m & f	hermaphrodite	hierba f mala	weed
hermético	airtight	hierba f alfombra	carpetgrass
hernia f de la col	clubroot	hierba f Bahía	Bahiagrass
herramienta f	tool	hierba f Bermuda	Bermudagrass
herramienta f mecánica	power tool	hierba f caballar	groundsel
herrumbre f	rust	hierba f callera	sedum
herrumbroso	rusty	hierba f cana	groundsel
hervir	boil, to	hierba f Dallis	Dallis grass
hesperidio m	hesperidium	hierba f de las pampas	pampas grass
heterocigosis f	heterozygosis	hierba f de marrano	pigweed
heterogamia f	heterogamy	hierba f de Natal	Natalgrass
heterosis f	heterosis	hierba f elefante	napiergrass
heterosis f	hybrid vigor	hierba f imperial	imperial grass
heterozigoto m	heterozygote	hierba f kikuyu	kikuyugrass
hexacloruro m de benzeno	BHC	hierba f sagrada	verbena
hibernar	hibernate, to	hierba f San Juan	St. John's wort
hibisco m	hibiscus	hierba m mora	black nightshade
hibridación f	hybridization	hierbabuena f	mint
hibrido m de injerto	graft hybrid	hierbajos m	forbs
hidracina f	hydrazine	hierbas f de cocina	culinary herbs
hidratado	hydrated	hierro m	iron
hidrato m de carbono m	carbohydrate	hierro m de marcar	branding iron
hidrazida f maleica	maleic hydrazine	hifa f	hypha

SPANISH - ENGLISH EQUIVALENTS

SPANISH	ENGLISH	SPANISH	ENGLISH
higiene f animal	animal health	homogeneización	homogenization
higo m	fig	homogeneizar	homogenize, to
higrometria f	hygrometry	homozigoto m	homozygote
higroscópico m	hygroscopic	homólogo m	homologue
higrotermógrafo m	hygrothermograph	hondonada	hollow
higrómetro m	hygrometer	hongo m	fungus
higuera f chumba	opuntia	hora f	hour
hijo m	slip	horario m	schedule
hijuelo m	sucker	horca f	pitchfork
hijuelo m	offset	horcón m	pitchfork
hilado	spinning	horizonte m	horizon
hilera f	row	hormiga f	ant
hileradora f	windrower	hormiga f cortadora	leaf cutting ant
hilo m	hilum	hormigón m pretensado	prestressed concrete
himenóptero m	hymenopteron	hormona f	hormone
hinchado	swollen	hornear	bake
hinchar	swell, to	horno m	oven
hincharse	bloat	horquilla f	fork (agricultural)
hincharse	swell, to (buds)	horquilla f	pitchfork
hinchazón f	swelling	hortaliza f de hoja	potherb
hinojo m	fennel	hortelano m	small truck farmer
hipertrofia f	hypertrophy	hortensia f	hydrangea
hipérico m	St. John's wort	horticultor m	horticulturist
hipocotilo m	hypocotyl	horticultora	horticulturist (woman)
hipoteca f	mortgage	horticultura f	horticulture
hipógea	hypogenous	hortaliza f	vegetable
hipógino	inferior (botanical)	hortalizas f verdes	leafy vegetables
hipógino	hypogynous	hortícola	horticultural
hipsómetro m	hypsometer	hospedero m	host
hirsuto	hirsute	hoyo m	hole
hisopo m	hyssop	hoz f	sickle
histología f	histology	hueco m	hollow
híbrido m	hybrid	hueco m	planting hole
híbrido m doble	double cross	huerta f	orchard
híbrido m línea variedad	inbred variety cross	huerta f familiar	kitchen garden
hídrico	hydric	huerto m frutal	orchard
hoja f	leaf	hueso m	pit
hoja f aislante	insulating film	huevo m	egg
hoja f electrónica	electronic leaf	huésped m	host
hoja f ornamental	cut foliage	humectante	wetting
hojas f	leaves	humectar	moisten, to
hojita f	blade (of grass)	humedad f	humidity
hojita f	small leaf	humedad f relativa	relative humidity
hojuela f	leaflet	humedecer	sok, to
hombre-día m	man-day	humedecible	wettable

SPANISH - ENGLISH EQUIVALENTS

SPANISH	ENGLISH	SPANISH	ENGLISH
humus m	humus	incremento m de la producción	yield increase
hundido	sunken	incubadora f	incubator
húmedo	moist	incubación f	incubation
húmedo	humid	indehiscencia f	indehiscence
húmedo	damp	indehiscente	indehiscent
identificación f espectrofotométrica	spectrophotometric identification	indicador m	indicator
igualar	level, to	indicador m	tracer
ilang-ilang m	ylang-ylang	índice	index
ilión m	ileum	índice m de precios	price index
iluminación f	lighting	indigeno	indigenous
iluminación f accesoria	supplementary lighting	indiviso	entire (bot.)
iluminación f cíclica	cyclic lighting	indización f	indexing
iluminación f energética	irradiance	inducción f	induction
iluminado	illuminated	indusio m	indusium
iluminar	illuminate, to	industria f	industry
imagen f del daño	pattern of damage	industria f conservera	preserving industry
imagen f radicular	root pattern	industria f de procesamiento	processing industry
imbibición f	imbibition	industria f pecuaria	cattle industry
impermeabilidad f	impermeabilty	industrialización f	industrialization
impermeable	impermeable	industrializar	industrialize, to
impermeable	waterproof	infeccioso	infectious
implantar	implant, to	infección f	infection
importación f	import	infectado	infected
importador m	importer	infectar	infect, to
importar	import	infectividad f	infectivity
impuesto m territorial	land taxation	infero	inferior (bot.)
impuestos m agrícolas	farm taxation	infestación f	infestation
impureza f	impurity	infestar	infest, to
impureza f anodina	inert matter	infiltración f	percolation
impureza f perjudicial	injurious impurity	infiltrar	percolate, to
impurificación f del aire	air pollution	inflamarse	bloat
inactivación f	inactivation	inflorescencia f	inflorescence
incidencia f	incidence	influencia f	influence
incidencia f de las plagas	pest incidence	influir en la floración	influence flowering
incienso m	incense	información f del mercado	market report
incisión f	incision	información f	information
inclinación f	inclination	infra-rojo	infrared
inclinarse	lean, to	infraespecífico	infraspecific
incomible	inedible	infructífero	unfruitful
incompatibilidad f	incompatibility	infructuosidad f	unfruitfulness
incompatible	incompatible	infundibuliforme	infundibular
incorporar	plow under	ingeniero m	engineer
incrementar	increase, to	ingeniero m	master of science
incremento m	increase	ingeniero m agrícola	agricultural engineer

SPANISH - ENGLISH EQUIVALENTS

SPANISH	ENGLISH	SPANISH	ENGLISH
ingenio m	sugar mill	injerto m inglés	whip and tongue grafting
ingestión f	ingestion	injerto m intermedio	double-working
ingrediente m	ingredient	injerto m lateral	side grafting
ingrediente m activo	active ingredient	injerto m nodrizo	nurse graft
ingresos m	income	injerto m por aproximación	graft, approach
ingresos m agrícolas	farm income	injerto por aproximación	
ingresos m netos	net income	en arco	graft, inarch
inhibidor m	growth retardant	inmaduro	immature
inhibidor m	inhibitor	inmaduro	unripe
inhibidor m de brotación	sprouting inhibitor	inmerso	immersed
iniciación f floral	flower iniciation	inmune	immune
iniciación f	initiation	inmunidad f	immunity
injertación f	grafting	inmunización f	immunization
injertador m	grafting knife	inmunizar	immunize
injertar	bud, to (graft)	inoculación f	inoculation
injertar	graft, to	inodoro	scentless
injerto m	graft	inodoro m	toilet
injerto m a caballo	saddle graft	inorgánico	inorganic
injerto m anular	budding, ring	inóculo m	inoculum
injerto m de arco	inarching	insecticida f	insecticide
injerto m de astilla	budding, chip	insectívoro m	insectivore
injerto m de chapa	veneer graft	insecto m	bug
injerto m de copa	topworking	insecto m	insect
injerto m de corona	graft, crown	insecto m vector de la	
injerto m de corteza	graft, bark	enfermedad	insect vector
injerto m de costado	graft, side	inseguridad f de tenencia	insecurity of tenure
injerto m de empalme	splice graft	inserción f	insertion
injerto m de escudete	shield budding	insertar	insert, to
injerto m de flauta	budding, flute	inserto	inserted
injerto m de fusta	whip graft	insípido	insipid
injerto m de fusta y lengua	whip and tongue graft	insolación f	insolation
injerto m de hendedura	graft, cleft	inspección f	inspection
injerto m de incrustación	graft, wedge	inspección f fitosanitaria	inspection for disease
injerto m de incrustación	inlay graft	inspector m	inspector
injerto m de lengüeta	graft, whip and tongue	instalación f de calefacción	heating plant
injerto m de ojo	shield budding	instar m	instar
injerto m de para	graft, cleft	instituto m	institute
injerto m de parche	patch budding	instrucción f	instruction
injerto m de pieze	patch budding	insumo m	input
injerto m de raíz	graft, root	intemperie f	inclement weather
injerto m de raíz-nodriza	graft, nurse root	intensidad f	intensity
injerto m de reconstrucción	topworking	intensidad f de plantación	plant density
injerto m de yema en "T"	budding, T	intensidad f luminosa	light intensity
injerto m en cabeza	top graft	intensificación f	intensification
injerto m en "T" invertida	budding, inverted T	interacción f	interaction

SPANISH - ENGLISH EQUIVALENTS

SPANISH	ENGLISH	SPANISH	ENGLISH
intercalamiento m	intercropping	invertebrado	invertebrate
intercambiable	interchangeable	invertir	invest, to
intercambio m	interchange	investigaciones f agronómicas	agricultural research
intercambio m de bases o cationes	base exchange	investigaciones f pecuarias	animal research
intercepción f	interception	investigación f	research
interferencia f	interference	investigador m	researcher
intermediario m	interstock	invierno	winter
internudo m	internode	involucrado	involucrate
interrupción f de la noche	night interruption	involucro m	involucre
interrupción f del crecimiento	interruption in growth	inyección f	injection
interruptor m	switch	inyectar	inject, to
interestatal	interstate	ion m	ion
intervalo m	interval	iónico	ionic
intervención f	intervention	ipecacuana f	ipecac
intestino m	bowel	ipomea f	morning glory
intestino m	intestine	iris m	iris
intestino m delgado	small intestine	irradiación f	irradiation
intestino m grueso	large intestine	irradiar	irradiate, to
introducción f	introduction	irregular	irregular
inundable	subject to flooding	irrigable	irrigable
inundación f	flood	irrigación f	irrigation
inundación f	flooding	irrigar	irrigate, to
inundación f regulada	controlled flooding	isoenzima f	isoenzyme
inundar	flood, to	isoenzimático	isoenzymatic
invadir	invade	isogénico	isogenic
invasión f	invasion	isoterma f	isothermal
invendible	unmarketable	isoyela	isoyelic
inventarización f	stock taking	isótopo m	isotope
invernación f	wintering	ixora f	ixora
invernadero m	glasshouse		
invernadero m	greenhouse		
invernadero m	hothouse		
invernadero m adosado	lean-to greenhouse		
invernadero m calentado	hothouse		- J -
invernadero m climático	growth chamber		
invernadero m de multiplicación	propagating greenhouse	jabalcón m	purlin
invernadero m multicuerpo	multispan greenhouse	jacinto m	hyacinth
invernadero m neumático	inflatable house	jacinto m racimoso	grape hyacinth
invernante	overwintered	jalar	to strip (i.e. thorns)
invernar	hibernate, to	jamón m	ham
invernar	overwinter, to	jaquimón m	halter
inversión f	inversion	jarabe m	syrup
invertasa f	invertase	jarabe m de manzana	apple syrup

SPANISH - ENGLISH EQUIVALENTS

SPANISH	ENGLISH	SPANISH	ENGLISH
jardinero m	gardener	lámina f de hoja	leaf blade
jardín m	garden	laminilla f	gill (mushroom)
jardín m de adorno	ornamental garden	laminilla f	lamella (mushroom)
jardín m de flores	flower garden	lámpara f fluorescente	fluorescent lamp
jardín m rocoso	rockery	lana f	fleece
jarrón m para flores	flower vase	lana f de vidrio	glass wool
jaula f	crate	lanchón m	barge
jefe m	boss	lanza f de pulverización	spray gun
jején	gnat	lanza-llamas f	flame gun
jeringuilla f	mock orange	laringe f	larynx
jornal m	wages	larva f	larva
joroba f	hump	larvicida f	larvicide
jugo m	juice	larvicida	larvicidal
jugo m	sap	lata f	can
jugo m de manzana	apple juice	látex m	latex
jugo m de uva	grape juice	latiguillo m	runner
jugoso	juicy	latitud m	latitude
junco m	reed	latón m	brass
junco m	rush	lavar	wash, to
juventud f	juvenile period	lavándula f	lavender
juzgar	judge, to	laya f	spade
		lazo m	knot
		lámpara f de incandescencia	incandescent lamp
- K -		lámpara f de vapor de mercurio de alta presión	high pressure mercury vapor lamp
		leche f de gallina	star of Bethlehem
kenaf m	kenaf	leche f descremada	skimmed milk
kentia f	kentia palm	leche f en polvo	powdered milk
kudzú m	kudzu	lechería f	dairy
		lechero m	dairyman
		lechón m	suckling pig
- L -		lechuga f	lettuce
		lechuga f repollada	lettuce, head
		legumbre f	legume
labiada f	labiate	leguminosas f	legumes
lábil	labile	lengua f azul	blue tongue
labio m	lip	lente m de aumento	magnifying glass
labor m agrícola	farm job	lenteja f	lentil
labranza	tillage	lentejilla f	lenticel
labranza f	plowing	lentícela f	lenticel
laburno m	laburnum	lenticula f	lenticel
lactación f	lactation	leña f proveniente de la poda	prunings
ladera f	hillside	leñosa	woody
lago m	lake	lepidio m	cress
lamburda f	mixed bud		

129

SPANISH - ENGLISH EQUIVALENTS

SPANISH	ENGLISH	SPANISH	ENGLISH
lesión f	lesion	lirio m	lily
lespedeza f	lespedeza	lirio m calla	calla
letrina f	latrine	lirio m de los valles	lily-of-the-valley
levadura f de cerveza desecada	Brewer's dried yeast	lirio m de San Juan	daylily
		lirio m de sangre	blood lily
liatris f	liatris	lirio m del Nilo	lily of the Nile
liberalización	liberalization	lirio m del valle	lily of the valley
libocedro m	incense cedar	lirio m kafir	clivia
libra f	pound	liriocalla f	lily, calla
licuación f	liquification	lisímetro m	lysimeter
ligero	lightweight	liso m	smooth (bot)
lignina f	lignin	lista f	chart
ligulado	strap shaped	lista f	stripe
ligustro m	privet	lista f de precios	price list
lila f	lilac	listón m de madera	lath
lima f	file (tool)	litera f	litter
lima f	lime	literatura f	literature
limar	file, to	lixiviación f	leaching
limbo m	blade (botanical)	lixiviar	leach, to
limo m	silt	lixiviar	lixiviate, to
limón	lemon	lobelia f	lobelia
limón m	lime (fruit)	lodícula f	lodicule
limonero m	lemon tree	lodo m	mud
limoso	muddy	lodo m de ciudades	sewage sludge
limpiadora f de semillas	seed cleaner	lodoso	muddy
limpiar	clean, to	loess m	loess
limpiar	wash, to	loma f	hill
limpiasemillas f	seed cleaner	loma f de arena	sand hill
linaje m	pedigree	lombriz f de tierra	earthworm
línea f	line	lomo m	loin
línea	row	lona f	canvas
línea f	strain (breeding)	longevidad f	longevity
línea f pura	pure line	longicornio m	long-horned beetle
lineal	linear	longitud f de onda	wavelength
lino m	flax	longitud f	longitude
lino m	linen	lote m	lot
liofilización f	freeze drying	lote m	plot
liofilización f	lyophilization	lote m de experimentos	experimental plot
liofílico m	lyophilic	lóbulo m	lobe (botanical)
lipólisis	lipolysis	lucha f contra la erosión	erosion control
líquen m	lichen	lucha f contra los insectos	insect control
liquidámbar m	sweet gum	lucrativo	profitable
liquidez f	liquidity	lugar m de clasificación	grading room
líquido m	liquid	lugar m de trabajo	workplace
líquido m desinfectante	liquid disinfectant	lunaria f	honesty plant

SPANISH - ENGLISH EQUIVALENTS

SPANISH	ENGLISH	SPANISH	ENGLISH
lunaria f	lunaria	madera f	wood
lupino m	lupin	madreselva f	honeysuckle
luxámetro m	lux-meter	maduración f artificial	after-ripening
luz artificial	artificial light	madurar	mature, to
luz f	light	madurar	ripen, to
luz f del día	daylight	madurez	ripeness
luz f del sol	sunshine	maduro	ripe
luz f diurna	daylight	maduro prematuro	prematurely ripe
		magnesia f	magnesia
		magnesio m	magnesium
		magnolia f	magnolia
		magulladura f	bruise
		magullar	bruise, to
- LL -		mahonia f	mahonia
		maíz m dulce	sweet corn
		majoramiento m genético	breeding
		majorca f	pod (of cacao)
		malanga f	caladium
llano	flat (level)	mal m de los semilleros	damping off
llano	level	mal m de semillero	damping off
llanos m	plains	maleza f	weed
llave f	faucet	malformación	malformation
llave f	hosebib	malva f	hollyhock
llave f	key	malva f	mallow
llenar	fill, to	malla f de gallinero	wire netting
lleno	full	manada f	herd
lleva f	cam (engine)	mancha f	stain
llover	rain, to	mancha f	spot
llovizna f	drizzle	mancha f	patch
lluvia f	rainfall	mancha f angular de la hoja	angular leaf spot
lluvia f de oro	laburnum	mancha f de la hoja	leaf spot
lluvia f efectiva	effective precipitation	mancha f ojival	eye spot
lluvia f torrencial	heavy rain	mancha f reticulada	net blotch
		manchar	stain, to
		manchita f	speck
		mandarina f	tangerine
- M -		maneja f del bosque	forest management
		manejar	handle, to
		manejar	operate, to
maceta f	flowerpot	manejo m	operation
maceta f	pot	manejo m de la finca	farm management
maceta f de barro	pot, clay	manejo m del suelo	soil management
maceta f de plástico	plastic pot	manejo m gerencial de la finca	farm management
macetas f de fibra de turba	pot, peat	manga f	chute
macollo m	cluster		

131

SPANISH - ENGLISH EQUIVALENTS

SPANISH	ENGLISH	SPANISH	ENGLISH
manga f	garden hose	masticar	chew
manga f de agua	hose	mata f	plant (esp. large herbaceous)
manganeso m	manganese		
mango m	handle	matabrozas f	brush killer
mango m	mango	matadero m	slaughterhouse
manguera f	garden hose	matanza f	slaughter
manguera f	hose	matar	slaughter, to
manipuleo m	handling	materia f fecal	foecal matter
manivela f	crank	materia f orgánica	organic matter
maní m	peanut	materia f seca	dry matter
mano f de obra	labor	material m aislante	insulating material
mano f de obra	manual labor	material m básico	foundation stock
mano f de obra familiar	family labor	material m de cobertura	covering material
mano f de obra utilizada	labor force	material m inicial	starting material
mano m	hand	materiales m de cementación	cementing materials
mano m de obra estacional	seasonal labor	materias f primas	raw materials
manómetro m	pressure gauge	matería f inorgánica	inorganic matter
mantequero m	churn	mayordomo m	foreman
mantillo m de hojas	leaf-mold	mayorista mf	wholesaler
manutisa f	sweet william	mazorca f	ear (of corn)
manzana f	apple	mazorca f	spadix
manzanila f silvestre	corn chamomile	mazorca f	pod of cacao
manzano m	apple tree	máquina f calibradora	grader
mapa f edafológico	soil map	máquina f clasificadora	grader
mapa m del suelo	soil map	máquina f de aire	wind machine
mapurito m	skunk	máquina f de sacadir	shaker (tree)
maquinaria f agrícola	farm machinery	máquina f deshojadora	defoliating machine
maravilla f	marigold	máscara f de gas	gas mask
marcador m	drill hoe	mástic m	putty
marcador m	marker	mecanización f	mechanization
marcador m	tracer	mechero m Bunsen	bunsen burner
marchitarse	wilt, to	medicamento m	drug
marchitarse	wither, to	medida f	measurement
marchitez f de la hoja	leaf blight	medida f de control	control measure
marchitez f temprana	early blight	medio m	medium
marchito	faded, withered	medio m ambiente	environment
marga f	marl	medio m de producción	production means
marga f calcárea	lime marl	medios m de conservación	preservatives
margarita f	daisy	medir	measure, to
margarita f	marguerite	mejora f	improvement
mariposa f	butterfly	mejoramiento m	improvement
marisma f costera	coastal marsh	mejoramiento m	improvement
martillo m	hammer	mejoramiento m del suelo	soil improvement
marrana f	sow	mejoramiento m por mutación	mutation breeding
masculino	staminate		

SPANISH - ENGLISH EQUIVALENTS

SPANISH	ENGLISH	SPANISH	ENGLISH
mejorana f	majoram	mildio m falso	downy mildew
mejorar	improve, to	mildiú m	downy mildew
mejoría f estructural del suelo	improvement of soil structure	milenrama f	yarrow
		milhojas f	yarrow
melocotonero m	peach tree	mimosa f	mimosa
melocotón m	peach	mimulo m	monkey flower
melón m	melon	mina f	mine
melón m	cantaloupe	minar	mine, to
melón m chino	honeydew melon	mineral	mineral
membrana f	membrane	minerales m	minerals
membrana f de la célula	cell membrane	mineralización f	mineralization
membranoso	membraous	minutisa f	sweet william
membrillero m	quince	mirto m	myrtle
membrillero m japonés	Japanese quince	mócher	mulcher
menta f	peppermint	modificación f	modification
menta f crespa	spearmint	modo m de empleo	directions for use
mercado m a término	futures market	moho m de la hoja	leaf mold
mercado m al por mayor	wholesale market	moho m gris	gray mold
mercado m de abasto	provision market	moho m	grey mold
mercurio m	mercury	mojante f	downy mildew
meristemo m	meristem	mojar	water, to
mermelada f	jam	mojar	wet, to
mermelada f	marmalade	moledora f	mulching machine
mesa f para plantas	greenhouse bench	molibdeno m	molybdenum
mesocarpio m	fruit flesh	molino m de harina	flourmill
mesófilo m	mesophyll	molino m de martillos	hammer-mill
metabolismo m	metabolism	monobásico	monobasic
metamorfosis f	metamorphosis	monocultivo m	monoculture
metodo m de siembra	growing method	monofásico m	single phase (current)
mezcla f de fertilizantes	fertilizer mixture	monopétalo	monopetalous
mezcla f de tierra	soil mixture	monoico	monoecious
mezcladora f	mixer	montecargas m	forklift
mezclar	mix, to	montón m de arena	sand drift
médula f	pith (bot)	montón m de abono vegetal	compost heap
microbios m	microbes	montón m de mantillo	compost pile
microclima m	microclimate	moquillo m	distemper
microelemento m	trace element	mora f	mulberry
microscopio m electrónico	electron microscope	mordaza f	clamp
microscópico	microscopic	moreado m	mottled
miel f	honey	morir	die, to
mijo m africano	finger millet	mortero m	mortar
mijo m japonés	barnyard grass	mosaico m	mosaic
mildeu m	mildew	mosaico m internerval	interveinal mosaic
mildio m	mildew	mosca f	fly
mildio m	powdery mildew	mosca f blanca	whitefly

SPANISH - ENGLISH EQUIVALENTS

SPANISH	ENGLISH	SPANISH	ENGLISH
mosca f de las cebollas	onion maggot		**- N -**
mosca f de sierra	saw fly		
mosca f mediterránea		nabo m	turnip
de las frutas	Mediterranean Fruitfly	nacer	shoot, to
mosca f minadora	leaf miner	nacimiento m	birth
moscardón m	botfly	nanismo	dwarfism
mosquito m de agalla	gall midge	napelo m	monkshood
mosto m	must	naranja f	orange
mostrador m	counter (i.e. in a shop)	naranja f de ombligo	navel orange
mota f	clod, (soil)	naranja f roja	blood orange
moteado	dotted	naranja f sanguínea	blood orange
motor m	engine	naranjilla f	naranjilla
motorizado	power-driven	naranjo m	orange tree
movimiento m de agua	water movement	naranjo m trifoliado	trifoliate orange
moyuelo m	pollard	narciso m	daffodil
mudar de tiesto	repot, to	narciso m	narcissus
muestra f	sample	narciso m arracimado	jonquil
muestra f de materia		narcótico m	narcotic
vegetal	plant sample	nariz f doble	double nose (bulb)
muestra f de semillas	seed sample	natalidad f	birth rate
muestra f del suelo	soil sample	naturaleza f	nature
muestra f seleccionada		navaja f	knife (folding)
al azar	random sample	navaja f para injerto	knife, grafting
muestra f testigo	control sample	navideño	storable until Christmas
muérdago m	mistletoe	nébeda f	catmint
multiplicación	propagation	neblina f	mist
multiplicación f asexual	asexual propagation	nebrina f	juniper
multiplicaciòn f con		nebulización f	mist (for propagation)
niebla artificial	mist propagation	nebulizador m	fog machine
multiplicación f sexual	sexual propagation	necesidades f de mano f	
multiplicar	propagate, to	de obra	labor requirements
multiplicar por división	divide, to (bot)	necrosado	necrotic
mullir	loosen up, to	necrosis f	necrosis
muro m	wall	néctar m	nectar
muscari m	grape hyacinth	nectarina f	nectarine
musgo m	moss	nectario m	nectary
musgo m de pantano	peat moss	negondo m	box elder
musgo m esfagníneo	sphagnum moss	negrón m	black mold
mutación f	mutation	negrón m	sooty mold
mutación f	sport	neguilla f	love-in-a-mist
mutación f en los brotes	bud sport	nelumbio m	lotus
mutación de yema	budsport	nematodo m de los prados	lesion nematode
mutageno	mutagenic	nematicida f	nematicide
mutante m	mutant	nemátodo m	eelworm
mycelio m	mycelium	nemátodo m	nematode

SPANISH - ENGLISH EQUIVALENTS

SPANISH	ENGLISH	SPANISH	ENGLISH
nemátodo m cecidio	cyst nematode	nogal m inglés	english walnut
nemátodo m de los prados	root lesion nematode	nogal m negro	black walnut
nenúfar m	water lily	nogueruela f	spurge
nepente m	pitcher plant	no laboreo	no tillage
nervadura	vein (plant)	nombre m generífico	generic name
nervaduras f	nerves (plant)	nomenclatura f	nomenclature
nervadura f	veination	nopal m	prickly pear cactus
nervio m	nerve	norma f de calidad	quality norm
nervio m central	midrib	norma f de vida	standard of living
neumático m	innertube	normalización f	standardization
neumoencefalitis m aviar	Newcastle disease	normalizar	standardize, to
neuróptero m	lace wing	novilla f	heifer
neutralización f	neutralization	novillo m castrado	steer
neutro	neutral	nube m de polvo	dust cloud
nevado	snowy	nucelar	nucellar
niacina f	niacin	nucleico	nucleic
nicotina f	nicotine	nucléolo m	nucleolus
niebla f	fog	nucleótido m	nucleotide
nieve f	snow	nudicaulo	leafless
nigua f	chigger	nudo m	node
ninfa f	pupa	nudosidad f	knottiness
ninfea f	water lily	nudoso	knotty
nitrato de calcio m	calcium nitrate	nuez f	nut
nitrato m amónico	ammonium nitrate	nuez f lisa	pecan
nitrato m	nitrate	nuez f moscada	nutmeg
nitrato m de cal	nitrate of lime	nutrición f	nutrition
nitrato m de potasa	nitrate of potash	nutrimento m digerible	digestible nutrient
nitrato m sódico	sodium nitrate	nutritivo	nutritious
nítrico	nitric	nutritivo	nutritive
nitrificación f	nitrification	núcleo m	nucleus
nitrificar	nitrify, to		
nitrogenado	nitrogenous		
nitrogenados m	nitrogen fertilizers		
nitroso	nitrous		
nitrógeno m	nitrogen	**- O -**	
nivel m	level		
nivelación f	levelling	obesidad f	obesity
niveladora f	bulldozer	oblongo	oblong
niveladora f	scraper	obrero m	worker
nivelar	level, to	obrero m agrícola	farm hand
no-laboreo	no-tillage	obrero m agrícola	hired hand
nocivo	noxious	obscurecer	darken, to
noctuela f	noctuid	obsolescencia f	obsolescence
nodulación f	nodulation	obstrucción f	obstruction
nogal m	walnut	obturación f	darkening

SPANISH - ENGLISH EQUIVALENTS

SPANISH	ENGLISH	SPANISH	ENGLISH
obtuso	blunt	orgánico	organic
ocalo m	bluegum	orientación f	orientation
ocotillo m	hopseed (Dodonea viscosa)	orientar	orient, to
ocozol m	sweet gum	oriente m	orient
ocre m	ochre, ocher	origen m	origin
oferta f	bid	orina f	urine
oferta f	supply	ormino m	clary sage
ofrecer	bid, to	orobanca f	broomrape
oídio m	powdery mildew	orobanche m	broomrape
ojaranzo m	hornbeam	orquídea f	orchid
ojo m	eye	ortiga f	nettle
okra f	okra	ortiga f	stinging nettle
oleaginoso m	oily	ortotropismo m	orthotropism
oleandro m	oleander	ortotrópico	orthotropic
oler	smell, to	oruga f	caterpillar
olericultura f	vegetable growing	oruga f	caterpillar tractor
oligoelemento m	trace element	oruga f	crawler tractor
olivicultor m	olive grower	oruga f	grub
olivo m	olive tree	oruga f	maggot
olmo m	elm	oscurecerse	darken, to
olor m	smell	oscuro m	dark
oloroso	fragrant	osmótico	osmotic
oloroso	scented	oval m	oval
ombligo m	hilum	ovalado	oval
ombligo m	navel	ovario m	ovary
ondulado	wavy	oveja f	ewe
ondulado	sinuate	ovicido	ovicidal
ontogenia f	ontogeny	oviforme	ovate
onza f	ounce	ovinos m	sheep
oosfera f	oosphere	oviponición f	egg laying
operario m	operator	ovipositor m	ovipositor
opio m	opium	oviscapto m	ovipositor
opuesto	opposite (bot)	oxiacanto	thorny
oreja f	ear	oxidación f	oxidation
oreja f de ratón	chickweed	oxidado	rusty (metal)
oreja f de gato	cat's ears (weed)	oxidar	rust, to
orégano m	marjoram	oxígeno m	oxygen
organelo m	organelle	ósmosis f	osmosis
organillo m	pennywort	óvulo m	ovule
organismo m	organism	óxido m	rust (metal)
organización f	organization		
organoclorado	organochlorine		
organofénesis f	organogenesis		
organofosforado	organophosphorus		
organoléptico	organoleptic		

SPANISH - ENGLISH EQUIVALENTS

SPANISH	ENGLISH	SPANISH	ENGLISH

- P -

SPANISH	ENGLISH
pacana f	pecan
padre m	sire
padre m no recurrente	non-recurrent parent
pago m	wages
pago m extraordinario	bonus
paisaje m	landscape
países m en vìa de desarrollo	developing countries
paja f	straw
paja f de cama	straw bedding
pajarilla f	columbine
pájaro m	bird (small)
pajuil m	cashew
pala f	shovel
pala f	spade
palanca f	lever
palatabilidad f	palatability
palay m	paddy (rice)
palear	shovel, to
palendra f	spade
paleta f	pallet
paleta f	phyllode (of succulent)
paleta f caja	bulk bin
palita f	dust pan
palma f datilera	date palm
palma f de aceite	oil palm
palmacristi f	castor plant
palmatifido	palmatifid
palmeado compuesto	digitate
palmeral m	date grove
palmeta f	palmette training
palminervado	palmate
palo m	pole
palo m	stick
paloma f	pigeon
palosanto m	persimmon
palpitación f	palpitation
pamplina f pajarera	chickweed
pamporcino m	cyclamen
pan m	bread
pandano m	pandanus
pandano m	screw pine
panícula f	panicle

SPANISH	ENGLISH
pánoja f	panicle
panel m	panel
paniculado	paniculate
panique sillo m	shepherd's purse
panizo m blanco	foxtail millet
pantano m	bog
pantano m	swamp
pantanoso	swampy
panza f	belly
paño m de Holanda	poinsettia
papa f	potato
papa f de siembra	seed potato
papagayo m	caladium
papaína f	papain
papal m	potato field
papaya f	papaya
papel m de esmeril	emery paper
papel m de filtro	filter paper
papel m de seda	tissue paper
papel m filtro	filter paper
papila f	papilla
papilionáceo	papilionaceous
papilla f	porridge
papiro m	papyrus
papo m	pappus
par m térmico	thermocouple
parabrisas m	windshield
parafina f	paraffin wax
paralelo	parallel
paralelo m	parallel
parálisis f	paralysis
paralizar	paralyze, to
parar	stop, to
pararrayos m	lightning arrestor
parasitación f	parasitism
parasitismo m	parasitism
parasitoide m	parasitoid
parasitología f	parasitology
parasítico	parasitic
parásito m	parasite
parasol m	umbel
paravientos m	windbreak
parcela f	lot
parcela f	parcel of land
parcela f	plot

SPANISH - ENGLISH EQUIVALENTS

SPANISH	ENGLISH	SPANISH	ENGLISH
parcela f subdividida	split-plot	pastos m comunales	communal pastures
parcelar	parcel out, to	pastura f	pasture
parcha f	passion flower	pastura f permanente	permanent pasture
parche m	patch	pata f	leg (animal)
pardeamiento m	browning	pata f de caballo	heel cutting
pared f	wall	pata f de gallo	orchardgrass
pared f celular	cell wall	patata f	potato
pared m de la célula	cell wall	patent m de plantas	patent, plant
parénquima f	parenchyma	patentarse	patent, to
paridera f	lambing season	pato m	duck
parietal	parietal	patogenicidad f	pathogenicity
parir	farrow, to	patol m	scarlet runner bean
parque m	park	patología f vegetal	pathology, plant
parra f	trellised vine	patotipo m	pathotype
parral m	arbor	patógeno	pathogenic
parriaz f	fox grape	patógeno m	pathogen
partenocarpia f	parthenocarpy	patólogo m	pathologist
partenogénesis m	parthenogenesis	patrón m	rootstock
partido	parted (bot)	patrón m	employer
parva f	heap	patrón m	pattern
pasa f	raison	patrón m	stock (grafting)
pasado	overripe	patrón m de vigor	vigorous rootstock
pasador m	pin	patrón m débil	weak rootstock
pasiflora f	passion flower	patrón m enanizante	dwarfing rootstock
pasionaria f	passion flower	patrón m intermedio	interstock
pasivos m	liabilities	paulonia f	paulownia
pasta f	paste	peca f	freckle
pasta f de manzana	apple sauce	pecana f	pecan nut
pasta f de tomates	tomato paste	peciolo m	petiole
pastadero m	feedlot	pectina f	pectin
pastar	pasture, to	pedazos m de macetas	pot shards
pasterizadora f	pasteurizer	pedicelo m	pedicel
pasterizar	pasteurize, to	pedir	borrow, to
pasteurizar	pasteurize, to	pedología f	pedology
pasteurización f	pasteurization	pedregoso	stony
pastinaca f	parsnip	pedúnculo m	flower stalk
pasto f azul de Kentucky	bluegrass	pedúnculo m	peduncle
pasto m bermuda	Bermudagrass	pedúnculo m	seed stalk
pasto m chato	knotgrass	pegado	taken (graft)
pastora f	poinsettia	pelado	peeled
pastorear	pasture, to	pelar	peel, to
pastoreo m abusivo	overgrazing	pelar	skin, to
pastoreo m diferido	deferred grazing	pelargonio m	pelargonium
pastoreo m irregular	spot grazing	pelechar	shed, to (animals)
pastoreo m selectivo	grazing, selective	peletizado	pelleted

SPANISH - ENGLISH EQUIVALENTS

SPANISH	ENGLISH	SPANISH	ENGLISH
película f	film	perfil m	profile
película f de contracción	shrinkage film	perfil m del suelo	soil profile
pelitre m	pyrethrum	perfoliado	perfoliate
pellizcar	pinch, to	perforador m	borer
pellizco m	pinching	perfumado	scented
pelo m	hair	perfumería f	perfumery
pelo m glandular	glandular hair	pergamino m	parchment (coffee)
pelo m radical	root hair	pérgola f	pergola
pelo m urticante	stinging hair	periantia m	perianth
pelos m radicales	root hairs	pericarpio m	pericarp
pelotilla f	pellet	perifolio m	chervil
penca f	fleshy leaf	perigonio m	perianth
pendiente	pendulous	periodicidad f	periodicity
pendiente	pitch (roof slope)	peristaltismo m	peristalsis
pendiente m	slope	peritecio m	perithicium
penetración f de las raíces	root penetration	peritoneo m	peritoneum
		período m de crecimiento	growing period
peniforme	pinniform	período m de incubación	incubation period
pensamiento m	pansy	período m de reposo	dormant period
pentaclorofenol m	pentachlorophenol	perjudicial	noxious
penumbra f	semi-darkness	perla f	yarrow
peonada f de una hora	man-hour	perlita f	perlite
peonía f	peony	permanente	persistent (bot)
peonía f arbórea	tree peony	permeabilidad f	permeability
peperomia f	peperomia	permeable	porous
pepinillo m	gherkin	peroxidasa f	peroxidase
pepino m	cucumber	perro m de las praderas	prairie dog
pepino m	gherkin	persistencia f	persistence
pepita f	kernal	perspectiva f	outlook
pepita f	seed (small)	pértiga f	pole
pera f	pear	pervinca f	periwinkle
peral m	pear tree	pesado	heavy
pérdida	loss	pesebre m	crib
pérdida f	leakage	peso m	weight
pérdida de calefacción	heat loss	peso m atómico	atomic weight
pérdida f de calidad	loss of quality	peso m bruto	gross weight
pérdida f de la cosecha	crop failure	peso m en canal	carcass weight
pérdida f de luz	loss of light	peso m específico aparente	apparent specific gravity
pérdida f de peso	weight loss	peso m excesivo	overweight
perecedero	perishable	peso m limpio	dead weight
peregrina f de Lima	alstroemeria	peso m molecular	molecular weight
peregrina f de Lima	peruvian lily	peso m neto	net weight
perejil m	parsley	peso m vivo	live weight
perenne	perennial	peste m aviar	fowl pest
perero m	fruit peeler	pesticida m	pesticide

SPANISH - ENGLISH EQUIVALENTS

SPANISH	ENGLISH	SPANISH	ENGLISH
pesticida m organoclorado	organochlorine pesticide	pimpollear	sprout, to
pesticida m organofosforado	organophosphorus pesticide	pimpollo m	sucker
		pina f	pine
pétalo m	petal	pinado	pinnate
petróleo m combustible	fuel oil	pinadolubulado	pinnately lobed
petunia f	petunia	pinatifido	pinnatifid
peyote m	peyote	pincel m	paintbrush
pez f	pitch	pinchudo	thorny
pezón m	stalk	pino m	pine
pezuña f	hoof	pinocha f	pine needle
pH	pH	pinta f	speck
pica f	tapping (rubber)	pinta f	pint
picadora f de heno	hay chopper	pintar	paint, to
picadura f	sting	pintura f	paint
picar	prick out, to	pinzamiento m	pinching
picea f	spruce	piña f	pine cone
picnidio m	pycnidium	piña f	pineapple
pico m	pick, spur	piñón m	pine nut
picudo m	weevil	piojillo m	thrip
picudo m del algodón	boll weevil	piojo m	louse
pie m	foot	piojos m	lice
pie m podrido	foot rot	pipeta f	pipette
piedra f	stone	piracanta m	pyracantha
piedra f calcárea	limestone	piretro m	pyrethrum
piedra f caliza	limestone	piriforme	pyriform
piedra f caliza molida	crushed limestone	pirola f	wintergreen
piedra f de cal	limestone	piscina f	fish pond
piedra f de esmeril	emery stone	piscina f	pool
piedra f pómez	pumice	piso m del arado	plowsole
piel f	leather	pistilado	pistillate
piel f	skin	pistilo m	pistil
piel f	peel	pistola f pulverizador	spray gun
pienso m	fodder	pistón m	piston
pienso m concentrado	concentrate	pitio m	PTO
pierna f	leg (human)	pitomba f	pitomba (Eugenia spp.)
pigmentación f	pigmentation	pitósporo m	pittosporum
pigmento m	pigment	pizcadora f	picking machine
pila f	dry cell battery	pivotante	tap-rooted
pila termoelélectrica	thermo-couple	placaminero m	persimmon
piloro m	pylorus	plaga f	pest
pilorriza f	root cap	plaga f	plague
pilosidad f	hairiness	plagiotropismo m	plagiotropism
piloso	hairy	plagiotrópico	plagiotropic
pimentón m	pimento	plan m	plan
pimienta f	pepper	plan m de cultivo	cropping plan

SPANISH - ENGLISH EQUIVALENTS

SPANISH	ENGLISH
plan m de cultivo	planting scheme
plan m de trabajo	work plan
plan m experimental reticular	lattice design
plancha f	iron (clothes)
plancheta f	plane table
planeamiento del aprovechamiento de la tierra	land use planning
planear	plan, to
planificación f del mercado	market planning
planificación f	planning
planificar	plan, to
plano m	blueprint
plano m de agua	water level
planta f	plant
planta f acuática	aquatic plant
planta f bulbosa	bulbous plant
planta f de adorno	decorative plant
planta f de balcón	balcony plant
planta f de bisagra	obedient plant
planta f de bisagra	physostegia
planta f de cuba	tub plant
planta f de día corto	short day plant
planta f de día largo	long-day plant
planta f de fresa	strawberry plant
planta f de hojas	foliage plant
planta f de invernadero	greenhouse plant
planta f de pantano	marsh plant
planta f de semilla	seed plant
planta f de tiesto	pot plant
planta f huésped	host-plant
planta f indicadora	indicator plant
planta f madre	mother plant
planta f madre	motherstock
planta f madre	stock plant
planta f ornamental	house plant
planta f ornamental	ornamental plant
planta f parásita	parasitic plant
planta f progenitora	mother plant
planta f suculenta	succulent plant
planta f tuberosa	tuberous plant
planta f venenosa	poison plant
plantación en hileras	row planting
plantacíon f	plantation
plantador m	dibble

SPANISH	ENGLISH
plantador m	planter
plantadora f	planter (machine)
plantar	plant, to
plantar en macetas	pot, to
plantas capaces de sobrevivir el invierno	hardy plants
plantas f leñosas	woody plants
plantas f medicinales	medicinal herbs
plantas f pl vivaces	herbaceous perennial
plantas f pl superiores	higher plants
plantilla f	seedling
plantilla f	plantlet
plantista m	gardener
plántula f	seedling
plasmólisis f	plasmolysis
plástico m	plastic
plasticidad	plastic
plasto m	plastid
plataforma f	platform
plataforma f recogedora	picking platform
plátano	plane tree
plátano m	plantain
plátano m	banana
plateado	silvery
platicerio m	staghorn fern
platino m	platinum
plazo m de seguridad	safety margin
pleguete m	tendril
pleno m	full
pluma f	feather
plúmula	plumule
plumilla f	plumule
plurilocular	multilocular
pluviometro m	rain gauge
población f	population
pobre de luz	light deficient
pobre en cal	deficient in lime
poco profundo	shallow
poda f	pruning
poda f severa	heavy pruning
podadera f	pruning knife
podar	lop, to
podar	prune, to
podazón f	pruning season
poder m adquisitivo	purchasing power

SPANISH - ENGLISH EQUIVALENTS

SPANISH	ENGLISH	SPANISH	ENGLISH
poder m de adsorción	adsorption capacity	polvo m	dust
podredumbre f	gray mold	polvo m de esmeril	emery powder
podredumbre f	grey mold	polvorear	dust, to
podredumbre f del corazón	heart rot	polvoroso	dusty
podredumbre f húmeda	soft rot	pomología f	pomology
podredumbre f radical	root rot	poner en latas	can, to
podredumbre f seca	dry rot	poner un clavo	hammer a nail
podrido	rotten	pontoneado m	bridging
podzol m	podzol	porcentaje de partes utilizables de un animal	dressing percent
poinsetia f	poinsettia	porción f	serving
polaridad f	polarity	poro m	pore
polea f	pulley	porosidad f	pore space
polen m	pollen	porosidad f	porosity
polenizar	pollinate, to	poroso	porous
poliamida f	polyamide	portador	payee
poliandro	polyandrous	portaútiles f	tool bar
policárpico	polycarpic	portayema f	budwood
poliembrionía f	polyembryony	porte m	habit (of plant)
poliester m	polyester	portillo m de escalones	stile
polietileno m	polyethylene	postclimatérico	post-climateric
polilla f	moth	postmaduración f	after-ripening
polimería m	polymer	postcosecha	postharvest
polímero m	polymer	poste m	post
polimorfismo m	polymorphism	postrado	prostrate
polinización f	pollination	potasa f	potash
polinización f cruzada	cross pollination	potasio m	potassium
polinizador m	pollinator	pote m	pot
polipétalo	polypetalous	potrero m	paddock
poliploide m	polyploid	potrillo m	colt
poliploidia f	polyploidy	potro m	colt
polipodia m	polypodium	pozo m	well
polipropileno m	polypropylene	pozo m absorbente	dry well
polisacárido m	polysaccharide	pradera f	prairie
polisépalo	polysepalous	precalentador m	pre-heater
polistireno m	polystyrene	precalentar	pre-heat, to
política f	policy	precintar	seal, to
polivalente	polyvalent	precio m indicativo	target price
polución f del aire	air pollution	precio m	price
polla f	pullet	precio m al contado	spot price
pollito m	chick	precio m de referencia	reference price
pollo m para freír	fryer (hen)	precio m de venta	selling price
pollo m para asar	broiler (chicken)	precio m del mercado	market price
polluelo m	chick	precio m garantizado	guaranteed price
polvificar	pulverize, to	precio m máximo	maximum price
polvillo m	fine dust		

SPANISH - ENGLISH EQUIVALENTS

SPANISH	ENGLISH	SPANISH	ENGLISH
precio m medio	average price	procedencia f	origin
precio m medio	mean price	procedimiento	process
precio m mínimo	minimum price	proceso m de fermentación	fermentation process
precio m sobre vagón	F.O.B.	procumbente	procumbent
precios m al productor	farm prices	procumbente	prostrate
precios m de sustención	support prices	producción f alterna	biennial bearing
precipitación f radioactiva	radioactive fall out	producción f	production
precipitación f	precipitation	producción f avícola	poultry production
precipitado m	precipitate	producción f bruta	gross yield
preclimatérico	preclimacteric	producción f vegetal	plant production
precocción f	precooking	producir	grow, to
precocer	precook, to	producir	produce, to
precocidad f	precocity	productividad f	productivity
precoz	early (precocious)	productividad f del trabajo	labor productivity
predator m	predator	productivo	productive
predicción f	prediction	producto m	commodity
predio m	estate	producto m	proceeds
preembalaje m	pre-packing	producto m animal	animal product
pregerminar	pre-germinate, to	producto m de protección	preservative
prenda f	pledge	producto m en polvo	dusting preparation
prender	to turn on (electrical)	producto m fitosanitario	pesticide
prensa f	press	producto m principal	staple
prensador m de paja	straw baler	productor	grower
prensar	press, to	productor m	producer
preñada f	pregnancy	productos m	produce
preparación f	preparation	productos m agroquímicos	agricultural chemicals
preparar	prepare, to	productos m de asimilación	assimilation products
prerrefrigeración f	precooling	productos m del vivero	nursery stock
preservar	preserve, to	productos m lácteos	dairy products
presiembra f	preplanting	productos m perecederos	perishable goods
presión f	pressure	profundidad f	depth
presión de vapor	steam pressure	profundidad f del drenaje	depth of drainage
presión f de agua	water pressure	profundidad f del suelo	depth of soil
presión atmosférica	atmospheric pressure	profundizar	deepen, to
presión f	pressure	progenie f	progeny
prestamista m	lender	progesterona f	progesterone
préstamo m	loan	programa m	program
presupuesto m	budget	programador m de riego	irrigation controller
pretratamiento m	pretreatment	prolífero	proliferous
primavera f	spring (season)	prolongar	stretch, to
primera generación f filial	F1 generation	promotor m	promoter
primordio m	primordium	pronosticación f	forecasting
primula f	primrose	pronóstico m	forecast
probabilidad f	probability	propagación f	propagation
probar	try, to (as in taste)	propagación f en niebla	mist propagation

SPANISH - ENGLISH EQUIVALENTS

SPANISH	ENGLISH	SPANISH	ENGLISH
propagador	propagator	pudrir	decay, to
propagar	propagate, to	pudrir	rot, to
propano m	propane	puente m de carga	loading bay
propenso m	susceptible	puente m de injerto	graft, bridge
propiedad f	property	puerca	sow (pig)
propiedad f colectiva	joint ownership	puerro m	leek
propietario m	land owner	puesto m meteorológico	weather station
propietario m	landlord	pulga f	flea
proplástico m	proplastic	pulgón m lanífero	mealy bug
proponer	bid, to	pulgón m	aphid
proporción f	proportion	pulgón m verde de manzana	apple aphid
propósito m	purpose	pulguilla f	flea beatle
protandria f	protandry	pulpa f	flesh (not meat)
protección f	protection	pulpa f	pulp
protección f contra el viento	windbreak	pulso m	pulse
proteger	screen, to	pulverización f	spraying
proteger	protect, to	pulverización aérea	aerial spraying
protegido de la helada	protected from frost	pulverizador m	sprayer
proteína f	protein	pulverizador m de aire comprimido	compressed air sprayer
proterógino	protogynous		
protoginia f	protogyny	pulverizador m para acoplar al tractor	tractor mounted sprayer
protoplasma m	cell sap		
protoplasma m	protoplasm	pulverizador m sobre toma de fuerza	PTO driven sprayer
prototipo m	prototype	pulverizadora f	duster
protozoario m	protozoan	pulverizar	dust, to (apply)
protozoarios m	protozoa	pulverizar	spray, to
protuberancia f	protuberance	pulverizar	pulverize, to
proveedor m de semillas	seed-dealer	puma m	cougar
proveer	supply, to	punta f de trabajo	peak load
provisiones f	supplies	puntal m	strut
proximal	proximal	punteado	dotted
proyecto m	project	punteado	spotted
prótalo m	prothallium	punteado m	leaf spot (symptom)
prótalo m	prothallus	punto m	stitch
prueba f	experiment	punto m de marchitamiento	wilting point
prueba f	trial	punto m de saturación	saturation point
prueba f del huésped	host indexing	pupa f	pupa
pruina f	bloom (wax on fruit)	pureza f	purity
pseudotallo m	pseudostem	pureza f de la variedad	varietal purity
psila f	psyllid	puré m	puree
psilas f	psylla	puré m de tomates	tomato paste
pteridófita f	pteridophyte	purificación f	purification
pubescente	pubescent	purificación f de agua	water purification
pudrición f negra	black rot	purificar	purify, to
pudricíon f seca	dry rot	purín m	liquid manure

SPANISH - ENGLISH EQUIVALENTS

SPANISH	ENGLISH	SPANISH	ENGLISH
puro	purebred		**- R -**
putrefacción f	decay		
putrefacción f	rot	rábano m	radish
putrefacción f	putrefaction	rábano m negro	black radish
putreficarse	putrefy, to	rábano m rusticano	horse radish
pútrido	rotten	rábano m picante	horse radish
púa f	scion	rabito m peludo	foxtail
púa f de injerto	scion	rabiza f	cowpea
		racimo m	raceme, bunch of grapes
		racimoso	racemose
		radiación f	radiation
	- Q -	radiación f ionizante	ionizing radiation
		radiación f visible	visible radiation
quelato m	chelate	radiación f gamma	gamma radiation
quema f	burning	radiador m	radiator
quemador m	burner	radicación f	rooting
quemador m de aceite	oil burner	radiculoso	radicular
quemador m de aire caliente	hot air heater	radioactividad f	radioactivity
quemador m de gas	gas burner	radioisótopo m	radioisotope
quemadura f	scorch	radiosensibilidad f	radiosensitivity
quemadura f del sol	sunscorch	radícula f	radicle
querria f	kerria	raer	abrade, to
queso m	cheese	rafia f	raffia
quiebra f	crack	rafia f	raphia palm
quilla f	keel (botanical)	raiceja f	rootlet
quimbombó m	okra	raices f	roots
quimera f	chimera	raíz f	root
quimera f mericlinal	chimera, mericlinal	raíz f aéria	aerial root
quimera f periclinal	chimera, periclinal	raíz f aéria de sostén	prop root
quimera f sectorial	chimera, sectorial	raíz f contráctil	contractile root
química f	chemistry	raíz f desnuda	bareroot
químico m	chemical	raíces f feculentas	starchy roots
químico m	chemist	raíz f fibrosa	fibrous root
quimiotropismo m	chemotropism	raíz f lateral	lateral root
quina f	quinine	raíz f penetrante	tap root
quincunce m	quincunx	raíz principal	main root
quingombó m	okra	raíces f tuberosas	tuberous roots
quinina f	quinine	raíces f superficiales	shallow rooted
quino m	cinchona	raleador m	thinner
quiste m	cyst	raleo m químico	thinner (chemical)
		ralé m	relay
		rallador m	rasp
		rallo m	rasp
		rama f	branch
		rama f	twig

SPANISH - ENGLISH EQUIVALENTS

SPANISH	ENGLISH	SPANISH	ENGLISH
rama f lateral	lateral branch	reacción f de Hill	Hill reaction
rama m principal lateral	main branch	reacción f química	chemical reaction
rambután m	rambutan	reactivo m	reagent
ramificación f	ramification	rebajar	cut back, to
ramificado	branched	rebrotar	regrow, to
ramificado	ramified	recalamiento	scald
ramificarse	branch out, to	recalce m	hilling (plants)
ramillete	cluster (bot)	recalzar	hill, to
ramillete	floral arrangement	receptáculo m	receptacle
ramillete m de flores	bouquet	recesivo	recessive
ramillete m	corsage	recipiente m	container
ramina f	ramie (fiber)	recogedora f	picker
ramio m	ramie (plant)	recogedora f de algodón	cotton stripper
ramo m de flores	bouquet of flowers	recogedora-enfardadora f	pick-up baler
ramonear	browse	recolección f	picking
rampa f de pulverización	spray boom	reconocimiento m	survey
rangpur m	rangpur lime	reconocimiento m aéreo	aerial survey
ranura f	groove	reconocimiento m edafológico	soil survey
ranúnculo m	ranunculus	reconocimiento m topográfico	land survey
raquis m	rachis	recortar	trim, to
raquítico	spindly	rectángulo m	rectangle
rastra f	harrow	recursos m naturales	natural resources
rastra f de discos	disk harrow	red f	net
rastra f de discos recortados	cutaway disk	red f de información	information network
rastrero	decumbent	reducción f	reduction
rastrero	rampant	reducir	reduce, to
rastrillar	rake in, to	reflector m	reflector
rastrillo m	rake	reflexión f	reflection
rastrillo m de descarga lateral	side delivery rake	reforestación f	reforestation
rastrojo m	stubble	reforma f agraria	land reform
rata f	rat	reforzado	reinforced
ratán m	rattan	reforzar	reinforce, to
ratón m	mouse	refractometría f	refractometry
ratón m campesino	field mouse	refractómetro m manual	refractometer, hand held
ravenala f	traveller's tree	refreno m del crecimiento	growth inhibition
raya f	streak	refrigeración f	cooling
raya f	stripe	refrigeración f al vacío	vacuum cooling
rayado	striated	refrigerador m	cooler
rayado	striped	refringente	refractive
rayo m	ray	refuerzo m	reinforcement
rayo m medular	pith ray (bot)	regadera f	watering can
raza f	strain	regador m de prado	lawn sprinkler
raza f	race	regaliz m	licorice
raza f fisiológica	physiological race		
reacción f	reaction		

SPANISH - ENGLISH EQUIVALENTS

SPANISH	ENGLISH	SPANISH	ENGLISH
regar	irrigate, to	reloj m de subasta	auction clock
regar	sprinkle, to	remanente m	carry over
regar	pour into, to	remate m, subasta f	auction
regar	water, to	remedio m	remedy
regata f	irrigation ditch	remoción f	removal
regeneración f	regeneration	remojar	soak, to
regime	régimen	remojar	pre-soak, to
régimen de aprovechamiento de la tierra	land use pattern	remolacha f	beet, redbeet
		remolacha f de azúcar	sugarbeet
régimen m alimenticio equilibrado	balanced diet	remontante	perpetual flowering
		remover	to rip (soil)
régimen m comunal agrario	communal land tenure	rendimiento m	yield
régimen m de tenencia de tierras	land tenure	rendimiento m bruto	gross yield
		rendimiento m medio	average yield
región f ciclonal	low pressure area	rendimiento m sostenido	sustained yield
registro m	damper	reniforme	reniform,
registro m de cultivos	crop records	renuevo m	flush (of growth)
registro m de semillas	seed registration	reparar	fix, to
registro m del trabajo	labor records	repelente m	repellent
registro m genealógico	herd book	repicadora f	transplanter
regla f de cálculo	slide rule	replantación f	replanting
reglas f pl de normalización	grading regulation	replantar	replant, to
regresión f	rgression	replicación f	replication
regresión f múltiple	multiple regression	repollo f de China	Chinese cabbage
regulación f de precios	price control	repollo m	cabbage
regulador m de crecimiento	growth regulator	repollo m morado	red cabbage
rehabilitación f de tierras	land reclamation	reposo m	rest
reina f margarita	China aster	reposo m invernal	dormancy
reinjertar	top work, to	reposo m invernal	winter dormancy
reinjerto m	topworking	represa f	dam
reino m vegetal	plant kingdom	reproducción f sexual	sexual reproduction
reja f	plough share	reproducirse	breed, to
reja f circular	disc coulter	repuestos m	spare parts
reja f de sembradora	drill coulter	requemarse	dry up, to
reja f del arado	coulter	requerimiento m	requirement
reja f del arado	plowshare	requerimiento m de abono	fertilizer requirement
rejilla f de madera	wooden strip	requerir	demand, to
rejuvenecimiento m	rejuvenation	requisito m de nutrición	nutritional requirement
relación f huésped-patógeno	host-pathogen relationship	resbaloso	slippery
		resecar	dry out, to
relámpago m	lightening	réseda f	mignonette
rellenar	fill in, to (gaps in a row)	residuo m	residue
rellenar	refill, to	residuo m de cosecha	crop residue
rellenar	replace plants, to	residuos m de matadera	offals
relleno	filled	resiembra f	reseeding

SPANISH - ENGLISH EQUIVALENTS

SPANISH	ENGLISH	SPANISH	ENGLISH
resina f	resin	riego m por inundación	flood irrigation
resistancia f a campo	field resistance	riego m por surcos	furrow irrigation
resistencia f	resistance	riego m subterráneo	subirrigation
resistencia f a las enfermedades	disease resistance	riego m superficial	surface irrigation
		rífer	reefer
resistencia f al desgarro	tear strength	rivalidad f	competition
resistente	resistant	rizado	curly
resistente a la helada	frost hardy	rizadura f	crinkle virus
resistente al choque	impact resistance	rizogénesis	rhizogenesis
resistente al frío	hardy	rizoide m	rhizoid
resíduo m de cosecha	crop residue	rizoma m	rhizome
resíduos m de matadera	offals	río m	stream
resorte m	spring (i.e. watch)	roble m	oak
respiración f	respiration	roca f	rock
respuesta f	response	roca f madre	bed rock
retardación f del crecimiento	growth reduction	roca f madre	parent rock
		roca f sedimentaria	sedimentary rock
retardación f	delay	rocalla f	rock garden
retardante m	growth retardant	rociador m	sprayer
retardante m de crecimiento	growth inhibitor	rociador m	sprinkler
retardar	slow down, to	rociar	drizzle, to
retoñar	ratoon, to	rociar	spray, to
retoño m	shoot	rociar	sprinkle, to
retoño m	sucker	rodal m	stand
retoño m	renewed growth	rodar	roll, to
retrasar	retard, to	rodillo m	roller
retraso m	delay	rodillo compactador m	cultipacker
retraso m de la cosecha	cropping delay	rodriga f	stake
retrocruza f	back-cross	rodrigón m	prop
retrocruzamiento m	back-crossing	roedor m	rodent
retrocruzar	back-cross, to	rollo m	roller
reverdecer	regreen, to	rolo m	cultipacker
revestimiento m	cladding	romboidal	rhombic
revestir	cover	romero m	rosemary
revista f	journal	romojo m	soak
revolución f verde	green revolution	rompenieve m	snowdrop
riboflavina f	riboflavin	romper	break, to
riego m	watering	romper	burst, to
riego m	irrigation	rompeviento m	windbreak
riego m de gotas	trickle irrigation	rompimiento m	breaking
riego m en casuela	basin irrigation	roña f	scab
riego m permanente	perennial irrigation	roñoso	rusty
riego m por aspersión	sprinkler irrigation	rosa f	rose
riego m por compartimientos	basin irrigation	rosal m	rose bush
		rosella f	roselle

SPANISH - ENGLISH EQUIVALENTS

SPANISH	ENGLISH	SPANISH	ENGLISH
rotación f de cultivos	crop rotation	salida f	outlet
rotenona f	rotenone	salida f del aire	air discharge
roya f	rust	salinidad f	salinity
roya f blanca	white rust	salinización f	salinizacion
roya f foliar	leaf rust	salino	saline
roya f lineal	stripe rust	salir del huevo	hatch, to
roya f vesicular	blister rust	salirse	leak, to
ruibarbo m	rhubarb	salitre m	saltpeter
ruptura f	rupture	saliva f	saliva
ruqueta f de Londres	London rocket	salmuera f	brine
rusco m	butcher's broom	salpicado	spotted
		salsedumbre f	saltiness
		salsero m	thyme
		salsifí m	salsify
	- S -	saltahoja f	leafhopper
		saltamontes m	grasshopper
sabana f	savanna	salud m	health
sabor m	flavor	salvado m	bran
sabor m	palatability	salvaje	wild
sabor m	taste	salvia f	sage
sabuco m	elder	sámago m	sapwood
sacarosa f	sucrose	sámara f	samara
saco	sack	sampsuco m	marjoram
saco m	bag	sándalo m	sandalwood
saco m de recolección	picking bucket	sandía f	watermelon
safra f	harvest (sugar cane)	sanidad f	health
sagitado	sagittate	sanidad f	sanitation
sagital	sagittate	sanidad f del suelo	soil sanitation
saguaro m	saguaro	sanidad f pecuaria	cattle sanitation
sagú m	sago palm	sanitario m	sanitary
sal f	salt	sano	healthy
sal f de higuera	magnesium sulfate	sano	undamaged
sal f de potasa	potash salt	santipaula f	African violet
sala f	hall	saprofítico	saprophytic
sala f	living room	saprófito	saprophyte
sala f de embalaje	packing station	sarna f de la papa	potato scab
salado	saline	saturación f	saturation
salario m	wages	saturación f en agua	waterlogging
salario m a destajo	piece work rate	saturar	saturate, to
salario m según tiempo	hourly rate	sauce m	willow
salchicha f	sausage	savia f	sap
saldo m	balance (financial)	sazonar	season, to
salegar f	salt lick	sazón f	ripeness
sales f solubles	soluble salts	scrubber m	scrubber
salida f	exit	secadero de verduras	dehydration plant

SPANISH - ENGLISH EQUIVALENTS

SPANISH	ENGLISH	SPANISH	ENGLISH
secado al aire	air dried	sembrar	spawn, to (mushrooms)
secado m	drying	sembrar	plant, to
secado m al aire	air drying	sembrar al voleo	broadcast seed, to
secadora f	dryer	sembrar al voleo	sow broadcast, to
secamiento m	drying	sembrar en fajas para	
secano m	dry land	evitar la erosión	strip-crop
secano m	unirrigated land	semen m	semen
secar	dehydrate, to	semi-automático	semi-automatic
secar	dry, to	semilla f	seed
sección f vertical de		semilla f de algodón	cottonseed
un suelo	soil profile	semilla f de ricino	castor bean
seco	dried	semilla f descascarada	hulled seed
secoya f	sequoia	semilla f escarificada	scarified seed
secreción f	secretion	semilla f original	original seed
secreción f azucarada	honeydew	semillas f oleaginosas	oilseeds
secreción f externa	external-secretion	semillero m	nursery bed
secreción f interna	internal secretion	semillero m	seed bed
sedativo m	sedative	semiprecoz	semi-early
sedimentación f	sedimentation	semitardío	medium-late
sedimento m	sediment	semitropical	semitropical
segadilla f	asparagus bean	sencillo	simple
segadora f	harvester	senda f	footpath
segadora f de hierba	lawn mower	sendero m	path
segadora f rotativa	rotary mower	senectud f	senescence
segregación f	segregation	seno m	sinus (botanical)
segunda generación f filial	F2 generation	senserina f	thyme
segunda siega f	aftermath	sensibilidad f	sensitivity
seguro m	insurance	sensible al frío	susceptible to frost
seguro m de cosechas	crop insurance	sensitiva f	sensitive plant
seleccionado	fancy (produce grade)	sentado	sessile
seleccionar	select, to	sentar	fit, to
selección f	selection	sépalo m	sepal
selectivo	selective	separación f	separation
selva f	jungle	separador m de agua	steam trap
sembrado m	crop	separar	separate, to
sembrador m de mano	hand seeder	septo m	septum
sembrador m de precisión	precision seeder	sequedad f	dryness
sembradora f	seed drill	sequero m	unirrigated land
sembradora f	seeding machine	sequía f	drought
sembradora f de papas	potato planter	serbal m	mountain ash
sembradora f de plantulas	transplanter	sericultura f	sericulture
sembradora f de surcos	drill (seeder)	serología f	serology
sembrar	grow, to	serpa f	runner
sembrar	seed, to	serpeta f del manzano	oystershell scale
sembrar	sow, to	serpiente f	snake

SPANISH - ENGLISH EQUIVALENTS

SPANISH	ENGLISH	SPANISH	ENGLISH
serpollar	sucker, to	sincarpo m	syncarp
serratula f	liatris	síndrome m	syndrome
serruchar	saw, to	sinergético	synergistic
servicio m de extensión	extension service	sinfín m	endless belt
servicio m de inspección	inspection service	sinonimia f	synonymy
sésamo m	sesame	sintetizar	synthesize, to
sésil	sessile	síntoma m	symptom
sesia f apiforme	hornet	síntoma f de carencia	deficiency symptom
seso m vegetal	akee	síntoma m de enfermedad	disease symptom
seto m	hedge	síntomas m carenciales	deficiency symptoms
seto m vivo	hedge	sintomatología f	symptomatology
seudotallo m	pseudostem	sinuoso	sinuate
sex-feromona f	sex pheromone	sisal m	sisal
sexo m	sex	sismografía f	seismography
sexo m femenino	female	sistema f radicular	root system
sicómoro m	sycamore	sistema m	system
sidra f	cider	sistema m de aspersión de tama	controlled droplet application
sidrería f	cider factory	sistema m de cultivos	cropping system
siembra f	sowing	sistemática f	systematics
siembra f	planting	sitio m	site
siembra f a nivel	contour planting	sobrante m	surplus
siembra f a voleo	broadcast seeding	sobre-maduro	over-ripe
siembra f aérea	aerial seeding	sobrealimentar	overfeed, to
siempreviva f	everlasting flower	sobreamiento m	shading
sierra f	saw	sobrearar	plow again, to
sierra f de cadena	chain saw	sobrecarga f de ganado por unidad de superficie	overstocking
sierra f mecánica	power saw	sobrecargar	overgraze, to
sierra f podadera	pruning saw	sobrecrecimiento m	overgrowth
sigatoka f	sigatoka disease	sobreinjertado	topworked
significado m	significance	sobreinjertar	topwork, to
silicio m	silica	sobrevivencia f	survival
silicona f	silicone	sobreinjerto m	topworking
silicua f	siliqua	sobrevivir	survive, to
silo m	silo	sociedad f	partnership
silo m pila	stack silo	sociedad f anónima (S.A.)	corporation
silvestre	wild	sociedad f colectiva	partnership firm
silvicultor m	forester	socio m	partner
simbiosis f	symbiosis	socolar	clear, to
simbiótico	symbiotic	soda f cáustica	caustic soda
simpétalo	sympetalous	sodio m	sodium
simplo	simple	soja f	soybean
sin calefación	unheated	sol m	sun
sin hilo	stringless (bean)	solanáceo	solanaceous
sin tratar	untreated		

SPANISH - ENGLISH EQUIVALENTS

SPANISH	ENGLISH	SPANISH	ENGLISH
solanina f	solanine	subsuelo m	subsoil
solar m	lot	subterráneo	underground
soldadura f	graft union	subterráneo	subterranean
soldadura f	solder	subtropical	subtropical
soldadura f	soldered joint	subvencionar	subsidize, to
soldar	solder, to	subvención f a los precios	price supports
soldar	weld, to	succionar	inarch
soleado	sunny	sucesión f de los trabajos	order of work
solidago m	golden rod	sucoso	juicy
solsticio m	solstice	suculenta f	succulent plant
soluble	soluble	suculento m	succulent
solubles m de pescado	fish solubles	suelo m	land
solución f	solution	suelo m	soil
solución f nutritiva	nutrient solution	suelo m arcillo-arenoso	sandy clay
solución f diluida	solution, diluted	suelo m arcilloso	clay soil
sombra f	shade	suelo m arenoso	sandy soil
sombreadero m	shadehouse	suelo m de grava	gravel soil
sombráculo m	shade house	suelo m forestal	forest floor
sombreado m	shading	suelo m franco	loam
sopladora f	blower	suelo m húmedo	wet soil
soplete m	blowtorch	suelo m margoso	marly soil
soporte m	trellis	suelo m pantanoso	marshy soil
sorgo m	sorghum	suelo m pesado	heavy soil
sorgo m Sudanensis	sudangrass	suelo m podsol	podzol
sorosis f	psorosis	suelo m secadero	drying-floor
soso	insipid	sueldo m	wages
soya f	soybean	suelto	loose
sótano m	cellar	sulfato m	sulfate
standardización f	standardization	sulfato m	sulphate
suave	tender	sulfato m amónico	sulphate of ammonia
suave	soft	sulfato m de cobre	copper sulphate
subalimentación f	underfeeding	sulfato m de hierro	ferrous sulphate
subasta f	auction	sulfato m de magnesia	magnesium sulfate
subespecie f	subspecies	sulfato m de potasa	sulphate of potash
subgénero m	subgenus	sulfato m doble de	sulphate of potash-
sublimado m	sublimate	potasio y magnesio	magnesia
submerge, to	sumergir	sulfito m	sulphite
subproducto m	by-product	sumergir	dip, to; to submerge
subsidio m	subsidy	suministrable	saleable
subsolada f	subsoiling	suministrar	furnish, to
subsoladora f	subsoiling	suministrar	supply, to
subsolar	subsoil, to	supeficie f del suelo	soil surface
substancia f orgánica	organic matter	superficial	shallow
substrato m	substrate	superficial	superficial
subsueladora f	subsoiler	superficie f	surface

SPANISH - ENGLISH EQUIVALENTS

SPANISH	ENGLISH	SPANISH	ENGLISH
superficie f de la hoja	leaf surface	tallo m principal	main stem
superficie f radiante	radiating surface	talo m	thallus
superfosfato m	superphosphate	talofítico	thallophytic
superior	superior (bot)	talófita f	thallophyte
supermercado m	supermarket	talón m	heel (of cutting)
supervivencia f	survival	talud m	slope
supresión f	deletion	tamaño m	size
surcar	furrow, to	tamaño m del grano	grain size
surcadora f	lister	tamarindo m	tamarind
surco m	crop row	tamarisco m	tamarisk
surco m	furrow	tambor m	brake drum
surfactante m	surfactant	tamiz m	sieve
surtido m	assortment	tamizar	sieve, to
surtido m de luz	light supply	tampón	buffer
susceptibilidad f	susceptibility	tangerina f	tangerine
sustancia f	substance	tanque m	tank
sustancia f activa	active ingredient	tanque m de expansión	expansion tank
sustancia f portadora	carrier	tanto m alzado	flat rate
sustrato m	substrate	tapado	plugged
sutura f	suture	tapar	cover up, to
		tapar	cover with a top, to
		tapar	put a lid on, to
		tapeadora f	topping machine
- T -		tapioca f	tapioca
		tapón m	plug
		tarea f	chore
tabla f	bench (greenhouse), tray	tarea f	task
tabla f	board	taro m	taro
tabla f	chart	tárrago m	clary
tabla f	plank	tasa f	rate
tablero m	instrument panel	taxonomía f	taxonomy
taladrador europeo del maíz	european corn borer	taxonomía f vegetal	plant taxonomy
taladrar	drill, to	tayota f	chayote
taladro m	drill	taza f	cup
talar	fell, to (tree)	té m	tea
talco m	talc	teca f	teak
talla f de los cereales	culm	techo m	roof
taller m	shop (repair)	técnica	technique
tallo de la flor	peduncle	técnica f del cultivo	growing technique
tallo m	stalk	técnica f de inmunosorbencia	immunosorbent technique
tallo m	stem	técnico m de la calefacción	heating technician
tallo m fructífero	seedstalk	tecnológico	technological
tallo m lateral	side shoot	tef m	teff
tallo m principal	leader (tree)	tegumento m	seed coat

SPANISH - ENGLISH EQUIVALENTS

SPANISH	ENGLISH	SPANISH	ENGLISH
tegumento m	tegument	termo-terapia f	heat treatment
tejido m	tissue	termocupla f	thermocouple
tejido m de empalizada	palisade tissue	termografo m	thermograph
tejido m vascular	vascular tissue	termopar m	thermocouple
tejo m	yew	termoperíodo m	thermoperiod
tela f	fabric	termostato m	thermostat
tela f de araña	cobweb	termómetro m	thermometer
tela f de embalar	packing cloth	termómetro m maxi-mini	max-min thermometer
tela f metálica	screen	ternero m	calf
tela f metálica	wire netting	terno	ternate
telaraña f	spider web	ternura f	tenderness
teleza f	plumbago	terraza f	terrace
temperatura f de conservación	storage temperature	terraza f de banco	bench terrace
temperatura f máxima	maximum temperature	terraza f de escalones	bench terrace
temperatura f mínima	minimum temperature	terraza f de escalón	step terrace
templado	temperate	terremoto m	earthquake
temporada f	season	terreno m de aluvión	flood plain
temporal	temporary	terreno m limpio	bare ground
tempranero	early	terreno m pantanoso de agua dulce	fresh water swamp
temprano	early	térreo	earthy
tendencia f	tendency	terrón m de tierra	clod (soil)
tender	stretch, to (wire)	terrón m	clod
tenedor m	payee	tetrapétalo	tetrapetalous
tensiometro m	tensiometer	tetraploide	tetraploid
tensión f	tension (voltage)	textura f	texture
tensión f de humidad	moisture tension	tiamina f	thiamine
tensión f capilar	capillary tension	tiempo m	weather
tensor m	turnbuckle	tienda f de flores	flower shop
tentredinido m	sawfly	tienda f de semillas	garden center
tentredino m	sawfly	tienda f por departamento	department store
teodolito m	quadrant level	tierra f	earth
teoría de la explotación agrícola	principles of farm management	tierra f	land
tépalo m	tepal	tierra f baja	lowland
tepe m	sod	tierra f calcárea	calcareous soil
terapia f	therapy	tierra f cultivable	cropland
teridófita f	pteridophyte	tierra f herbosa	sod
termes m	termite	tierra f incultivable	waste land
terminación f	completion	tierra f labrantía	arable land
terminal m	terminal	tierra f para maceta	potting soil
terminar	finish, to	tierra f turba	peat soil, muck soil
terminarse	end, to	tiesto m	flower pot
termita f	termite	tigmotaxia f	thigmotaxis
térmite m	termite	tigmotropismo m	thigmotropism
		tijera f de podar	pruning shears

SPANISH - ENGLISH EQUIVALENTS

SPANISH	ENGLISH	SPANISH	ENGLISH
tijera f podadera	pruning shears	topo m	mole
tijeras f	shears	topografía f	topography
tijeras f de jardinero	hedge shears	tormenta f de nieve	blizzard
tijeras f de podar	secateur	tornasol m	litmus
tijeras f para setos vivos	hedgeshears	tornillo m	screw
tijereta f	earwig	toro m	bull
tila f	linden	toro m probado	proved sire
tilo m	lime tree	toronja f	grapefruit
timón m de arado	shank (plow)	torta f de algodón	cottonseed cake
tinte f	dye	torta f oleaginosa	oilcake
tipo m	type	tortrix m	leaf roller
tipo m de finca	farm type	tortrix m	tortrix moth
tipo m del suelo	soil type	toxicidad f	toxicity
tipos m de suelos	soil types	toxicología f	toxicology
tira f	band	tóxico m de contacto	contact poison
tirar	pull, to	tórsalo m	botfly
tisanóptaro m	thrip	trabajado	grafted
titulación f	titration	trabajar	work, to
tiza f	chalk	trabajar el jardín	garden, to
tizón m	blight	trabajo m	labor
tizón m polvoriento	powdery mildew	trabajo m contratado	contract work
tizón tardío	late blight	trabajo m de equipo	team work
título m calificativo de propiedad	deed	trabajo m estacional	seasonal labor
tobaco m	nicotiana, tobacco	trabajo m manual	manual labor
tocino m	bacon	tracción f	traction
tocón	tree stump	tractor m	tractor
tocón m	stump	tractor m de oruga	caterpillar tractor
toldo m	awning	tractor m de orugas	crawler tractor
tolerancia f	tolerance	tragar	swallow, to
tolerante	tolerant	trailla f mecánica	earthmover
tolva f	hopper	traje m protector	spray suit
toma f de fuerza	power take-off (PTO)	trampa f	trap
toma f de tierra	ground wire	trampa f de luz	light trap
tomar muestras	sample, to	trampa f para insectos	insect trap
tomar prestado	borrow	transecto m	transect
tomate m	tomato	transformación f	processing
tomatillo m falso	ground cherry	transformación f	transformation
tomento m	tomentum	transformador m	transformer
tomentoso	tomentose	translocación f	translocation
tomillo m	thyme	transluciente	translucent
tonel m	barrel	transmisión f luminosa	light transmission
tonel m	cask	transmisión f	transmission
tonelada f	ton	transpiración f	transpiration
topiaria f	topiary	transpirar	transpire, to
		transportador m de paletas	pallet truck

155

SPANISH - ENGLISH EQUIVALENTS

SPANISH	ENGLISH	SPANISH	ENGLISH
transportador m por rodillos	roller conveyer	triploide	triploid
transporte m interior	internal transport	triploidía f	triploidy
trapiadora f	mop	trípode m	tripod
trapo	rag	tristeza f de los cítricos	tristeza
tráquea f	trachea	tritoma f	red hot poker plant
traqueida f	tracheid	trituradora f de martillos	hammer mill
trasovado	obovate	triturar	crush, to
trasplantación f	transplantation	tronco m	stump
trasplantador m	garden trowel	tronco m	trunk
trasplantar	transplant, to	tronco m guía	central leader
trastorno m fisiológico	physiological disorder	tronco m intermedio	intermediate stock
tratamiento m	treatment	tropismo m	tropism
tratamiento m con agua caliente	hot water treatment	troquita f	hand truck
		trozo m	log
tratamiento m con agua templada	warm-water treatment	trufa f	truffle
		terapia f	therapy
tratamiento m de día corto	short day treatment	tuberculos m	tubercles
tratamiento m de días largos	long-day treatment	tubería f	pipes
		tubería f	tubing
tratamiento m de las semillas	seed treatment	tuberoso	tuberous
tratamiento m del suelo	soil treatment	tubérculo m	tuber
tratamiento m por calor	heat treatment	tubérculo m caulino	corm
tratamiento m térmico	heat treatment	tubiforme	tubular
tratar	try, to	tubo m	hose
traza f	trace	tubo m	pipe
trazador m	tracer	tubo m	tube
trazo m	layout	tubo m criboso	sieve tube
trébol m	clover	tubo m de acoplamiento	quick coupling pipe
trébol m de carretilla	bur clover	tubo m de admisión	suction tube
trementina f	turpentine	tubo m de alimentación	feed pipe
tren m del volante	steering mechanism	tubo m de drenaje	drain pipe
trepador m	climbing	tubo m flexible perforado	soaker hose
trepadora f	vine	tubo m para vapor	steam pipe
trepar	climb, to	tuerca f	locknut
triangular	triangular	tuétano m	pith
tribásico	tribasic	tufo m	haze
tricoma f	trichome	tule m	bullrush
trifoliado	trifoliate	tulipán m	tulip
trigo m	wheat	tumor m	tumor
trigo m de primavera	spring wheat	túnel m	tunnel
trillado	threshing	túnica f	tunic (bulb)
trillador m	thresher	tung m	tung
trilladora	threshing machine	tupinambo m	Jerusalem artichoke
trip m	thrip	turba f	peat
tripétalo m	tripetalous	turbal m	peat bog

SPANISH - ENGLISH EQUIVALENTS

SPANISH	ENGLISH	SPANISH	ENGLISH
turbera f	bog	vagoneta f	pick-up (truck)
turbinto m	California pepper tree	vaina f	sheath
turbonada f	squall	vaina f	spathe
turgencia f	turgidity	vaina f	pod
turgente	turgid	vainilla f	vanilla
turgescencia f	turgidity	vainita f	string bean
tusa f de maíz	corncob	valor de la tierra	land value
tutor m	stake	valor m añadido	added value
tutorado m	staking	valor m comercial	trade value
tuza f	gopher	valor m contable	book value
		valor m de adquisición	original value
		valor m de sustitución	replacement value
		valor m en nuevo	new value
- U -		valor m en venta	sale value
		valor m nutritivo	nutritive value
uchuba f	cape gooseberry	valor m residual	residual value
ultravioleta	ultraviolet	válvula	valve
umbela f	umbel	válvula f de bola	ball valve
umbral m económico	economic threshol	válvula f de desagüe	drain valve
umbrático	shady	válvula f de retorno	return valve
umbrío	shady	válvula f de seguridad	safety valve
unicelular	unicellular	válvula f de tres vias	three way valve
uniculular	one-celled	válvula f derecha	globe valve
unidad f	unit	válvula f flotante	float valve
unilocular	unilocular	válvula f reductora	reducing valve
unión f	union	válvula f solenoide	solenoid valve
unión f del injerto	graft union	vapam f	vapam
unisexual	unisexual	vapor m	steam
uña f	finger nail	vaporación f	vaporization
urea f	urea	vaquería f	cowshed
urea-formol m	urea formaldehyde	vaquero m	cowboy
uredospora f	urediospore	vaquita f de San Antón	ladybird
uso m	use	vara f	scape
utilización f	utilization	vara m de oro	goldenrod
uva f	grape	varear	knock down, to (fruit)
		variabilidad f	variability
		variacíon f	variation
		variancia f	variance
- V -		variedad de madurez tardía	late maturing variety
		variedad f	variety
vaca a	cow	variedad f enana	dwarf variety
vaciar	to empty	variedad f temprana	early variety
vacío m	vacuum	varilla f de tensión	tension rod
vacunos m	cattle	varita f	stirring rod
vacuola f	vacuole		

SPANISH - ENGLISH EQUIVALENTS

SPANISH	ENGLISH	SPANISH	ENGLISH
vasiforme	cup shaped	verificar	check, to
vasiforme	urn-shaped	vermiculita f	vermiculite
vasiforme	vasiform	vernación f	vernation
vaso m	vessel (bot)	vernalización f	vernalization
vaso m capilar	capillary vessel	verónica f	veronica
vaso m con pequeño pico	beaker	versátil	versatile
vaso m de captación	catchment basin	vertedera f	moldboard
vaso m leñoso	xylem	vertedera f	mouldboard
vaso m para flores	flower vase	verticilado	whorled
vástago	shoot	verticilo m	whorl
vástago m	scion	vervena f	verbena
vástago m	stem	vesícula	vesicle
vástago m	root sucker	veta f	streak
vecería f	biennial bearing	vetiver m	vetiver
vecero m	alternate bearer	veza f velluda	hairy vetch
vecindario m	neighborhood	viabilidad f	viability
vector m	vector	viable	viable
vega f	fertile plain	víbora	snake
vegetación f	vegetation	vibrador m	vibrator
vegetar	vegetate, to	vibrar	vibrate, to
vejiga f	blister	vicia f	vetch
vellocino m	fleece	vida f útil	usefull life
vellón m	fleece	vidrio m	pane
vellosidad f	fuzziness	vienos m reinantes	wind, prevailing
velloso	hairy	viga f laminada	laminated beam
velloso	hirsute	vigor m germinativo	rate of germination
velloso	pilose	vigor m híbrido	heterosis
vena f	vein, streak	vigor m híbrido	hybrid vigor
venación f	veination	vigoroso	vigorous
vender	sell, to	vilano m	pappus
veneno m	poison	vinagre m	vinegar
veneno m estomacal	stomach poison	vinagrillo m	wood sorrel
venenoso	poisonous	vinca f	periwinkle
ventana f	sash	vinicultor m	viticulturist
ventana f	window	viña f	vineyard
ventanilla f	damper	viñal m	vineyard
ventas f para entregar	future trading	viñedo m	vineyard
ventilación f	ventilation	violáceo	violet
ventilador m	blower	violeta f	violet
ventilador m	fan	violeta f africana	African violet
ventilador m	ventilator	violeto m	peach (clingstone)
ventilar	ventilate, to	virología f	virology
verde oliva	olive-green	virosis f	virus disease
verdolaga f	purslane	viruela f	leaf spot
verduras f	vegetable greens	viruela f	pox

SPANISH - ENGLISH EQUIVALENTS

SPANISH	ENGLISH	SPANISH	ENGLISH
viruela f aviar	fowl pox	yema f axilar	axillary bud
virulencia f	virulence	yema f dormida	dormant bud
virus m transmisible por el suelo	soil-borne virus	yema f floral	flower bud
		yema f foliar	leaf bud
viruta f	shaving	yema f mixta	mixed bud
viruta f de madera	wood shaving	yema f principal	main bud
viscosidad	viscosity	yema f radicular	root bud
viscoso	viscous	yema f terminal	terminal bud
vistaria f	wistaria	yerba f	herb
vitamina f	vitamin	yerba f búfalo	buffalo grass
viticultura f	viticulture	yerbaluisa f	lemongrass
vivaz	perennial	yeso m	gypsum
vivero m	nursery	yesquero m	globe thistle
vivienda f	dwelling	ylang-ylang m	ylang-ylang
volar	fly, to	yodo m	iodine
volatilizarse	volatilize, to	yuca f	cassava
volátil	volatile	yute m	jute
voltage m	tension (voltage)	yuyuba f	jujube
voluble	twining		
volumen m	bulk		
volumen m	volume		
volumen m de poros	pore space		
volúbilis m	bindweed		
vuelco m	lodging (plants)		
vuelco m de un cultivo	lodging		

- Z -

SPANISH	ENGLISH
zacate m de empaque	excelsior
zafra f	sugar crop
zamboa f	sour orange
zanahoria f	carrot
zanahoria f silvestre	wild carrot
zángano m	drone
zanja f	ditch
zanja f	surface drain
zanja f	trench
zanja f de desagüe	drainage ditch
zanja f de desvío	diversion ditch
zanjadora f	ditchdigger
zanjar	trench, to
zanjón	creek
zapa f	spade
zapallo m	gourd
zapapico m	mattock
zapatillo m de Venus	lady's slipper
zapatillo m de Venus	paphiopedilum
zapote m	sapodilla
zapato m	brake shoe, shoe

- X -

SPANISH	ENGLISH
xilema f	xylem
xylem m	xylem

- Y -

SPANISH	ENGLISH
yaque m	mesquite
yautía f	cocoyam
yedra f	ivy
yema f	bud
yema f	egg yolk
yema f adventicia	adventitious bud

SPANISH - ENGLISH EQUIVALENTS

SPANISH	ENGLISH	SPANISH	ENGLISH
zaranda f	screen		
zaranda f	sieve		
zarapico m	candytuft (perennial)		
zarapico m anual	candytuft (annual)		
zarcillo m	tendril		
zarza f	bramble, blackberry plant		
zarza f japonesa	Japanese wineberry		
zarzamora f	blackberry (fruit)		
zarzamora f	brambleberry		
zarzo m	hurdle		
zinc m	zinc		
zinia f	zinnia		
zona f algodonera	cotton belt		
zona f del maíz	cornbelt		
zona f experimental	experimental area		
zootecnia f, producción pecuaria	animal production		
zumaque m	sumac		
zumo m de uva	grape juice		
zuzón m	groundsel		